Library of Davidson College

ATHANASIUS:
CONTRA GENTES

PHILOSOPHIA PATRUM

INTERPRETATIONS OF PATRISTIC TEXTS

EDITED BY

J. H. WASZINK AND J. C. M. VAN WINDEN

VOLUME VII

LEIDEN
E. J. BRILL
1984

ATHANASIUS: CONTRA GENTES

INTRODUCTION, TRANSLATION AND COMMENTARY

BY

E. P. MEIJERING

Reader in Latin Patristics in the University of Leyden

LEIDEN
E. J. BRILL
1984

Published with financial support from the Netherlands Organzation for the Advancement of Pure Research (Z.W.O.).

Also by E. P. Meijering:

Orthodoxy and Platonism in Athanasius. Synthesis of Antithesis?, E. J. Brill, Leiden 1974², 201 pp.
God Being History. Studies in Patristic Philosophy, N.H.P.C., Amsterdam-Oxford 1975, 185 pp.
Tertullian contra Marcion. Gotteslehre in der Polemik (Adversus Marcionem I-II), E. J. Brill, Leiden 1977, 183 pp.
Theologische Urteile über die Dogmengeschichte. Ritschls Einfluss auf von Harnack, E. J. Brill, Leiden 1978, 101 pp.
Augustin über Schöpfung, Ewigkeit und Zeit. Das elfte Buch der Bekenntnisse, E. J. Brill, Leiden 1979, 127 pp.
Calvin wider die Neugierde. Ein Beitrag zum Vergleich zwischen reformatorischem und patristischem Denken, B. de Graaf, Nieuwkoop 1980, 122 pp.
Hilary of Poitiers on the Trinity. De Trinitate, 1, 1-19, 2, 3, E. J. Brill, Leiden 1982 (in close cooperation with J. C. M. van Winden), 199 pp.
Der "ganze" und der "wahre" Luther. Hintergrund und Bedeutung der Lutherinterpretation Adolf von Harnacks, N.H.P.C., Amsterdam-Oxford 1983, 45 pp.
Melanchthon and Patristic Thought. The Doctrine of Christ and Grace, the Trinity and the Creation, E. J. Brill, Leiden 1983, 166 pp.

ISBN 90 04 07226 8

Copyright 1984 by E. J. Brill, Leiden, The Netherlands

All rights reserved. No part of this book may be reproduced or translated in any form, by print, photoprint, microfilm, microfiche or any other means without written permission from the publisher

PRINTED IN THE NETHERLANDS BY E. J. BRILL

HENRICO BERKHOF
XIV LUSTRA COMPLENTI
D.D.D.
AUCTOR

CONTENTS

Preface	ix
Introduction	1
Athanasius: Contra Gentes. Translation and Commentary	
Contents of the 'Contra Gentes'	7
Introduction	9
Part I. The origin of evil: man's sin	14
Part II. The refutation of idolatry	38
Part III. Man has a soul and a reason	98
Part IV. The Creator and Creation	115
Some Final Observations	155
Indices	
I. Index of quotations from ancient authors	156
II. Index of Subjects and names	165
III. Index of modern authors	167

PREFACE

Athanasius' *Contra Gentes* is probably his least original piece of writing, – it seems therefore most suitable to form the subject of a commentary. For this commentary we made use of R. W. Thomson, *Athanasius, Contra Gentes and De Incarnatione, Edited and Translated*, Oxford 1971.

I want to thank E. J. Brill's for editing the book and the *Netherlands Organization for the Advancement of Pure Research (Z.W.O.)* for providing a subsidy.

I want to express my gratitude to Mrs. T. C. C. M. Heesterman-Visser, Oegstgeest, for typing the manuscript and my nephew Mr F. N. Marshall, London, for correcting my English.

In *C.G.* 39 Athanasius says: καὶ γὰρ καὶ τεχνίτην ἐν ἀνθρώποις οὐκ ἄν τις εἴποι τέλειον, ἀλλὰ ἀσθενῆ, εἰ μὴ μόνος, ἀλλὰ μετὰ πολλῶν ἓν ἀποτελοίη τὸ ἔργον. Working together with Professor Van Winden one certainly realizes one's own weakness, but one also discovers that Athanasius underestimated the value and pleasure of cooperation, because he falsely believed perfection to be at all possible.

The book has been dedicated to Professor H. Berkhof, the dogmatician with a lively interest in the history of Christian thought. I agree with him on the importance of Platonic ontology to Athanasius (see *Die Theologie des Euseb von Caesarea*, Amsterdam 1939, p. 68 and p. 100), I disagree with him on the date of Athanasius' apologetic treatise (see Athanasius' De Incarnatione Verbi, *Kerkelijke Klassieken*, Wageningen 1949, p. 23), but during the last twenty-five years I have both agreed and disagreed with him on more important matters as well.

November 1983   E.P.M.
Oranjelaan 11
2341 CA *Oegstgeest* / The Netherlands

I want to thank my colleague and friend Professor J. C. M. van Winden for his very thorough correction of the original manuscript.

INTRODUCTION

The fact that there is no reference to the Arians in Athanasius' apologetic treatises *Contra Gentes - De Incarnatione Verbi* has usually been interpreted as an indication that these treatises were written before the Arian controversy was in full progress (see the brief survey given by J. C. M. van Winden, On the Date of Athanasius' Apologetic Treatises, *Vigiliae Christianae* (29), 1975, pp. 291 f.), but it has also been argued that any reference to the Arians was avoided on purpose and that the treatises were written during Athanasius exile in Trier (335-337). This would explain why he did not have, as he says in the opening chapter, the writings of his teachers at hand (*C.G.* 1: ...ἐπειδὴ τὰς τῶν διδασκάλων συντάξεις ἐν χερσὶν νῦν οὔκ ἔχομεν). The most recent advocate of this latter view is Ch. Kannengiesser (see his papers, Le témoignage des *Lettres Festales* de saint Athanase sur la date de l'Apologie *Contre les Paiens*, *Sur l'Incarnation du Verbe*, Recherches de Science Religieuse (52), 1964, pp. 91 ff. and *Recherches de Science Religieuse* (58) 1970, pp. 383 ff.). J. C. M. van Winden argues strongly in favour of an early dating of the treatises before the peak of the Arian controversy. In *C.G.* 6 and *De Inc.* 2 Athanasius refers to the view held by *the* heretics that besides the good God there is also the evil Creator of the evil creation, see *C.G.* 6: Οἱ δὲ ἀπὸ αἱρέσεων, ἐκπεσόντες τῆς ἐκκλησιαστικῆς διδασκαλίας, καὶ περὶ τὴν πίστιν ναυαγήσαντες, καὶ οὗτοι μὲν ὑπόστασιν τοῦ κακοῦ παραφρονοῦσιν εἶναι, ἀναπλάττονται δὲ ἑαυτοῖς παρὰ τὸν ἀληθινὸν τοῦ Χριστοῦ Πατέρα θεὸν ἕτερον, καὶ τοῦτον ἀγέννητον τοῦ κακοῦ ποιητὴν καὶ τῆς κακίας ἀρχηγόν, τὸν καὶ τῆς κτίσεως δημιουργόν. This view is held by the Gnostics and Marcionites and not by the Arians. We believe Van Winden to be right in drawing the conclusion that this shows that Athanasius did not think of the Arians at all when he wrote his apologetic treatises, because at that time there was no formal Arian heresy as yet. We want to elaborate this argument a little more.

One might suggest that this remark about the dualistic views held by *the* heretics (which were, in fact, not held by the Arians) betrays a certain carelessness on the part of Athanasius and therefore does not necessarily imply that there was no formal Arian heresy as yet. But Athanasius usually is sufficiently precise in his references to heretical doctrines to differentiate between views held by *some* heretics and *the* heretics. In *C.G.* 30 he opposes the doctrine held by *some* heretics that man has no reasonable soul (see *infra*, 101). When in his Anti-Arian writings he opposes various doctrines of creation he clearly differentiates between Gnostic (Marcionite) and Arian views: see e.g. *De Decretis Nicaenae Synodi* 19 (PG 25, 449B) where he says that *some* heretics say that there is another Creator (besides the good God) and that others say that the universe was created by angels: ἢ ὥς τινες τῶν αἱρετικῶν ἄλλον δημιουργὸν λέγουσι· ἢ ὡς πάλιν ἄλλοι ὑπό τινων ἀγγέλων λέγουσιν εἶναι τὴν τῶν πάντων σύστασιν. In *Contra Arianos* 1, 56 (PG 26, 129C) he says that the Arians adopted their doctrine that the Son is no more than an angel from the Gnostic Carpocrates, who taught that the angels created the world. It is significant that he does *not* accuse the Arians of saying that the angels created the world (which was not their doctrine), but that they degrade Christ, who is the mediator in creation, to the status of angels, and in this respect resemble Carpocrates to whom the angels are the creators of the world (cp. *Contra Arianos* 2, 21, PG 26, 192A). In *Contra Arianos* 2, 40 (PG 26, 232) he attacks the Arian doctrine that there are two Wisdoms of God, one which is eternally in God and one which appeared in Jesus. According to Athanasius in saying this they deny the true Wisdom of God (Christ) and invent a non-existing one; just as the Manicheans imagine there is another god besides the true one. It was usual for the orthodox to trace the heresies which they attacked back either to earlier heresies or to Greek philosophers (cp. *infra*, 32). In this particular case Athanasius is well aware that he cannot accuse the Arians of teaching an evil creator besides the true God, therefore he must content himself with stating that their doctrine of Christ (who is not God's eternal Wisdom) shows some similarity with Gnostic dualism. That there is a plurality in heretical views on creation is clearly stated in the (anti-Arian writing) *De Synodis*, see ch. 35 (PG 26, 756B): τῶν δὲ αἱρετικῶν ἕκαστος ὡς ἠθέλησεν ἀνεπλάσατο, καὶ περὶ τῆς κτίσεως μυθολογεῖ.

There remains the question of why Athanasius says that he does not have the books of his teachers at hand. Van Winden says that Athanasius argues in the opening chapter in a typically rhetorical way (*op. cit.*, p. 295; on rhetoric in Athanasius' writings in general see G. C. Stead, Rhetorical Method in Athanasius, *Vigiliae Christianae* (30) 1976, pp. 121 ff.). He draws attention to the fact that Athanasius does not complain about the fact that he does not have the books of his teachers at hand, but that the reason why he writes is "that we do not now have the writings of our teachers at hand" (τὰς τῶν διδασκάλων συντάξεις ἐν χερσὶ νῦν οὐκ ἔχομεν). Then the "we" must include the reader as well. Now it is hardly conceivable that at the time both Athanasius and the person (or persons) addressed were in exile. Why did the reader and the writer of the treatise not have the books of earlier Christian writers at hand? This question simply cannot be answered. But elaborating on Van Winden's remark that Athanasius argues in a typically rhetorical way we want to suggest the following: the purpose of an *exordium* is to make the reader *attentive*, *docile* and *benevolent* towards the writer (see H. Lausberg, *Handbuch der literarischen Rhetorik*, München 1973, pp. 152 ff.). In order to make the reader attentive one must surmount the reader's possible *teadium*. This *taedium* may be caused by supersaturation: too much has already been said or written about the subject. Ways of surmounting this *taedium* are: to underline the importance of the subject, to promise brevity and to give the impression of humility or modesty. It appears that this is exactly what Athanasius does (for more details see also *infra*, 9 ff.): in the opening sentence he says that knowledge of religion and the universe does not need instruction from men, since it reveals itself daily through creation and the teaching of Christ more clearly than the sun. Here humility or modesty is expressed in admitting that the piece of writing is in itself unnecessary, and at the same time the importance of the subject is underlined: it deals with nothing less than what God and Christ reveal daily. Then Athanasius goes on to say that despite this clear revelation the reader nevertheless wants to hear (more) about it. This is a way of making him docile: he who is told that he is already docile will certainly become docile. But then the difficulty arises that Scripture and earlier Christian writers already testify sufficiently to God's revelation. So how can the readers' *taedium* be overcome? Pagan writers may claim to say more clearly what was not said clearly enough before, but Athanasius cannot promise to improve the knowledge which one has already received from Scripture and Christian tradition. Here the fact that both Athanasius and the reader do not have the writings of Christian writers at hand shows a way out: the knowledge which Athanasius and the reader already have can be refreshed by re-reading the books of earlier Christian writers, but since they do not have these books at hand it is necessary for Athanasius to write down what he has learned from just these books (see further *infra*, 10 f.). Here again modesty is expressed (Athanasius does not claim to present a new doctrine), but also the importance of the book is underlined (it contains a summary of what Christian writers have written down). The reader need not fear he will be burdened up with lengthy and tedious expositions, since brevity is promised (...ὀλίγα τῆς κατὰ πίστεως ἐκθώμεθα). It seems to us that the in itself inexplicable fact that both Athanasius and his reader (or readers) did not have the books of earlier Christian writers at hand, was used as a means to 'sell' the book to an attentive Christian public.

One objection against an early dating remains: Athanasius' dependence on Eusebius' *Praeparatio Evangelica* which was written between 312 and 322 (see on this matter T. Kehrhahn, *De Sancti Athanasii quae fertur contra gentes oratione*, Berlin 1913). But we do not regard this objection as decisive: the parallels between arguments given by

Athanasius in his apologetic treatises and the ones given by Eusebius in the *Praeparatio Evangelica* are usually commonplaces in Christian and Pagan writers, as we shall try to show in the commentary. Furthermore it could be possible that the apologetic treatise was written between 322 and 325 at a time when discussions between Arius and Ecclesiastical leaders in Alexandria were going on, but when there was no formal Arian heresy as yet (cp. J. C. M. van Winden, *op. cit.*, p. 294), as there was after the condemnation of Arianism at the Nicene Synod.

Ch. Kannengiesser (see *Recherches de Science Religieuse* (52) 1964, pp. 91 ff.) believes that the remark made against the heretics in *De Inc.* 24, that they want to divide the body of Christ, i.e. the church, is a hidden attack on the Arians. But this need not apply to the Arians, since it is a traditional argument against the heretics (see e.g. Clement of Rome, *Ad Cor.* 46 and Irenaeus, *Adv. Haer.* 4, 53, 1, cp. E. P. Meijering, *Orthodoxy and Platonism in Athanasius. Synthesis or Antithesis?*, Leiden 1974², pp. 111 f. – On *C.G.* 46 where the doctrine is opposed, that Christ is the Son by participation, see *infra*, 149).

Furthermore it seems to us rather difficult to think of a plausible reason why Athanasius should not mention the Arians if the treatises were written at the height of the Arian controversy, but it seems even more difficult to think of a reason why he should not freely refer to the fact that he was in exile. Being in exile was a *topos* in ancient literature (see A. Giesecke, *De philosophorum veterum quae ad exilium spectant sententiis*, Leipzig 1891), and in those pieces of writing which were written in exile Athanasius does explicitly refer to this fact (see *Ad Serapionem* 1, 1, cp. Hilary of Poitiers, *De Trinitate* 10, 4). If the apologetic treatises had been written in exile and this was the reason why he did not have the books of his teachers at hand, one would certainly expect Athanasius to say in the opening chapter something like: "They may deprive us of freedom and of our books, but they cannot deprive us of knowledge of the truth, since we can remember what we learned from our teachers and this is what we shall write down on your behalf." Since the fact that Athanasius and his reader (or readers) do not have the books of his teachers at hand remains unexplicable (we do *not* suggest that this statement is made by Athanasius for purely rhetorical reasons and is in fact untrue), nothing can be said with absolute certainty about the dating of his apologetic treatises. We regard it as most likely that they should be dated rather early when the Arian doctrine was no formal heresy as yet. But even if they were written during the exile in Trier, this would hardly alter our view on the purpose of the treatises.

Turning to this purpose we want first of all to stress that *Contra Gentes* forms a unity with *De Incarnatione Verbi*. Towards the end of *De Incarnatione*

Verbi (ch. 56) he says he has written a στοιχείωσις or χαρακτὴρ τῆς κατὰ Χριστὸν πίστεως, i.e. an elementary instruction in and an outline of faith in Christ. This elementary instruction is given the traditional form of an apology against the Pagans. It cannot have been Athanasius' primary purpose to convince as many Pagans as possible, since he addresses himself to a Christian reader (see *C.G.* 1 and *De Inc.* 56, *infra*, 10). This Christian reader is instructed about the main aspects of Christian faith and provided with a refutation of Pagan objections against this faith, so that he can be sure that he was not misled when he put confidence in truth by knowing Christ.

The heretics pose no threat to Christian faith either, since they can easily be refuted, as Athanasius shows in connection with the cosmological views held by the Gnostics and Marcionites, or even be ignored, as Athanasius would show in connection with the Arians if he wrote his treatise when he was in exile in Trier (which we regard, however, as unlikely).

ATHANASIUS: CONTRA GENTES. TRANSLATION AND COMMENTARY

CONTENTS OF THE 'CONTRA GENTES'

Introduction (1).
I. The origin of evil: man's sin (2-7).
   1) Man's original, sinless state in Paradise: the true life with God (2).
   2) Man's fall from his original state, exemplified in Adam's fall (3).
   3) Man uses his free will in the wrong way and turns to evil, i.e. non-being (4).
   4) Further description of the sinner's activities (5).
   5) Attack on the dualistic views held by some Greek philosophers and some heretics (6).
   6) Further polemics against Marconite dualism. – Evil has no substance of its own, but finds its origin in the human soul which turns away from God (7).

II. The refutation of idolatry (8-29).
   1) As a sinner man imagines as good what is not, and he deifies bodily things (8).
   2) Catalogue of the various forms of idolatry (9).
   3) Attack on the deification of men (10).
   4) Refutation of deification from Scripture. Attack on the ways of life of the Greek gods (11).
   5) Further attack on the Pagan gods' way of life (12).
   6) Attack on the images of gods (13).
   7) Scriptural proof against the worship of idols (14).
   8) Recapitulation of the attack on idolatry given so far (15).
   9) Attack on the attempt made by some Pagans to explain the myths away (16).
   10) The myths show that the so-called gods are in fact mortal men (17).
   11) Continuation of the refutation of the euhemeristic interpretation of gods (18).
   12) Attack on the images of the gods and on attempts to justify them (19).
   13) Refutation of the first defence of images given by Greek philosophers (20).
   14) Attack on the Neo-Platonic defence of images of the Divine (21).
   15) Attack on the various forms of the images of the Divine (22).
   16) Attack on the variety of the gods of the Pagans (23).
   17) Attack on the fact that the sacrifices offered to the gods are deified themselves (24).
   18) Attack on human sacrifices (25).
   19) Attack on the sexual practices associated with idolatry and on the bad example of behaviour which the gods set (26).
   20) Attack on the deification of parts of the universe (27).

21) The parts of the universe are not divine and the universe as a whole is not divine (28).
22) The conflicting parts of creation cannot be gods and cannot give harmony (29).

III. Man has a soul and a reason (30-34).
1) In his soul man can find the way to the true God (30).
2) The fact that man can distinguish between good and evil shows that he has a rational soul (31).
3) Further proof that man has a rational soul (32).
4) Proof of the soul's immortality (33).
5) Refutation of idolatry and exhortation to turn towards the true God on the basis of the immortal soul (34).

IV. The Creator and creation (35-46).
1. God's revelation through the harmony of the universe (35-45a).
a) The works of creation reveal the Creator (35).
b) The harmony of the opposite proves the existence of a Creator (36).
c) Elaboration of the harmony of the opposite and attack on the doctrine of the survival of the fittest (37).
d) The harmony of the universe proves that there is one Creator (38).
e) The one universe proves that there is one Creator (39).
f) The Creator of the world is the Father of Jesus Christ. Jesus Christ is the Word of the Father (40).
g) The reason why God created and rules the world in His Word (41).
h) The Word of the Father establishes the harmony of the universe (42).
i) Comparisons for the relation between the Word of God and the universe (43).
j) The ruling power of the Father's Word behind what happens in the world (44).
k) The relation between the Word and the Father (45a).
2. Scriptural testimony to God's revelation through the harmony of the universe (45b-46).
a) Scriptural warnings against idolatry (45b).
b) Scriptural instruction about God and His Word (46).
Peroration (47).

INTRODUCTION

CHAPTER 1

The reason why the treatise is written: Athanasius does not have the writings of his teachers at hand. The purpose of the treatise: a refutation of the objections made by the Greeks against the cross of Christ.

Translation and Commentary:

(1) "Instruction about the worship of God and the true nature of the universe need not so much be taught by men as it makes itself known."

True religion is linked with knowledge of the true nature of the universe, i.e. creation: The apologetic treatise will show that false religion consists of deification of (parts of) the universe. - It is, of course, a theological commonplace to say that God is only revealed by Himself and can only be known if He gives testimony of Himself, see e.g. Tertullian, *Apologeticum* 17, 2-3, *Adv. Marc.* 1, 18, 3, Irenaeus, *Adv. Haer.* 4, 34, 5, Hilary of Poitiers, *De Trinitate* 1, 18; 4, 14, 36; 5, 21; 6, 17; 7, 30, 38. - On the possible rhetorical background of this statement see *supra*, 13.

"For every day it almost loudly proclaims itself through its works and it displays itself more clearly than the sun through the doctrine of Christ."

It is not entirely clear whether "the works" are the works of God in creation or the works of the risen Christ in the Christian believers; the former possibility appears in *C.G.* 27: ... ἀρκεῖ τὴν κτίσιν αὐτὴν κατ' αὐτῶν μονονουχὶ βοῆσαι, καὶ δεῖξαι τὸν αὐτῆς ποιητὴν καὶ δημιουργὸν θεόν cp. *C.G.* 34 (*infra*, 114), *Contra Arianos* 2, 25 (PG 26, 200B) (on this 'crying out' of creation cp. Gregory of Nyssa, *De anima et resurrectione* (PG 46) 25A, *In Sanctum Pascha* GNO IX 257, Augustin, *Confessiones* 11, 4, 6), the latter in *De Inc.* 32: εἰ δὲ τὰ ἔργα βοᾷ καὶ δείκνυσιν ἐναργῶς, διὰ τί ἑκόντες ἀρνοῦνται τὴν τῆς ἀναστάσεως οὕτως φανερῶς ζωήν (cp. Origen, *Contra Celsum*, *Praef.* 2: Ἰησοῦς ... ἀπολογεῖται δὲ ἐν τῷ βίῳ τῶν γνησίων ἑαυτοῦ μαθητῶν, κεκραγότι τὰ διαφέροντα καὶ πάσης ψευδομαρτυρίας ὄντι κρείττονι ...). Here in the opening chapter of the treatises the former seems more likely: the works of Christ in the believers are here separately named ("it displays itself more clearly than the sun through the doctrine of Christ"), these will be discussed in the second treatise, the first treatise deals with God's works in the creation, so these should be referred to in the opening chapter as well. - The knowledge of God and the universe is *displayed* (ἐπιδείκνυται) through the doctrine of Christ. The word ἐπιδείκνυσθαι is used in a different sense elsewhere, *viz.*, in the sense of a rejectable 'showing off' which Christ did not come to do, see *De Inc.* 43: ... γιγνωσκέτωσαν ὅτι οὐκ ἐπιδείξασθαι ἦλθεν ὁ Κύριος, ἀλλὰ θεραπεῦσαι καὶ διδάξαι τοὺς πάσχοντας, ἐπιδεικνυνένου μὲν γὰρ ἦν μόνον ἐπιφανῆναι καὶ καταπλῆξαι τοὺς ὁρῶντας (this is what the Greek 'sons of God' do, see Origen, *Contra Celsum* 3, 22 and 1, 67, cp. C. Andresen, *Logos und Nomos. Die Polemik des Kelsos wider das Christentum*, Berlin 1955, pp. 53 f.).

"Nevertheless, since you want to hear what can be said about this, well my friend, let us expound, as far as we are able to do, a few things about faith in Christ, for although you can find it in Holy Scripture, yet you like to hear it in a scholarly way from others as well."

The reader is made docile by telling him that he already is docile, see *supra*, 3; cp. also *De Inc.* 56 ... μεταδίδομεν καὶ τῇ σῇ φιλομαθείᾳ. This reader is a Christian: he knows Christ, *C.G.* 1, see *infra*, 13, he is called φιλόχριστος, *C.G.* 47, *De Inc.* 1, 56 (see further P. Th. Camelot, *Athanase d'Alexandrie, Contre les Païens* (S.C. 18bis), Paris 1977[2], p. 12). - Brevity in the expositions is promised to overcome the reader's *taedium*, see *supra*, 3 (for further examples of brevity expressed by early Christian writers see E. P. Meijering (in close cooperation with J. C. M. van Winden), *Hilary of Poitiers on the Trinity. De Trinitate 1, 1-19, 2, 3*, Leiden 1982, pp. 143 ff.).

"For the Holy and divinely inspired Scriptures are in themselves sufficient to proclaim the truth, but there are also many treatises of our blessed teachers composed for this purpose. If somebody reads them, he will somehow receive an idea about the interpretation of Scripture and will be able to acquire the knowledge he desires."

On the sufficiency of Biblical revelation, cp. *De Inc.* 56: ἐκεῖναι μὲν γὰρ διὰ θεολόγων ἀνδρῶν παρὰ θεοῦ ἐλαλήθησαν καὶ ἐγράφησαν, *Vita Antonii* 16 (PG 26, 868A) where he makes Antony say: τὰς μὲν γραφὰς ἱκανὰς εἶναι πρὸς διδασκαλίαν, and *Ad Ser.* 1, 19 (PG 26, 573B) ... μόνον τὰ ἐν ταῖς Γραφαῖς μανθανέτω. Αὐτάρκη γὰρ καὶ ἱκανὰ τὰ ἐν ταύταις κείμενα ... (for further examples of this Biblicism see e.g. Irenaeus, *Adv. Haer.* 2, 40, 1; 2, 41; Hilary of Poitiers, *De Trinitate* 2, 5; 4, 14; 9, 44; 11, 1; 12, 26). To go beyond this Scriptural revelation is fallacious *curiosity*, see *Contra Arianos* 3, 1 (PG 26, 324A); *Ad Ser.* 1, 17, 18; 4, 5 (PG 26, 572/573, 644B/C). - In the previous sentence it was said that the reader himself wanted to learn from Christian writers as well, despite the fact that Scripture contains the whole truth. These Christian writers can add nothing new to Scriptural revelation but only expound more extensively and explain what is said in Scripture. They only say what they read in Scripture, see *De Inc.* 56: ἡμεῖς δὲ παρὰ τῶν αὐταῖς (sc. ταῖς γραφαῖς) ἐντυγχανόντων θεολόγων διδασκάλων ... μαθόντες.

> "But since we do not right now have the writings of our teachers at hand, we must proclaim and write to you what we learned from them (I mean the faith in the Saviour Christ)."

It was the reader's own desire to read more than Scripture, i.e. to read the writings of the Christian teachers. Since Athanasius and his reader cannot consult those writings, Athanasius must write down on behalf of his reader what he remembers of those writings. So writing his treatise means granting a wish expressed by his reader (see further *supra*, 2 ff.). Towards the end of his apologetic treatise Athanasius will make it clear (with the modesty required in this context) that Scripture says more clearly the things Athanasius has said in his piece of writing, see *De Inc.* 56: ... εἰ ἐντυγχάνοις τοῖς τῶν γραφῶν γράμμασι, γνησίως αὐτοῖς ἐφιστάνων τὸν νοῦν γνώσῃ παρ' αὐτῶν τελειότερον μὲν καὶ τρανότερον τῶν λεχθέντων τὴν ἀκρίβειαν.

> "That nobody may regard the instruction of our doctrine as worthless and presume our faith in Christ to be unreasonable. In this way the Greeks ridicule with slander and loudly laugh at us, coming forward only with the cross of Christ."

On the general charge that Christian faith is unreasonable see e.g. Origen, *Contra Celsum* 1, 9 where Celsus calls the Christians τοὺς ἀλόγως πιστεύοντας, cp. J. C. M. van Winden, Notes on Origen, Contra Celsum, *Vigiliae Christianae* (20) 1966, pp. 207 ff., see also Eusebius, *Praeparatio Evangelica* 1, 5, 2 (see G. Ruhbach, *Apologetik und Geschichte. Untersuchungen zur Theologie Eusebs von Caesarea*, Heidelberg 1962, pp. 42 f. and 69). Athanasius often refers to the fact that the Greeks mock the Christian doctrine about the cross and the incarnation of Christ, see *De Inc.* 1, 33, 41, 48, 49, 53, 54; *Ad Maximum Phil.* 1 (PG 26, 1088A); *Contra Arianos* 3, 35 (PG 26, 400A); *Vita Antonii* 74 ff. (PG 26, 944 ff.). One of the major objections made by Celsus against the incarnation is that it would imply that God is changeable - a completely false idea, see Origen, *Contra Celsum* 4, 14: εἰ δὴ ἐς ἀνθρώπους κάτεισι, μεταβολῆς αὐτῷ δεῖ, μεταβολῆς δὲ ἐξ ἀγαθοῦ εἰς κακόν ... Τίς ἂν οὖν ἕλοιτο τοιαύτην μεταβολήν; καὶ μὲν δὴ τῷ μὲν ἀλλάττεσθαι καὶ μεταπλάττεσθαι φύσις, τῷ δ' ἀθανάτῳ κατὰ τὰ αὐτὰ καὶ ὡσαύτως ἔχειν. Athanasius obviously knows about this objection and counters it by asking whether it is better to say that God's Logos did not change, or that He, remaining the same, took upon himself a body for the sake of human salvation, in order to make men participants of the divine and intelligible nature, see *Vita Antonii* 74 (PG 26, 945B/C): Ἔπειτα τί βέλτιόν ἐστι, λέγειν, ὅτι ὁ τοῦ Θεοῦ Λόγος οὐκ ἐτράπη· ἀλλ' ὁ αὐτὸς ὤν, ἐπὶ σωτηρίᾳ καὶ εὐεργεσίᾳ τῶν ἀνθρώπων ἀνείληφε σῶμα ἀνθρώπινον, ἵνα, τῇ ἀνθρωπίνῃ γενέσει κοινωνήσας, ποιήσῃ τοὺς ἀνθρώπους κοινωνῆσαι θείας καὶ νοερᾶς φύσεως.

> "It is for this reason that one would particularly have to pity their lack of perception, because, slandering the cross they do not see that its power has filled the whole world and that through it the works resulting from the knowledge of God have been revealed to all."

The only argument that the Pagans produce, *viz.*, the cross, proves to be an invalid one, therefore they ought to be pitied. The fact that the Greeks ought to be pitied does not imply any excuse, since in the next sentence it will be made clear that they could have seen what they did not see, cp. *C.G.* 12 (*infra*, 55), 13 (*infra*, 57), 26 (*infra*, 87). – One of the aspects of the power of the cross is the victory over death, so that Christians show with their lives that they do not fear death any more, see *De Inc.* 26-30, *Vita Antonii* 75 (PG 26, 948B), cp. Eusebius, *Demonstratio Evangelica* 3, 6. The difference between Christ and the gods of the Greeks is that the latter are confined to certain places, whilst Christ is adored everywhere, see *De Inc.* 46, cp. *C.G.* 23, *infra*, 79 ff., and *Vita Antonii* 79 (PG 26, 953A). – The works of the knowledge of God through the cross are the demolition of idolatry, the routing of the demons and the conversion of men to Christianity which are mentioned later in this chapter. In the *De Incarnatione Verbi* these are the works of the risen Christ.

> "For if they, too, had sincerely applied their minds to His divinity they would not mock such a great thing."

The divinity of Christ appears from the power which the risen Christ exerts in breaking the power of the demons and in ruling the hearts of the Christians, as will be made clear in the present chapter and extensively in *De Incarnatione Verbi*.

> "But they, too, would rather acknowledge Him as the Saviour of the universe and would realize that His cross did not harm but cure creation."

It seems strange that somebody should object to the incarnation that it harms creation; one might expect the criticism that it cannot take place or does not help. The word 'harm' could either be used by Athanasius as a mere antithesis of 'cure'; in that case not too much should be read into it, since antitheses are common in Greek; or it could be a reference to one of Celsus' objections against Christianity, *viz.*, that in the view of the Christians God has deserted the motion of the heavens and disregarded the vast earth to give attention to the Christians alone, see Origen, *Contra Celsum* 4, 28: ... τὴν οὐράνιον φορὰν ἀπολιπόντα τὸν θεὸν καὶ τὴν τοσαύτην γῆν παριδόντα ἡμῖν μόνοις ἐμπολιτεύεσθαι.

> "For if after the event of the cross all idolatry has been abolished, through this sign all false appearance of demons is routed, only Christ is worshipped, through Him the Father is known, the opponents are put to shame, and He invisibly converts every day the souls of His opponents, then one may reasonably say to them, how one can still regard this as something human and not rather confess that it is the Word of God and the Saviour of the universe who ascended the cross?"

So the works of Christ are the proof of His divinity. On the abolition of idolatry see further *De Inc.* 30, 46. On the routing of the demons *De Inc.* 30, 48, 50. That only Christ is worshipped means that polytheism is abandoned and all people adore the true God revealed in Christ, see *supra*, 12; on the putting to shame of the opponents see especially *De Inc.* 47, 50, 53 where Christ's triumph over Greek philosophers is stressed. On the invisible persuasion by the Logos see further *De Inc.* 1, 30, 53, – the idols cannot even persuade those near by, Christ persuades the whole world, see *De Inc.* 46: καὶ ὃ μὴ δεδύνηται τῶν εἰδώλων ἡ ἀσθένεια ποιῆσαι, ὥστε κἂν τοὺς πλησίον οἰκοῦντας πεῖσαι, τοῦτο ὁ Χριστὸς πεποίηκεν, οὐ μόνον τοὺς πλησίον ἀλλὰ καὶ πᾶσαν ἁπλῶς τὴν οἰκουμένην πείσας ἕνα καὶ τὸν αὐτὸν Κύριον σέβειν, καὶ δι' αὐτοῦ Θεὸν αὐτοῦ Πατέρα. – Whilst in this context the miraculous working of the sign of the cross is a proof of His divinity, elsewhere the miracles of the earthly Christ prove His divinity, see *De Inc.* 18 f., *Contra Arianos* 2, 12 (PG 26, 172); 3, 31 f. (PG 26, 212 f.), *Ad Ser.* 4, 16 (PG 26, 660 f.), – see on this subject more in general R. M. Grant, *Miracle and Natural Law in Graeco-Roman and Early Christian Thought*, Amsterdam 1952, pp. 188 ff.

> "For they seem to me to experience something similar to somebody slandering the sun because it is hidden by clouds, but admiring its light on seeing that the whole creation is illuminated by it. For as light is good, and the sun, the source of light, is better, so when it is a divine matter that the whole world is filled with the knowledge of Him, the Author and Principle of such an achievement must be God and the Word of God."

In order to make the reader attentive an author should give in the introduction a brief comparison, see H. Lausberg, *op. cit.*, p. 155. On this comparison see *infra*, 36, *C.G.* 7. On the idea that the cause is more than what is caused see *C.G. 9*, *infra*, 47. On the word 'achievement' and its background and use, see P. Th. Camelot, *op. cit.*, p. 51, R. W. Thomson, *Contra Gentes and De Incarnatione*, Oxford 1971, p. 27 n. 5.

> "So we go on speaking according to our ability, first having refuted the ignorance of the unbelievers, that lies having been refuted, truth may henceforth shine by itself and you, too, my friend may have confidence that you put trust in truth and were not misled in knowing Christ. I believe it to be becoming to you, as a Christian, to discuss the things concerning Christ, for I trust that you regard knowledge of and faith in Him as the most precious of all."

The main purpose of these words is to make the reader benevolent: the unbelievers' ignorance (ἀμαθία) contrasts unfavourably with the reader's φιλομάθεια (*De Inc.* 56, see the quotation given *supra*, 10). The reader is assured that he will have confidence that he was not misled in knowing Christ. Athanasius may here have in mind Celsus' claim that the Christians do not follow reason in accepting doctrines and are certain to be deceived, see Origen, *Contra Celsum* 1, 9. That knowledge about Christ is regarded as most precious by the reader appears from the fact that he wants to know what Christian writers said about this despite the fact that Scripture already contains the truth, see *supra*, 10. – There seems to be no difference between γνῶσις and πίστις in this sentence. We regard it as unlikely that the difference between the faith of the simple believer and the knowledge of the theologian who reflects about faith is presupposed.

Part I

(2-7)

THE ORIGIN OF EVIL: MAN'S SIN

Before Athanasius can attack idolatry he must trace its origin. This origin is human sin. But then the question immediately arises: what is the cause of human sin? Athanasius at all costs wants to avoid the idea that God is the cause of sin. God is good and in His goodness created man in such a way that man could turn his attention towards God. Original man is portrayed both as a Christian ascetic and as a Platonic mystic (2). But man forsakes his original destination, the contemplation of God, and turns towards evil (3). Man can do this because he has been created with a free will. It is significant that Athanasius does not discuss the question (which was raised by the Marcionites) whether the gift of free will was a bad gift and shows that man's Creator is an evil Creator. Athanasius simply states that man has a free will and that this free will appears in the fact that the human soul can move. But the human soul fails to make in its movements a distinction between a right and a wrong direction and therefore in fact moves towards evil. Evil is called 'non-being' in typically Platonic language, but Athanasius does not betray much knowledge of the many subtleties behind this Platonic doctrine. Non-being here means to Athanasius: evil has not been created by God, but it has been invented by man who in doing so misused his freedom (4-5). This doctrine having been established Athanasius attacks both Greeks and heretics who claim that evil is a substance of its own. The Greeks attacked here are most probably the Platonists (whose views are somewhat distorted and simplified), the heretics are the Marcionites. As the idea that evil has been created by God contradicts God's goodness, so the idea that evil is a substance of its own, and thereby a second principle besides God, contradicts God's omnipotence. In his refutation of Platonic and Marcionite views on evil Athanasius makes use of traditional material (6-7). After it has been made clear that man is exclusively responsible for his sin the attack on one of the consequences of sin, *viz.*, idolatry, can begin. In a sense the sin which Athanasius describes is already a kind of idolatry: in sinning man turns away from God and focuses his attention on the bodily world, – and this is what idolatry is: the deification of parts of creation.

CHAPTER 2

Man's original, sinless state in Paradise: the true life with God.

Tanslation and Commentary:

(2) "Evil has not existed from the beginning."

This is a reference to *Sap. Sal.* 14:13 (quoted in *C.G.* 11, *infra*, 50), but there evil is idolatry, whilst Athanasius here speaks of evil in general (which according to him leads to idolatry). That evil has not existed from the beginning implies that it had not been created by God, see *C.G.* 7, *infra*, 36, cp. *Vita Antonii* 22 (PG 26, 876A).

"For even now it does not exist in the saints and does not exist at all in their sphere."

The saints are the angels, see P. Th. Camelot, *op. cit.*, p. 52 n. 1, further *infra*, 17 f.

"But men started to conceive of it later on and to imagine it against themselves."

The 'conceiving' (ἐπινοεῖν, cp. E. C. E. Owen, 'Ἐπινοέω, ἐπίνοια and allied words, *Journal of Theological Studies* (35) 1934, p. 369 and p. 373) is often used in connection with evil, see e.g. *C.G.* 4, 7, 8. This is the wrong activity of the human mind. When men conceive of evil against themselves this means that when they do evil they live below their original destination, which is to live as a creature created in God's image.

"Hence they shaped for themselves the idea of the idols, regarding as being what is not."

Idolatry is caused by sin in general, cp. C.G. 7: ... ἡ τῶν εἰδώλων εὕρεσις οὐκ ἀπὸ ἀγαθοῦ, ἀλλ' ἀπὸ κακίας γέγονε. Athanasius' words here in C.G. 2 are obviously influenced by Sap. Sal. 14:12 (quoted in C.G. 11): ἀρχὴ πορνείας ἐπίνοια εἰδώλων.

"For God, the Creator and King of the universe who is beyond all being and beyond human imagination, since He is good and supremely beautiful, made through His own Word, our Savior Jesus Christ, human race in His own image."

When it says of God, the Creator, that He is ὑπερέκεινα πάσης οὐσίας καὶ ἀνθρωπίνης ἐπινοίας ὑπάρχων, on the surface this looks like the famous Neo-Platonic 'definition' of God (which goes back to Plato, *Republic* VI 509B) as ἐπέκεινα τῆς οὐσίας καὶ τοῦ νοῦ. (On the use of this expression in the history of Platonism see J. Whittaker, Ἐπέκεινα νοῦ καὶ οὐσίας, *Vigiliae Christianae* (23) 1969, pp. 91 ff.) But Athanasius cannot mean here that God is beyond the being of the ideas which cannot be seen with bodily eyes but only with the eyes of the human mind. As appears from C.G. 35 (where it says that God is ἐπέκεινα πάσης γενετῆς οὐσίας ὑπάρχων) and C.G. 40 (where we read the almost identical words ὑπερεπέκεινα πάσης γενετῆς οὐσίας) οὐσία here must have the meaning 'created substance'. The word ἐπίνοια having the meaning of 'figment' of 'fancy' Athanasius can only want to say that the true God is beyond creation and human fancy and sharply differs from the idols which are parts of creation and invented as 'gods' by men. This seems to be a common adaptation of Plato's famous words in the *Republic*; it also appears in Justin, *Dial.* 4, 1 (cp. J. Whittaker, *op. cit.*, pp. 91 f. and J. C. M. van Winden, *An Early Christian Philosopher. Justin Martyr's Dialogue with Trypho, Chapters One to Nine*, Leiden 1971, p. 73), Irenaeus, *Epideixis* 3, cp. also Clement of Alexandria, *Stromateis* 2, 2, 6, 1; 5, 6, 38, 6 (P. Th. Camelot, *op. cit.*, p. 53 n. 4). – Athanasius does not betray any profound knowledge of Neo-Platonism. There is a fairly general reference to the doctrine of the three divine Principles, see *De Decretis Nicaenae Synodi* 28 (PG 25, 468B): ... ὃν λέγουσιν ἐκ τοῦ ἀγαθοῦ νοῦν καὶ τὴν ἐκ τοῦ νοῦ ψυχήν ... There are some other possible reminiscences of Neo-Platonic ideas (see e.g. C.G. 34, *infra*, 113 ff.), but these could also stem from Middle Platonism. On the goodness of the Creator see C.G. 41, *infra*, 135 f., on Athanasius' thoughts on man as God's image see also J. B. Schoemann, Eikon in den Schriften des hl. Athanasius, *Scholastik* (16) 1941, pp. 340 f.

"And through the likeness to Him He made man in such a way that he could behold and know that which is really, giving him also an idea and knowledge of his own eternity, that, preserving his identity, he may never abandon the contemplation of God and never turn away from life with the saints, but, keeping the grace of the Giver, keeping also his own power which he received from the Father's Word, may rejoice in and communicate with the Divine living the truly immortal life which knows no sorrows and is blessed."

Man is not only created in God's image but also in God's likeness (*Genesis* 1:26), ὁμοίωσις. Just like other Christian writers Athanasius seems to interpret *Genesis* 1:26 *inter alia* in the light of the famous statement made by Plato, *Theaetetus* 176A-B, that the goal of human life is to flee from here to the ideas and that this flight is to become like God as far as possible: διὸ καὶ πειρᾶσθαι χρὴ ἐνθένδε ἐκεῖσε φεύγειν ὅτι τάχιστα. Φυγὴ δὲ ὁμοίωσις θεῷ κατὰ τὸ δυνατόν (see on this subject H. Merki, ΟΜΟΙΩΣΙΣ ΘΕΩ, *Von der platonischen Angleichung an Gott zur Gottähnlichkeit bei Gregor von Nyssa*, Freiburg 1952; J. H. Waszink, Der Platonismus und die altchristliche Gedankenwelt, *Entretiens sur l'Antiquité classique* III, Vandoeuvres-Genève 1955, pp. 29 ff., C. W. Müller, *Gleiches zu Gleichem. Ein Prinzip frühgriechischen Denkens*, Wiesbaden 1965, pp. 180 ff.). Here in *C.G.* 2 Athanasius explains man's being created in God's likeness as implying that man can contemplate and know τὰ ὄντα. The Biblical background may be *Sap. Sal.* 7:17: αὐτὸς γάρ μοι ἔδωκεν τῶν ὄντων γνῶσιν ἀψευδῆ, but there τὰ ὄντα seems to stand for 'created things' whilst Athanasius, as appears from τὰ νοητά and τὰ θεῖα which are used as synonyms of τὰ ὄντα further on in this chapter, must think of the truly Divine which cannot be seen by bodily eyes, but by the human mind which transcends the physical world. Similar statements appear in the writings of Platonists, see e.g. Albinus, *Epit.* 3, 1, who says that theoretical life lies ἔν τε τῇ θέα καὶ τῇ τῶν ὄντων γνώσει, Numenius, *fragment* 2 (ed. Des Places, = *fr.* 11 ed. Leemans): δεῖ τινα ἀπελθόντα πόρρω ἀπὸ τῶν αἰσθητῶν ὁμιλῆσαι τῷ ἀγαθῷ μόνῳ μόνον, Porphyry, *Sent.* 33, 3 who says that one can speak of ἀρεταὶ πρὸς θεωρίαν which are καθάρσεις ... τῆς ψυχῆς ἀφισταμένης πρὸς τὸ ὄντως ὄν. So original man is here portrayed by Athanasius as a Platonic mystic. – Man's immortal life is made dependent on the preservation of his identity which is directed towards God. This is said more clearly in *De Inc.* 3: ... ἔδωκεν (sc. ὁ θεὸς) αὐτοῖς νόμον· ἵνα εἰ μὲν φυλάξαιεν τὴν χάριν καὶ μένοιεν καλοί, ἔχωσι τὴν ἐν παραδείσῳ ἄλυπον καὶ ἀνώδυνον καὶ ἀμέριμνον ζωήν ... εἰ δὲ παραβαῖεν καὶ στραφέντες γένοιντο φαῦλοι, γινώσκοιεν ἑαυτοὺς τὴν ἐν θανάτῳ κατὰ φύσιν φθορὰν ὑπομένειν ...; a similar idea is expressed by e.g. Theophilus, *Ad Autolycum* 2, 27. – Original man is not only portrayed as a Platonic mystic, but also as a Christian ascetic, as appears from the remark that he should live with the saints, i.e. the angels. The Christian ascetic is meant to lead an angelic life, cp. Clement of Alexandria,

Stromateis 7, 12, 78, 6 and 7, 14, 84 (see also *C.G.* 33, *infra*, 109). – Athanasius uses θεός and θεῖον indiscriminately, unlike the author of Ps. Justin, *Cohortatio ad Graecos* 22, who claims that the difference between Moses and Plato is that God is called by Moses ὁ ὤν and by Plato τὸ ὄν.

> "For since he has no obstacle to the knowledge of the Divine, through his own purity he always contemplates the Image of the Father, God the Word in whose image he was made."

The obstacle which original man does not have to knowledge of God is, of course, sin, see *C.G.* 34 (*infra*, 113 f.), where Athanasius says that if man wants to know God in the way he was originally created, then he has to cleanse his soul of the stain of sin, cp. *De Inc.* 57. – Man is created in God's Εἰκών, i.e. the Word. So man is the εἰκών Εἰκόνος, see *De Inc.* 13 where the following reason for the incarnation is given: ὅθεν ὁ τοῦ Θεοῦ Λόγος δ' ἑαυτοῦ παρεγένετο, ἵνα ὡς εἰκὼν ὢν τοῦ Πατρὸς τὸν κατ' εἰκόνα ἄνθρωπον ἀνακτίσαι δυνηθῇ (on man as the εἰκών of God's Εἰκών see also Philo, *De opif. mundi* 25).

> "And he marvels at the knowledge of the providence which is extended through Him to the universe, whereby he is above what can be perceived by senses and all bodily perception and is through the power of his mind tied to the divine and intelligible things in heaven."

In *C.G.* 34 (see *infra*, 114 f.) Athanasius says that when man fails to know God with the purity of the soul which is created in God's image and likeness he can know God through the harmony of the cosmos (which testifies to God's providence). Since it says here in *C.G.* 2 that original man already marvels at the knowledge of God's providence it is clear that knowledge through providence (which is dealt with in *C.G.* 35 ff.) does not come *after* knowledge through the soul, but is possible at the same time.

> "For when the mind of men does not converse with the bodies and has nothing which stems from the desire of the bodies mingled with itself from outside, but in its totality is above, being with itself as it was created from the beginning, then, transcending what is sensible and all that is human, it is exalted to heaven, and seeing the Word it sees in Him also the Father, rejoicing in His contemplation and being renewed in the desire for Him."

Since Athanasius speaks about created man he does not mean that this man has no body, but that his mind is not hindered by bolidy desires. The mind of original man can preserve its identity by concentrating exclusively on God. Desire is evil (see *infra*, 20 ff.), therefore the soul of original man should not be mingled with desire, since God should not be mingled with evil, see *C.G.* 6: οὐ γὰρ ἐκ τοῦ καλοῦ τὸ κακόν, οὐδὲ ἐν αὐτῷ ἐστιν, οὐδὲ δι' αὐτοῦ· ἐπεὶ οὐκέτι καλὸν ἂν εἴη μεμιγμένην ἔχον τὴν φύσιν ...

Original man sees the Logos in His relation with the Father by transcending the physical world, – this is also stressed by Athanasius against the Arians: one has to go beyond the physical realm and one should not speak about the Father and the Son in a bodily and earthly way, see *De Decr.* 24 (PG 25, 457B): Ἐξηρήσθω δὲ πάλιν ἐν τούτοις πᾶς λογισμὸς σωματικός· φαντασίαν τε πάσης αἰσθήσεως ὑπερβάντες, καθαρᾷ τῇ νοήσει καὶ μόνῳ τῷ νῷ νοῶμεν Ψιοῦ πρὸς Πατέρα τὸ γνήσιον, *Contra Arianos* 1, 21 (PG 26, 56), *Ad Serapionem* 4, 6 (PG 26, 476). – It seems strange that Athanasius should say that original man's desire for God was renewed, since such a renewal might imply that the desire was not perfect. Since in original man there was no sin or lack of knowledge of God this can only mean that the desire was constantly being renewed so that it could not decrease at any time. This desire for God is also typical of the Christians, see *De Inc.* 31 (where it says that they are brought to this desire by the risen Christ), and especially of the Christian ascetic, see *Vita Antonii* 45 (PG 26, 909A).

> "In this way then, according to Holy Scripture, the first created man, who is called Adam in Hebrew, had his mind fixed on God in the beginning with an unashamed frankness and lived with the saints in the contemplation of the intelligible, a contemplation which he possessed in that place which the holy Moses figuratively called Paradise."

We regard it as unlikely that Athanasius here in *C.G.* 2-3 treats Adam as a symbolic and not as a historical figure and regards his fall as a timeless example of the fall of any man, whilst in *De Incarnatione Verbi* he bases his expositions on Adam as a historical figure (this view is advanced by A. Louth, The Concept of the Soul in Athanasius, *Studia Patristica* XIII, Berlin 1975, pp. 27 ff.). Adam is not a symbolical figure, but as the place in which he lives is *called* figuratively 'paradise' (a remark with which Athanasius avoids taking sides in the question of where Paradise should be located, in heaven or on earth), so the Hebrew name Adam has the symbolic meaning of '(first) man'. Adam's life and fall in Paradise are treated as both historical and timeless events: the Christian who realizes that his soul has been created in God's image can live in the same way as Adam before the fall, the sinner is a servant of his bodily desires just as Adam was after the fall (we agree with the expositions given by P. Athanasius Recheis, Sancti Athanasii Magni doctrina de primordiis seu quomodo explicaverit Genesin 1-3, *Antonianum* (28) 1953, pp. 244 f.). On Adam's unembarrassed frankness (ἀνεπαίσχυντος παρρησία) see apart from P. Th. Camelot, *op. cit.*, pp. 56 f. n. 1, H. Jaeger, Παρρησία et fiducia, *Studia Patristica* I, Berlin 1957, p. 233 and R. Joly, Sur deux thèmes mystiques de Grégoire de Nysse, *Byzantion* (36) 1966, pp. 127 ff., and *C.G.* 47, *infra*, 152.

"And the purity of the soul has the ability to see through itself even God as in a mirror, as also the Lord says: 'Blessed are the pure in heart, for they shall see God' (*Matthew* 5:8)."

This is a general statement and does not only apply to Adam before the fall. Any man who believes that his soul is created in God's image can know God, see especially *C.G.* 30, *infra*, 99 f. Matthew 5:8 is used by Origen for the same purpose, see e.g. *De Princ.* 1, 1, 9: *Quod si proponat nobis aliquis, quare dictum est: "Beati mundi corde, quoniam ipsi deum videbunt", multo magis etiam ex hoc, ut ego arbitror, assertio nostra firmabitur; nam quid aliud est 'corde deum videre', nisi mente eum intellegere atque cognoscere* (cp. 2, 11, 7. On the comparison of the soul with a mirror see *C.G.* 34, *infra*, 114).

CHAPTER 3

Man's fall from his original state, exemplified by Adam's fall.

Translation and Commentary:

(3) "So, as has been said, the Creator made the human race in this way and wanted it to remain such."

This refers to the fact that man's soul is created in God's image and likeness and that therefore man can contemplate God and can, if he does so, live eternally.

"But men, negligent of the better reality and shrinking from grasping it with their minds sought rather the things which were nearer to them, and what was nearer to them was the body and its sensations. Hence they turned away their mind from the intelligible and started to contemplate themselves and contemplating themselves and preceiving the body and other perceptible things, and so to speak misled in what was their own, fell into the desire for themselves preferring what is their own to the contemplation of the Divine."

Whilst before the fall man transcended in his mind the physical world (including his own body), the fall manifests in itself in the fact that man concentrates on himself (no longer regarding himself as being created in God's Image) and on his body and that he replaces the desire for God by the desires of his body, cp. *C.G.* 8, *infra*, 40 f., and Clement of Alexandria, *Protrept.* 11: ὁ πρῶτος ἐν παραδείσῳ ἔπαιζε λελυμένος, ἐπεὶ παιδίον ἦν τοῦ θεοῦ· ὅτε δὲ ὑποπίπτων ἡδονῇ (ὄφις ἀλληγορεῖται ἡδονὴ ἐπὶ γαστέρα ἔρπουσα, κακία γηΐνη, εἰς ὕλας τρεφομένη) παρήγετο ἐπιθυμίαις, Eusebius, *Praeparatio Evangelica* 7, 2: οἱ μὲν δὴ λοιποὶ πάντες ἄνθρωποι ... τῇ τῶν σωμάτων προσανασχόντες αἰσθήσει τῷ μηδὲν περὶ τῆς ἐν αὐτοῖς ψυχῆς διειληφέναι πλέον τε οὐδὲν τῶν ὁρωμένων ἐν τοῖς οὖσιν ὑπάρχειν ἡγησάμενοι, τὸ καλὸν καὶ συμφέρον καὶ μόνον ἀγαθὸν τῇ τῶν σωμάτων ἀνέφηκαν ἡδονῇ.

"Having spent their time with this and unwilling to withdraw from what is closer to them, they locked their soul in the pleasures of the body, their soul which had been disordered and mixed up with all kinds of desires, and they completely forgot the power which they received in the beginning from God."

In the previous chapter it was stressed that before the fall original man did *not* have his mind mixed up with bodily desires, see *supra*, 17. In itself it is typically Platonic terminology to say that the fall means that man *forgot* about his original destination, since Plato (in connection with the doctrine of *anamnesis*) says that the human soul forgot what it saw in its pre-existence (see e.g. E. Zeller, *Die Philosophie der Griechen in ihrer geschichtlichen Entwicklung* 2, 1, Darmstadt 1963[6], pp. 823 ff.). Most Christians attacked this Platonic doctrine (see e.g. Irenaeus, *Adversus Haereses* 2, 51-2, 52; Tertullian, *De anima* 24, see J. H. Waszink's edition, pp. 303 ff.), but they adopted Plato's terminology by saying that created man forgot his original destination, see here *C.G.* 3 and e.g. Lactance, *Divinae Institutiones* 2, 1, 5. But the difference with Plato is that man forgot *after* having been created, material existence itself is no fall. (It should, however, in this context be noticed that Plato and the Platonists were not dualists in the sense that they spoke exclusively negatively about bodily existence, see A. H. Armstrong, Neoplatonic Valuations of Nature, Body and Intellect. An Attempt to understand some Ambiguities, *Augustinian Studies* 1972, pp. 35 ff. and C. J. de Vogel, Was Plato a Dualist?, *Theta-Pi* (1) 1972, pp. 4-60.)

"One could see this to be true also from the very first created man, as Holy Scripture tells about him. For he, too, as long as he had his mind fixed on God and His contemplation, turned away from contemplation of the body."

As in the previous chapter the historical character of the first man is not doubted and his conduct is portrayed as typical of man in general.

"But when at the instigation of the serpent he stopped directing his mind towards God and began to contemplate himself, then they fell into the desire of the body and realized that they were naked and realizing this they were ashamed. They realized that they were not so much devoid of clothes, but that they had become divested of the contemplation of the Divine and that they had transferred their mind to the opposite."

The serpent is, of course, the devil, see *De Inc.* 5: οἱ δὲ ἄνθρωποι, ἀποστραφέντες τὰ αἰώνια, καὶ συμβουλίᾳ τοῦ διαβόλου εἰς τὰ τῆς φθορᾶς ἐπιστραφέντες ... Adam and Eve were ashamed when they realized that they were naked, i.e. divested of the contemplation of the Divine. This is the opposite of original man before the fall who had his mind directed towards God with unashamed frankness, see *supra*, 19 (see also *C.G.* 47, *infra*, 152).

> "For having turned away from the contemplation of and desire for the One and the Being, I mean God, they furthermore embarked on desires different from the desire for God, especially on the separate desires of the body."

The characterization of God as the Being goes back to *Exodus* 3:14 (cp. *Sapientia Salomonis* 13:17): Ἐγώ εἰμι ὁ Ὤν, which the Christians used to interpret in a Platonic way, cp. P. Munz, Sum qui sum, *Hibbert Journal* (50) 1951/52, p. 147. – The desire of the one God is contrasted with the multitude of bodily desires. On the difference between the one and the many cp. *C.G.* 23, *infra*, 82: ἐκπεσόντες γὰρ ἀπὸ τῆς πρὸς τὸν ἕνα θεὸν κατανοήσεως εἰς πολλὰ καὶ διάφορα καταπεπτώκασιν, *C.G.* 39: (λόγος φυσικὸς) τὸ ἓν καὶ τέλειον τῶν διαφόρων κρεῖττον εἶναι. Biblical background may be *Ecclesiastes* 7:30: Ὁ θεὸς τὸν ἄνθρωπον ἐποίησεν εὐθῆ· αὐτοὶ δὲ ἐζήτησαν λογισμοὺς πολλούς, quoted in *C.G.* 7, see *infra*, 37, and *Sapientia Salomonis* 9:15: φθαρτὸν γὰρ σῶμα βαρύνει ψυχήν, καὶ βρίθει τὸ γεῶδες σκῆνος, νοῦν πολυφρόντιδα. The philosophical background consists of Plato's expositions on the one and the many in the *Parmenides* which were well known in Neo-Platonism (see E. F. Osborn, *The Philosophy of Clement of Alexandria*, Cambridge 1957, pp. 17 ff. and P. Merlan's paper, The old Academy, *The Cambridge History of Later Greek and Early Medieval Philosophy*, ed. by A. H. Armstrong, Cambridge 1970[2], p. 22). Origen describes creation itself as a fall from an original unity into a diversity, see *De Princ.* 2, 1, 1; this is not Athanasius' view: the fall from contemplation of the one God to contemplation of the many bodily desires takes place *after* creation.

> "Then, as tends to happen, having received a desire for each separate thing and a multitude of things they began to adopt the corresponding attachment towards them so that they were also afraid of losing them."

Desire for material possession may be (temporarily) satisfied, but it leads to the fear of losing again what one possesses, cp. Hilary, *De Trinitate* 1, 1.

> "Hence the soul became in addition subject to anxiety, fear, pleasure and thoughts of mortality. For being unwilling to turn away from desires it fears death and the separation from the body."

Desire inevitably leads to fear of death, since in death one will definitively lose all one has acquired. In *De Inc.* 28 Athanasius argues that the sinners' natural fear of death is overcome by Christ. Death as a separation (of the soul) from the body is a Stoic definition, see *Stoicorum veterum fragmenta* 2, fr. 604: ἐπεὶ γὰρ ὁ θάνατος μέν ἐστι χωρισμὸς ἀπὸ τοῦ σώματος, cp. J. H. Waszink's edition of Tertullian, *De anima*, p. 527.

> "And desiring again but not obtaining similar things it learned to murder and commit injustice. It is right to indicate, as best we can, how it does this, too."

Once a desire is satisfied, one desires again similar things, i.e. more. Since not all desires can be fulfilled man becomes frustrated and aggressive and turns against his fellow men.

CHAPTER 4

Man uses his free will in the wrong way and turns to evil, i.e. non-being.

Translation and Commentary:

(4) "Having turned away from the contemplation of the intelligible things and misusing the separate faculties of the body, delighting in the contemplation of the body, and seeing that pleasure is something good for itself, it erroneously misused the word 'good' and thought that pleasure is the really good."

It should be noted that Athanasius does not, of course, regard the created world as bad – it is good since it has been created by the good Creator (see *C.G.* 6, *infra*, 32 f.). The bodily realm becomes evil when it is regarded as the only reality and turns away man's attention from God; on bodily pleasure as evil see *supra*, 20 ff.

> "It is as if somebody, deranged in his mind and asking for a sword to use against whoever he meets regards this behaviour as showing self-control."

When the human soul behaves in such a way it does not exert its power to distinguish between good and evil, see *C.G.* 31 (*infra*, 103): ἀμέλει καὶ ξίφους λαβέσθαι δύναται ἡ χείρ ... ἀλλ' οὐκ οἶδεν ὅτι βλάπτει ταῦτα, εἰ μὴ ὁ νοῦς διακρίνῃ. As has been noticed (see L. Leone, *Sancti Athanasii Archiepiscopi Alexandriae Contra Gentes. Introduzione-Testo critico-Traduzione.* Napels 1965, p. 7; P. Th. Camelot, *op. cit.*, p. 60, n. 1), this image is derived from Plato, *Republic* I 331 C, who says that it is not right to give back weapons to somebody who gave the weapons when he was sane and wants them back at a time when he is insane (Cicero, *De Officiis* 3, 25, 95 replaces 'weapons' by 'a sword', just as Athanasius does here in *C.G.* 4). A reader who knew about this background might interpret ἀπαιτῶν as 'asking back'.

"And having become a lover of pleasure it started practising it in various ways. For being in its nature easily moved, it does not stop moving although it has turned away from the good. So it moves no longer in accordance with virtue and not in such a way as to contemplate God."

Athanasius calls the soul εὐκίνητος, this may be a reminiscence of Plato, *Phaedrus* 245 C, where the souls is called ἀεικίνητος. But there this word appears in the context of the doctrine of pre-existence, to which Athanasius is opposed, see *infra*, 109, *C.G.* 33. Plotinus, too, says of the weakness of the human soul that this appears from the fact that it is εὐκίνητος πρὸς ἐπιθυμίας, see *Enn.* 1, 8, 14, 3, cf. Origen, *De Princ.* 1, 8, 4 (ed. Görgemanns/Karpp, p. 282).

"But reflecting on what is not it changes its own power, misusing it for the desires it imagined, since it was also created with a free will. For as it can verge towards the good, it can also turn away from the good."

Man's original power, which he received in being created in God's image and likeness was that he could contemplate the good God (see *supra*, 16 ff.), he misuses this power when he starts contemplating evil. He can turn his attention in both directions, since he has been created with a free will. All early Christian theologians stress free will against Gnostic determinism (see e.g. the list given by L. Leone, *op. cit.*, p. 7). In *Contra Gentes* Athanasius uses free will for apologetic purposes: in *C.G.* 34 he says that as man could turn to evil he can turn to good again as well: δύνανται γάρ, ὥσπερ ἀπεστράφησαν τῇ διανοίᾳ τὸν Θεὸν καὶ τὰ οὐκ ὄντα ἀνεπλάσαντο εἰς θεούς, οὕτως ἀναβῆναι τῷ νῷ τῆς ψυχῆς, καὶ πάλιν ἐπιστρέψαι πρὸς τὸν θεόν. In his polemics against the Arians Athanasius denies that Christ and God have a free will as man has, and the reason he gives is that man's free will means ambiguity: he can want this today and the opposite tomorrow. The technical term which expresses this ambiguity is τὴν ῥοπὴν εἰς ἑκάτερα ἔχειν, see e.g. *Contra Arianos* 1, 52 (PG 26, 121A); 3, 62 (PG 26, 453C); 3, 66 (PG 26, 464B). If God had a free will in the same way, there would be arbitrariness in God, a completely unacceptable idea. A similar evaluation of free will appears in Albinus who places the possible (τὸ δυνατόν) between what is true and what is false and says that free will (τὸ ἐφ' ἡμῖν) so to speak rides on the possible which cannot be determined, see *Epitome* 26, 3: ἡ δὲ τοῦ δυνατοῦ φύσις πέπτωκε μέν πως μεταξὺ τοῦ τε ἀληθοῦς καὶ τοῦ ψευδοῦς, ἀορίστῳ δὲ ὄντι αὐτῷ τῇ φύσει ὥσπερ ἐποχεῖται τὸ ἐφ' ἡμῖν. He then goes on to say that the possible, being undecided in free will, can be realized in several ways which can be opposite to each other: ἀοριστοῖνον (sc. τὸ δυνατὸν) δὲ τῷ ἐφ' ἡμῖν κατὰ τὴν ἐφ' ὁπότερον ῥοπὴν λαμβάνει τὸ ἀληθεύειν ἢ μή.

"And turning away from the good it necessarily considers the opposite. For it cannot completely stop its motion, since it is, as I said before, in its nature easily moved. And knowing its free will, it sees that it can use its bodily members in both directions towards what is and towards what is not. What is is the good, what is not is the evil. And I call the good what is, since it has its exemplars from God who is. And I call the evil what is not, since, having no reality, it has been fashioned by the imagination of men."

Athanasius wants to exclude the idea that evil is a created substance, see *C.G.* 6, *infra*, 30 ff. Evil is the wrong use of free will manifesting itself in the wrong use of the body. It is false imagination to think that this wrong use of the body for pleasure is a reality. – The good is what is, since it has its exemplars from God who is. This statement could be a reminiscence of the Middle Platonic doctrine of the ideas. Plato himself already uses παράδειγμα as a synonym for 'idea' (see *Timaeus* 28A, 37C) and in later Platonism it appears to be a technical term for 'idea'. This can be gathered from Albinus who calls the second principle in Plato (besides matter and God) the ἀρχὴ παραδειγματική, τουτέστι ἡ τῶν ἰδεῶν (see *Epit.* 9, 1). Similarly Irenaeus and Hippolytus, obviously following a Middle-Platonic manual, call Plato's second principle, i.e. the ideas, παράδειγμα (see *Refutatio* 1, 19, 1 and *Adversus Haereses* 2, 18, 3). In Middle-Platonism and in Philo the ideas are not outside the Creator, but are the thoughts of the Creator (cp. W. Theiler, *Die Vorbereitung des Neuplatonismus*, Berlin/Zürich 1964² (Vorwort)). Christians adopted this doctrine (see H. A. Wolfson, *The Philosophy of the Church Fathers*, Cambridge 1956, pp. 257 ff.; J. H. Waszink, Bemerkungen zum Einfluss des Platonismus im frühen Christentum, *Vigiliae Christianae* (19), 1965, pp. 139 ff.). Athanasius says here obviously something similar. – Evil is qualified as non-being. On the surface this is Neo-Platonic thought, but in fact only Neo-Platonic terminology is adopted. Athanasius does not produce Plotinus' view that matter as the absolute non-being is evil (see on this A. H. Armstrong, Plotinus, *The Cambridge History of Later Greek and Early Medieval Philosophy*, pp. 256 ff.; see also *infra*, 29 ff.). Athanasius is here in line with Origen, *De Principiis* 2, 9, 2: ... *desidia et laboris taedium in servando bono et aversio ac neglegentia meliorum initium dedit recedendi a bono. Recedere autem a bono non aliud est quam effici in malo. Certum namque est malum esse bono carere*, see also *In Joann.* 2, 13.

"For although the body has eyes to see creation and to know the Creator through this harmonious order, and although it also possesses hearing in order to hear the divine words and the laws of God, and although it also has hands in order to do what is necessary and in order to spread them out towards the prayer to God, the soul having turned away from the contemplation of the good, and from the movement in the good, it further erroneously moves in the opposite direction."

When the soul turns to evil it no longer exerts its power over the body in order to make the body do the right things and avoid the wrong things. This will be stated extensively in *C.G.* 31-32, see *infra*, 102 ff. Original man contemplated God's providence over the creation, the sinner sees no longer that this world has been created and therefore points towards the Creator. Man has ears to hear the divine words and laws: it seems unlikely that this applies to the Old Testament, rather to the fact that the soul, by being created in God's image, knows the laws of good and evil, see *C.G.* 32, *infra*, 107. The body has hands to do the necessary things and to pray. These 'necessary things' could be the things which are absolutely necessary for life and which man needs to do without occupying himself with these things more than necessary, cp. Clement of Alexandria, *Stromateis* 6, 12, 99, 6 f.: αἱ κτήσεις γὰρ καὶ χρήσεις τῶν ἀναγκαίων οὐ τὴν ποιότητα ἔχουσι βλαβεράν, ἀλλὰ τὴν παρὰ τὸ μέτρον ποσότητα. διόπερ τὰς ἐπιθυμίας ὁ γνωστικὸς περιγράφει κατά τε τὴν κτῆσιν κατά τε τὴν χρῆσιν, οὐχ' ὑπερβαίνων τὸν τῶν ἀναγκαίων ὅρον. But in *Strom.* 4, 5, 21, 1 ff. he calls contemplation and pure sinlessness necessary and says that poverty is an obstacle for this (cp. also Augustin's distinction between *res necessaria* which is necessary for the body and temporal, and *res permansura* which concentrates on the eternal good, *De Civ.* 10, 14, Martha is occupied with the *res necessaria*, Mary with the *res permansura*, see *Sermo* 255, 2, 2; 255, 6, 6; *De Trin.* 1, 10, 20, – the *vitae necessaria* are eating and drinking and procreation, see *Sermo* 51, 14, 23-24). So when Athanasius says that man no longer used his hands for the necessary things and prayer, he either means with the 'necessary things' contemplation of which man forsook (and in that case 'prayer' would be an exposition), or he means the things which are necessary in order to survive, but then wants to say that man did more than was necessary, since he was a slave of bodily desire.

> "Then seeing its power, as I said before, and misusing it, it realized that it could also move the bodily members in the opposite direction."

The power of the soul is free will, as was said earlier in this chapter.

> "And therefore instead of looking at the creation, it turns its eye away towards desires, showing that it can do that, too, and thinking that by just being in motion it preserves its own dignity and does not sin in doing what it can do, not knowing that it was not created in order merely to move but to move towards what it should do. Therefore the apostolic saying commands: *All things are allowed, but not all things are expedient* (*1 Cor.* 6:12)."

The possibility to move is not good in itself. The right use of this possibility is needed (cp. Albinus' remarks on the possible and free will, quoted *supra*, 24). A man who misuses his liberty by failing to distinguish between good and evil lives on the level of the animals which have no ψυχὴ λογική, see *C. G.* 31, *infra*, 102 ff. - Irenaeus, too, uses *1 Cor.* 6:12 in explaining man's free will, see *Adv. Haer.* 4, 60, 2: *Et propter hoc Paulus ait*: *Omnia licent, sed non omnia expediunt; et libertatem referens hominis, quapropter et omnia licent, non cogente eum Deo; et id, non expedit, ostendens, ut non ad velamen malitiae abutamur libertate, non enim hoc expedit.*

CHAPTER 5

Further description of the sinner's activities.

Translation and Commentary:

(5) "But the audacity of men, having fixed its eye not on what is expedient and becoming but on its own ability, started doing the opposite."

Here the word 'audacity', τόλμα, which is of some importance in the writings of Plotinus (see A. H. Armstrong's paper, Plotinus, *The Cambridge History* etc., pp. 242 ff., who says that this thought should neither be overestimated nor underestimated in Plotinus and who shows that in the thought of Plotinus man's existence is not only caused by this illicit self-assertion, but is also the result of the giving out of the One) is used (cp. *C. G.* 9, *infra*, 44). But this is not a τόλμα which leads to existence, but it is a τόλμα in man who has already received his existence from God. - The audacity started to do the opposite of what is expedient.

"Hence, moving the hands in the opposite direction it made them kill and it turned its hearing to disobedience and its other members towards adultery instead of lawful procreation."

The hands were meant for doing necessary things and for prayer, the ears for hearing the words and laws of God, see *supra*, 26. Here it says that man received his sexual organs for lawful procreation, a similar view is e.g. expressed by Clement of Alexandria, *Paedagogus* 2, 10, 83-115, *Stromateis* 2, 23, 137, 1: Ἐπεὶ δὲ ἡδονῇ καὶ ἐπθυμίᾳ ὑποπίπτειν γάμος δοκεῖ, καὶ περὶ τούτου διαληπτέον. γάμος μὲν οὖν ἐστι σύνοδος ἀνδρὸς καὶ γυναικὸς ἡ πρώτη κατὰ νόμον ἐπὶ γνησίων τέκνων σπορᾷ; cp. 3, 3, 12 ff.; Tertullian, *Ad Ux.* 1, 2. Orthodox Christians wanted to take an in-between position between the rigorous sexual asceticism of Marcion and the licentiousness which they detected in the gods of the Pagans and many of their worshippers, see *infra*, 45 ff., 86 ff.

"And it turned its tongue instead of the use of good words towards blasphemy, abuse and perjury, and again the hands towards stealing and beating fellow men, its sense of smell towards all kinds of erotic perfumes, and the feet for quick bloodshed, and the stomach towards drunkenness and insatiable surfeit."

This catalogue of actions by the various members of the body reoccurs in *C.G.* 31, see *infra*, 102 ff., it is presented in the form of a "Lasterkatalog" also in *De Inc.* 5 (for literature on the subject of "Lasterkataloge" see O. Michel, *Der Brief an die Römer*, Göttingen 1963[12], p. 70, n. 1). Some of these sinful actions are discussed extensively by Clement of Alexandria: on the use of improper language see *Paedagogus* 2, 6, 49-52, on erotic perfumes see *Paedagogus* 2, 67, 2, on gluttony and drinking see *Paedagogus* 2, 1, 1-2, 2, 34. Athanasius says that man's stomach has an insatiable gluttony. Elsewhere he says more in general that man is insatiable in inventing evil, see *C.G.* 8: καὶ κόρον οὐ λαμβάνοντες τῶν πρώτων ἄλλοις πάλιν ἐνεπίμπλαντο κακοῖς, προκόπτοντες ἐν τοῖς αἰσχίστοις, *De Inc.* 5: ... ἀκόρεστοι περὶ τὸ ἁμαρτάνειν γεγόνασι. The background could be Origen's doctrine that the fall of the soul is caused by the fact that the soul has lost its desire to be filled with the good by contemplation, see *De Princ.* 1, 3, 8 (and the quotation given *supra*, 22). Then Athanasius might suggest that whilst man loses his desire for the good, his desire for evil is insatiable (see on this subject M. Harl, Recherches sur l'origénisme d'Origène: la "satiété" (κόρος) de la contemplation comme motif de la chute des âmes, *Studia Patristica*, VIII, Berlin 1966, pp. 373 ff. (on Athanasius, *C.G.* 8 see p. 384).

> "All this is evil and sin of the soul. And this has as its only cause the abandoning of what is better. For it is as when a charioteer mounting the horse wagon in the statium neglects the goal to which he ought to drive and, turning away from it, simply drives his horse as he can, and he can as he wants to."

For the abandoning of what is better see also *C.G.* 3, *supra*, 20. The soul's relation to the body is here compared with the relation of the charioteer to his horses. This image reappears in *C.G.* 32 where it says that the body is driven by the nod of somebody else: τὸ σῶμα ... καὶ πρὸς τὸ ἐκείνου νεῦμα ἡνιοχεῖται ... ὥσπερ οὐδὲ ἵππος ἑαυτὸν ὑποζεύγνυσιν, ἀλλ' ὑπὸ τοῦ κρατοῦντος ἐλαύνεται. This seems to be a combination of Plato, *Phaedrus* 246/247, where the reasonable part of the soul is compared with a charioteer who drives two horses, a good one and a bad one (these are the two lower parts τὸ θυμοειδές and τὸ ἐπιθυμητικόν) and Plato, *Timaeus* 69C: ὄχημά τε πᾶν τὸ σῶμα ἔδοσαν (sc. τῇ ψυχῇ οἱ θεοί), the former place is quoted e.g. by Clement of Alexandria, *Strom.* 5, 8, 52 f. (who quotes Plato as speaking of *one* horse), also the latter place was well known amongst Christians (see J. H. Waszink's edition of Tertullian, *De anima*, p. 542, commentary on *De anima* 53, 3). Athanasius leaves out the tripartition of the soul and speaks about the body as Plato speaks about that part of the soul which is ἐπιθυνητικόν. – The charioteer drives the horse as he can and he can as he wants to: there is a clear element of arbitrariness in this *will* of the charioteer, cf. *C.G.* 7: ... ἄνθρωποι κατὰ στέρησιν τῆς τοῦ καλοῦ φαντασίας ἑαυτοῖς ἐπινοεῖν ἤρξαντο καὶ ἀναπλάττειν, καὶ ἅπερ βούλονται.

> "And often he moves towards those who meet him, and often he drives over the edges, carried wherever he carries himself with the speed of the horses, thinking that if he races in this way, he does not miss the goal, for he only looks at the track and does not see that he has got out of the direction towards the goal. Similarly the soul, having turned away from the road towards God and moving the bodily members improperly, or rather being moved itself by itself together with the bodily members, sins and creates evil for itself, not seeing that it has gone off the road and got outside the goal of truth, which the blessed Paul, the bearer of Christ, envisaged when he said: *I press towards the goal for the price of the call above of Jesus Christ* (Phil. 3:14)."

Since the missing of the goal is a life ruled by bodily pleasures, the goal must be ascetic life, the purity of heart, cp. M. Harl, Le Guetteur et la Cible: Les deux sens de *skopos* dans la langue religieuse des Chrétiens, *Revue des études grecques* (74), 1961, especially pp. 456 ff. – The motive is again that the soul does not exert its ability to direct the body towards the good and to make it avoid evil, *C.G.* 31, *infra*, 102 ff.; instead it is ruled itself by the body. – The road towards God is the soul itself, *viz.*, when it realizes that it has been created in God's image in order to contemplate God, see *supra*, 16 ff., *C.G.* 2, and *infra*, 99 ff., *C.G.* 30.

"So the holy man, fixing his eyes on the good, never worked evil."

Knowing the nature and destiny of the soul Paul did not sin.

CHAPTER 6

Attack on the dualistic views held by some Greek philosophers and some heretics.

Translation and Commentary:

> (6) "Now some of the Greeks, having gone off the road, and not knowing Christ, gave as their opinion that evil is a substance and exists by itself, thereby erring for the following two reasons: either they deprive the Creator of being the Maker of what is, for He will not be the Lord of what is, if, at least in their view, evil has a substance and being by itself, or, on the other hand, if they want Him to be the Maker of all things, they will necessarily admit that He is also the Maker of evil, for in their view evil, too, belongs to what is. But this would appear to be absurd and impossible, for evil does not stem from what is good, neither is it in the good or through the good. For it would no longer be good if its nature were mixed or if it were the cause of evil."

So Athanasius argues that if one believes evil to exist by itself one has either to deny that God is the Creator of all things (since then He would be the Creator of evil as well) or one has indeed to assert that God is the Creator of evil. – Whom does Athanasius attack here? R. W. Thomson, *op. cit.*, p. 15 n. 1 to ch. 6, thinks that here the Gnostics and Manicheans are attacked; P. Th. Camelot believes that Athanasius has the Gnostics, especially the Marcionites, in mind: *op. cit.*, pp. 64 f. n. 1. We regard this as unlikely. In *De Inc.* 2 Athanasius makes a similar attack on the cosmology of Greek philosophers and heretics; there he attacks the heretics for introducing a creator of all things besides the Father of Jesus Christ. Here in *C.G.* 6 (see *infra*, 32) he accuses them of introducing a creator of evil besides the Father of Jesus Christ. Before mentioning the heretics he attacks in *De Inc.* 2 Greek philosophers, *viz.*, the Epicureans who deny creation and providence and Plato who teaches a creation out of an already existing matter, in *C.G.* 6 he attacks before the heretics 'some of the Greeks' who teach that evil is a substance of its own. As Athanasius says in *De Inc.* 1 he repeats in the opening chapters of the *De Incarnatione Verbi* what was said in the *Contra Gentes* (Εἰς δὲ τὴν περὶ τούτων διήγησιν, χρεία τῆς τῶν προειρημένων μνήμης). If the attack on the Greeks and the heretics in *De Inc.* is meant as a repetition of what was said before, then these attacks must appear in the *Contra Gentes* as well. The heretics are clearly attacked in both *C.G.* 6 and *De Inc.* 2. In *De Inc.* 2 both the Epicureans and Plato are explicitly mentioned. The Epicureans are attacked in *C.G.* 37 f. as well (see *infra*, 122 ff.), so it is most likely that the 'some of the Greeks' mentioned here in *C.G.* 6 must be Plato and his followers. They teach, according to Athanasius, that evil is a substance of its own. He says that the heretics introduce a creator of evil, besides the Father of Jesus Christ, 'evil' can here only mean 'the world'. So Athanasius in the case of the Greeks attacks the doctrine that evil, i.e. the world, is a substance of its down ('evil' must mean in both cases 'the world', since no distinction is made). A difficulty is that the Platonists do not say that the world is evil, on the contrary, Plato says in the *Timaeus* that the good Creator created the world, which is as good as possible (see *Timaeus* 29E, a section which Athanasius knew, see *C.G.* 41, *infra*, 135 ff.). But then was a controversy in Platonism as to whether Plato regarded matter as the source of evil or the wrong movements of the soul (see C. Baeumker, *Das Problem der Materie in der griechischen Philosophie*, Münster 1890, pp. 110 ff., 371 ff.; F. P. Hager, Die Materie und das Böse im antiken Platonismus, *Museum Helveticum* (19) 1962, pp. 73 ff.; and *Die Vernunft und das Problem des Bösen im Rahmen der platonischen Ethik und Metaphysik*, Bern 1963, pp. 230 ff.). Athanasius, having stated as his own position that the wrong movements of the soul are the cause of evil, here obviously ascribes to Plato and his followers the view that matter is (the cause of) evil (cp. Ps-Justin Martyr, *Cohortatio ad Graecos* 20 and Lactance, *Epit.* 63). And since the evil 'some of the Greeks' and the heretics speak of must be the same as the evil only the heretics speak about, and since the evil the heretics have in mind is the world, Athanasius even goes even a step further and accuses the Platonists of holding the view that the world is evil (which they do not say). Athanasius may have felt justified in making this accusation by believing that if the world has been created out of an evil matter, then the world itself must be evil. Like many ancient writers, Athanasius uses to pin down his opponents consequences of their views, which they themselves would not have drawn (cp. G. C. Stead, Rhetorical Method in Athanasius, pp. 128 ff.). Athanasius lists two objections against the Platonic view that evil, i.e. matter and the world, is a substance of its own. Either God is not the Creator of the world; the same argument appears in *De Inc.* 2 in his opposition against the doctrine that the world has been created out of pre-existent matter: καθόλου γὰρ οὐδὲ κτίστης ἂν λεχθείη, εἴ γε μὴ κτίζει τὴν ὕλην ἐξ ἧς καὶ τὰ κτισθέντα γέγονεν. Or they will have to admit that God is the cause of evil (if matter or the world, i.e. evil) has been created by God. Athanasius will certainly have known that Plato and the Platonists were opposed to the idea that God is the cause of evil, see e.g. *Rep.* X 617E: αἰτία ἑλομένου θεὸς ἀναίτιος (quoted by Justin Martyr *Apol.* I 44), Plutarch, *De an. procr.* 1015C: ... Πλάτων ... τοῦ θεοῦ τὴν τῶν κακῶν αἰτίαν ἀπωτάτω τιθέμενος, Porphyry, *Epist. ad Marc.* 24: κακῶν ἀνθρώπῳ οὐδεὶς θεὸς αἴτιος, ἀλλὰ αὐτὸς ἑαυτῷ ὁ ἑλόμενος, Celsus is quoted by Origen, *Contra Celsum* 4, 66: ἐκ τοῦ μὲν οὐκ ἔστι κακά, ὕλῃ δὲ πρόσκειται. So Athanasius may want to show that the Platonists' doctrine that evil, i.e. matter and the world, is a substance of its own forces them into an idea which they oppose: God is the cause of evil, if at least they want to maintain their doctrine that God is the Creator of the world. The Platonists are confronted with the crude dilemma: either God is not the Creator or He is the Creator of evil. The differentiated view of the Platonists that the world is as good as possible, but that it has been created out of evil matter, is not discussed. (Similarly he will present the Arians with the crude dilemma: either Christ is fully God or He is merely a man, their differentiated view that He is God's first and most outstanding creature not being taken seriously, cp. G. C. Stead, *op. cit.*, p. 129.) – When Athanasius says that according to some Greeks evil is ἐν ὑποστάσει καὶ καθ' ἑαυτήν his formulation comes close to αὐθυπόστατον, a word which the Platonists use for good and evil, see H. Dörrie, Ὑπόστασις. Wort und Bedeutungsgeschichte, *Nachrichten der Akademie der Wissenschaften in Göttingen*, Phil.-hist. Klasse (1955), p. 66. – For the statement that evil is neither out of nor in nor through the good cp. *C. G.* 7: τὸ κακὸν οὐ παρὰ Θεοῦ οὐδὲ ἐν Θεῷ οὔτε ἐξ ἀρχῆς γέγονεν οὔτε οὐσία τίς ἐστιν αὐτοῦ.

"But those who belong to the heretics, having lapsed from the ecclesiastical instruction, and having suffered shipwreck in their faith, they, too, hold the wrong view that there is a substance of evil. And they shape for themselves in contrast to the true Father of Christ another god and regard him as the unbegotten Maker and Source of evil and the Creator of creation."

The Marcionites are obviously meant here, cp. the brief summary of Marcion's doctrine given by Irenaeus, *Adv. Haer.* 1, 25, 1: *Marcion Ponticus ... impudorate blasphemans eum qui a lege et prophetis annunciatus est Deus, malorum factorem ... Jesum autem ab eo Patre, qui est super mundi fabricatorem Deum*, Hippolytus, *Ref.* 10, 19: οἱ δὲ πάντες τὸν μὲν ἀγαθὸν οὐδὲν ὅλως πεποιηκέναι, τὸν δὲ δίκαιον, οἱ μὲν τὸν πονηρόν, οἱ δὲ μόνον δίκαιον ὀνομάζουσι, πεποιηκέναι δὲ τὰ πάντα φάσκουσιν ἐκ τῆς ὑποκειμένης ὕλης, πεποιηκέναι γὰρ οὐ καλῶς, ἀλλ' ἀλόγως. Tertullian, too, says that Marcion taught a creation out of matter, *Adv. Marc.* 1, 15, 4. We regard it as likely that Athanasius here ascribes the same doctrine to Marcion, and in naming Marcion after 'some of the Greeks', i.e. Plato, he can suggest that Marcion adopted his doctrine from Greek philosophy. This was a usual charge made against the heretics; their patriarchs are Greek philosophers, see Tertullian, *De anima* 3, 1, cp. J. H. Waszink's edition, p. 115; Athanasius makes the same charge against the Arians, see *Contra Arianos* 1, 30 ff. (PG 26, 73 ff.), *De Decr.* 28 (PG 25, 468 f.) (in connection with the word ἀγένητος).

"But one could easily refute these people both from Scripture and from human reason itself out of which they shaped these ideas, too, in their mad imagination."

The Marcionites cannot, of course, base their doctrine on Scripture, only on reason which has gone mad. Therefore they can easily be refuted with Scripture and sound reason. Similarly Irenaeus refutes the Gnostics (and Marcion) both with reasonable arguments (in the second book of the *Adversus Haereses*) and with Scriptural ones (in the third, fourth and fifth book, see the *Praefatio* to book III).

"Now our Lord and Saviour Jesus Christ says in His gospels confirming the words of Moses: '*The Lord God is one*' (*Mark* 12:29, *Deut.* 6:4) and '*I confess Thee, Father, Lord of heaven and earth*' (*Matth.* 11:25). But if God is one, and if He is the Lord of heaven and earth, how could there be another god in contrast to Him?"

It is important that Jesus confirms the words of Moses, since hereby

He indicates that the God of the Old Testament is His Father as well. Irenaeus refers to the same texts when he wants to show that Christ called the Creator His Father, see *Adv. Haer.* 4, 2. Athanasius draws a reasonable conclusion from these two texts by saying that if there is only one God, the Creator, there can be no other God besides Him.

> "And where will their god be, since the only and true God fills all things embracing heaven and earth."

The same argument appears in Athenagoras, *Leg.* 8: εἰ δὲ ἰδίᾳ ἕκαστος αὐτῶν, ὄντος τοῦ τὸν κόσμον πεποιηκότος ἀνωτέρω τῶν γεγονότων καὶ ὑπὲρ ἃ ἐποίησέ τε καὶ ἐκόσμησεν, ποῦ ὁ ἕτερος ἢ οἱ λοιποί; Tertullian, *Adv. Marc.* 1, 11, 3: *Denique si universitas creatoris est, iam nec locum video dei alterius. Plena et occupata sunt omnia suo auctore*; Irenaeus, *Adv. Haer.* 2, 1: *Quemadmodum enim poterit super hunc alia plenitudo, aut initium, aut potestas, aut alius Deus esse: cum oporteat Deum horum omnium pleroma in immenso omnia circumcontinere, et circumcontineri a nemine?*

> "And how could there be also another Maker of those things of which the God and Father of Christ is Lord according to the Saviour's word? Or it would have to be that they say that the evil god can become the Lord of the creation of the good God as well, as if these two have equal power. But if they say this, look how great the impiety is into which they fall! For amongst those who have equal power that which surpasses and is stronger could not be found. For if the one exists against the will of the other one, the weakness and strength of both is equal. Their strength is equal, because they prevail in their existence over each other's will, but also they are both weak, for things happen without and against their will. For both the good one exists against the will of the bad one and the bad one exists against the will of the good one."

(We regard it as likely to read, as Thomson does, τῶν τοῦ ἀγαθοῦ Θεοῦ τὸν φαῦλον δύνασθαι γενέσθαι κύριον εἴποιεν and not to leave out τῶν as Leone and Camelot do. If Athanasius opposed the idea that the evil god becomes the Lord of the good God he could not do so by opposing the idea that they have equal power. But they do have equal power if the evil god, too, becomes, just like the good God, the Lord of the good God's creation. (Although it should be noticed that Athanasius confuses his own view, *viz.*, that the good God is the Creator, with the Marcionites' view that the evil god is the creator, this is caused by the previous sentence in which Athanasius argues that the evil god cannot be the creator of the good God's creation.)) It is an impiety to say that there are two gods with equal power, since it is a generally held view that God is all-powerful, dominating all things and dominated by nothing, see *C.G.* 29: ... ὁ περὶ θεοῦ κρατεῖ λόγος, δυνατὸν αὐτὸν εἶναι κατὰ πάντα, καὶ μηδὲν αὐτοῦ κρατεῖν, αὐτὸν δὲ τῶν πάντων κρατεῖν καὶ δεσπόζειν. The possibility that the two gods are in peace with each other is, of course, excluded by the fact that they are as good and evil opposed in nature, see *C.G.* 7, *infra*, 35. Similarly Athanasius opposes polytheism: the many gods destroy each other, *C.G.* 24: διαφόρων γὰρ ὄντων καὶ πολλῶν κατὰ πόλιν καὶ χώραν θεῶν, καὶ τοῦ ἑτέρου τὸν τοῦ ἑτέρου ἀναιροῦντος θεόν, οἱ πάντες παρὰ πάντων ἀναιροῦνται. It is absurd to suppose two gods with equal power and equal weakness who exist against each other's will. So there can only be the one Creator who is also the Father of Jesus Christ and who is almighty. In a similar way Tertullian refutes the existence of Marcion's god besides the Creator: as the *summum magnum* God must be one, two gods cannot be the *summum magnum* at the same time, see *Adv. Marc.* 1, 3 ff., where he says that all are agreed that God must be the *summum magnum* (*Adv. Marc.* 1, 3, 3). This could go back to Xenophanes' criticism of polytheism, see Diels, *Fragmente der Vorsokratiker*, 21, A31: τὸ γὰρ ἓν τοῦτο καὶ πᾶν τὸν θεὸν ἔλεγεν ὁ Ξενοφάνης, ὃ ἕνα μὲν δείκνυσιν ἐκ τοῦ πάντων κράτιστον εἶναι· πλειόνων γάρ, φησίν, ὄντων ὁμοίως ὑπάρχειν ἀνάγκη πᾶσι τὸ κρατεῖν· τὸ δὲ πάντων κράτιστον καὶ ἄριστον θεός. (On the influence of Presocratic philosophy on early Christian theology in general see R. M. Grant, Early Christianity and Pre-Socratic Philosophy, *H. A. Wolfson Jubilee Volume*, American Academy for Jewish Research, Jerusalem 1965, pp. 376 ff.).

CHAPTER 7

Further polemics against Marcionite dualism. Evil has no substance of its own, but finds its origin in the human soul which turns away from God.

Translation and Commentary:

(7) "Furthermore – for one could also say this to them –: if what is visible is the work of the evil god, what is the work of the good one? For nothing can be seen expect only the creation of the Creator. And what makes us know that there is also the good God, when there are no works of Him, through which He could be known? For the Creator is known through His works."

The same argument is used against the dualism of the Manicheans, see *Epistola ad ep. Aeg. et Lib.* 16 (PG 25, 573A/B): Καὶ γὰρ κἀκεῖνοι μόνον ἄχρι ὀνόματος ἀγαθὸν θεὸν ὀνομάζουσι, καὶ ἔργον μὲν αὐτοῦ οὔτε βλεπόμενον οὔτε ἀόρατον δεικνύειν δύνανται, *Contra Arianos* 2, 39 (PG 26, 229C): κἀκεῖνοι γάρ, τὰ μὲν ἔργα τοῦ Θεοῦ βλέποντες, ἀρνοῦνται αὐτὸν μόνον ὄντα καὶ ἀληθινὸν Θεόν, ἕτερον δὲ ἑαυτοῖς ἀναπλάσσουσιν, οὗ μήτε ἔργον, μήτε τινὰ μαρτυρίαν ἀπὸ τῶν θείων λογίων δεικνύειν δύνανται. This seems to be a common argument against the Marcionites, see Irenaeus, *Adv. Haer.* 3, 12, 14: *Si autem et erat super hunc alius Deus, ex abundanti per comparationem diceremus, hic illo melior est. Melior enim ex operibus apparet, quemadmodum et praediximus,* (see *Adv. Haer.* 2, 46, 1, 2, 4): *et cum illi nullum Patris sui opus habeant ostendere, hic solus ostenditur Deus,* Tertullian, *Adv. Marc.* 1, 11, 9: *Quando etiam insigniora et superbiora opera debuisset condidisse, ut et deus ex operibus cognosceretur secundum creatorem, et ex honestioribus potior et generosior creatore.* The Marcionites were obviously impressed by this argument, since they claim that their good God is the Creator of the invisible things, see Tertullian, *Adv. Marcionem* 1, 16, 1.

> "But how could there at all be two creators in contrast with each other, or what is the dividing principle between these two in order that they are separated? For it is impossible that they are together, since they annihilate each other."

First Athanasius argues that a good and a bad creator cannot exist at the same time, since they would annihilate each other, cp. the argument with which Irenaeus opposes the existence of word and silence in the pleroma, *Adv. Haer.* 2, 14, 1: *Haec enim consumptibilia sunt invicem, quemadmodum lumen et tenebrae in eodem nequaquam erunt.* A third and dividing god would be required. Then Athanasius also excludes the possibility that they exist in each other:

> "Nor could one (god) be in the other one, since their nature cannot be mingled and is dissimilar. So there will appear a third dividing principle and that will be God."

The same argument appears in Irenaeus, *Adv. Haer.* 2, 1, 2: *Si autem hoc dixerint* (sc. *in immensum distare et separata esse ab invicem, id est pleroma et quod est extra illud*), *tertium quid erit, quod in immensum separat pleroma et hoc quod est extra illud; et hoc tertium circumfinit et continebit utraque, et erit maius tertium hoc et pleromate et eo quod est extra illud.* Irenaeus develops this argument *ad infinitum*. (In a similar way Athanasius opposes the Arian doctrine that Christ is God's mediator through whom God created the world by saying that a mediator would be required for the creation of Christ the mediator and so on, *ad infinitum*, see *Contra Arianos* 2, 26 (PG 26, 201B/C), 24 (PG 26, 197B), *De Decr.* 8 (PG 25, 437A/B).

> "But of which nature will also this third principle be? Of the nature of the good one or of the nature of the bad one? That will be unclear. For it is impossible that it is of the nature of both."

Since there is no in between between good and evil and since nothing transcends the antithesis of good and evil, and since this third principle cannot be both good and evil, it follows that it does not exist at all. And if the dividing principle does not exist, then there can be no second God besides the One creator, the Father of Jesus Christ. With this argument the reasonable refutation of the Marcionite doctrine ends.

Athanasius now gives a summary of what has been said about the origin of sin:

> "So since it appears that this kind of reasoning of theirs is unsound, the truth of the church's knowledge must shine that evil does not stem from God, and is not in God and has not existed from the beginning and that there is no substance of it."

In *C.G.* 6 Athanasius made the claim that the Marcionite doctrine was based on a reason which had gone mad (see *supra*, 32, he now has provided the proof of this. On the statement that evil is not from God and in God see *C.G.* 6, *supra*, 29; that it has not existed from the beginning see *C.G.* 2, *supra*, 15; that it has no substance, see *C.G.* 6, *supra*, 31 f.

> "But men, depriving themselves of the contemplation of the good, started to imagine and shape for themselves in an arbitrary way what is not."

This was discussed more extensively in *C.G.* 4, see *supra*, 23 ff.

> "For it is as when somebody, whilst the sun is shining and the whole earth is illuminated by its light, closes his eyes and imagines for himself darkness whilst there is no darkness, and from then on wanders around as if there were darkness, often falling and stumbling over precipices, supposing that there is no light but darkness, for believing that he looks he does not see at all."

The sun which illuminates the earth is here compared with God who illuminates the human minds; this comparison occurs frequently in the apologetic treatises, see *C.G.* 1, 23, *De Inc.* 29, 32, 40. Interesting is *De Inc.* 32, where Athanasius says that a blind man may not see the sun, but feels its warmth and therefore knows that it is above the earth: ἐπεὶ καὶ τυφλὸς ἐὰν μὴ βλέπῃ τὸν ἥλιον, ἀλλὰ κἂν τῆς ὑπ' αὐτοῦ γενομένης θέρμης ἀντιλαμβανόμενος, οἶδεν ὅτι ἥλιος ὑπὲρ γῆς ἐστιν. So man can never deprive himself completely of knowledge of God and therefore cannot be excused. This comparison goes back to Plato, *Republic* VI, 508C ff., a famous passage where Plato compares those who direct their attention to the ideas to people who see in bright sunshine, and those who direct it to the sensible world, to people who see in the darkness. Origen adopts this comparison in *De Princ.* 1, 1, 5 (see the edition of H. Görgemanns and H. Karpp, p. 109 n. 11), cp. Theophilus, *Ad Autolycum* 1, 2: οὐ παρὰ τὸ μὴ βλέπειν τοὺς τυφλοὺς ἤδη καὶ οὐκ ἔστιν τὸ φῶς τοῦ ἡλίου φαῖνον, ἀλλὰ ἑαυτοὺς αἰτιάσθωσαν οἱ τυφλοί, and Irenaeus, *Adv. Haer.* 4, 64, 3: οὔτε τὸ φῶς ἐξασθενεῖ διὰ τοὺς ἑαυτοὺς τυφλώττοντας· ἀλλ' ἐκείνου μένοντος ὁποῖον καὶ ἐστίν, οἱ τυφλωθέντες παρὰ τὴν αἰτίαν τὴν ἑαυτῶν ἐν ἀορασίᾳ καθίστανται.

> "In the same way the soul of man, having closed its eye through which it can see God, imagined for itself evil things and whilst it moves around in these things it does not know that although it believes to do something it does nothing at all."

On the eye of the soul see *C.G.* 2, *supra*, 18; on the movement in evil see *C.G.* 4, *supra*, 25.

> "For it shapes for itself what is not."

See on this *C.G.* 4, *supra*, 25.

> "And it did not remain in the way it was made. But in the way in which it defiled itself it is also seen. For it was made in order to see God and to be illuminated by Him."

On the original destination of the soul see *C.G.* 2, *supra*, 16 ff.

> "But instead of God it sought what is corruptible and darkness, as also the Holy Spirit says somewhere in Scripture: *God made man righteous, but man sought many notions*" (*Eccl.* 7:30).

On the difference between the one God who really is and the many things see *C.G.* 3, *supra*, 22.

> "So this is the way in which the invention and imagination of evil initially took place and found its shape in man."

Hereby Athanasius has completed his expositions on the origin of sin. Now he can turn to a description of how idolatry developed out of sin:

> "But now it is necessary to say how they embarked on the way downwards to the folly of the idols, that you may know that the invention of the idols does not at all stem from the good, but from evil. And that of which the beginning is evil could not possibly be judged good in any respect, since it is bad in its totality."

This is the opening statement in the attack on Pagan idolatry which is to follow. This statement makes it clear *a limine* that nothing good can be expected in the idolatry of the Pagans.

Part II

(8-29)

THE REFUTATION OF IDOLATRY

Introduction

The theme of the attack on the various forms of idolatry is set in the first chapter of this part of the treatise: instead of looking upwards and adoring the true God man looks downwards and adores what is below him: the material world (8). Athanasius stresses time and again that the Pagan gods and their idols are below man, at least below the original destination of man and that they pull man downwards to unacceptable way of life.

The description of the development of idolatry, which is a development to the worse, which is given is in itself logical: idolatry begins with the deification of heavenly bodies, and then it goes slowly downwards: the ether, air, elements of the earth, men, animals, beings which are half men half animals, the pleasures of the flesh (9). Athanasius does not follow this development in his refutation of idolatry. He begins with an attack on the gods who are in fact deified men. These gods are below men for two reasons: man has deified them and he who deifies is more than he who has been deified; in the second place the gods' lack of morality (as becomes clear in the stories told about them) shows that they are on a lower level than beings which can distinguish between good and evil by making use of their reason (10-12). The images of the gods are the products of men's skill and therefore below men. Whilst man is a living being these images are lifeless and immobile (13-15). All attempts made by the Greeks to rationalize and defend the mythological stories about the gods and their images are brushed aside by Athanasius, whereby he likes to make use of the argument by elimination: when the Greeks claim that the myths do not mean to tell the truth, but that their purpose is merely to please the audience, Athanasius asks whether they lie about the nature of the gods or about their acts or about both. If the Pagans are consistent they must admit that the poets lie about both the natures and the acts of the gods. But then Athanasius proves that things are even worse: what the poets say about the nature of the gods is false, since they are not gods but men, what they say about their immoral acts is right (16-17). It is not correct to say that the gods are men who have rightly been deified because they were inventors of arts. By making use of the generally accepted theory that art is an imitation of nature Athanasius shows that art is below human nature and is therefore no reason for deification, or if it is, all inventors and not only some of them ought to be deified (18). Then Athanasius resumes the attack on the images of gods. These images prove them to be men or even living beings below men, i.e. animals. The Greeks try to defend these images by saying that these images are not themselves gods, but that God is represented through them and that in them divine messengers appear. Athanasius confronts those who say this with the dilemma of whether God is made known through the material or through the form of the images. In either case one of the two is superfluous. If the images are meant to make divine messengers appear it is false to call these images gods and thereby put them on the same level as or even on a higher one than what they signify (the subtle Platonic way of arguing about the images and the Divine is here completely ignored) (19-21). The forms in which the Divine is represented vary from each other and in any case make God a bodily being, subject to suffering and destruction (22). Various people adore various gods and this variety leads to dissensions and factions. This variety becomes even more apparent in the various sacrifices: some people offer as sacrifices the very beings which other people adore as gods (23-24). The worst forms of idolatry are human sacrifices, whereby men are offered to beings which are below men, and further prostitution, self-castration and homosexuality. All these evil things men learned from their gods. The implication of this is that men first created gods who are a perversion of their own likeness and then imitated these gods, hereby sinking themselves to a lower level than their original destination of men who have been created in God's image (25-26). After the worst forms of idolatry a seemingly less specious form of it is attacked: the deification of heavenly bodies and of elements of the earth; this is the kind of idolatry with which the road downwards began. By making use of doxographical material Athanasius shows that the various heavenly bodies and elements of the earth can only function together and are therefore in need of each other's help. This can also be expressed in another way: the heavenly bodies, the elements and the seasons confine each other and thereby (at least temporarily) exert power over each other. What needs the help of something else and what is in its power confined by something else cannot be called almighty and therefore cannot be god. This shows that the parts of the universe are not divine but created beings. Athanasius here makes use of the natural laws as seen by ancient physiologists in order to be able to reject the divinity of parts of the universe or of the whole universe (27-29).

Chapter 8

As a sinner man imagines as good what is not, and he deifies bodily things.

Translation and commentary:

> (8) "Not satisfied with the imagination of evil the human soul started to extend itself slowly to the things which are even worse."

Since it was announced in the last sentence of the previous chapter that idolatry would now be discussed (see *supra*, 39) this remark indicates that idolatry is the worst form of sin.

> "For having learned varieties of pleasures and having girded itself with the forgetfulness of things divine, taking pleasure in the passions of the body and fixing its eyes only on things of the moment and on the impressions they give, it thought that nothing more existed than what is visible, but that only the temporal and bodily things are good."

On the varieties of pleasure see *C.G.* 3, *supra*, 22. – In *C.G.* 3 it is said that Adam and Eve realized, when they were naked, that they were more divested of knowledge of God than of clothes, see *supra*, 21. When Athanasius now says that man girded himself with forgetfulness (which manifests itself in taking pleasure in bodily passions), this is obviously meant as an allegorical interpretation of the fig-leaves with which Adam and Eve girded themselves – on this not unusual interpretation of the fig-leaves see H. Koch, Die Feigenblätter der Stammeltern bei Irenäus und bei Tertullian und die Nachwirkung ihrer Erklärungen, *Theologische Studien und Kritiken* (105) 1933, pp. 39-50, and J. H. Waszink's edition of Tertullian, *De anima*, pp. 436 f. – When man fixes his eye only on what is present, he does not make use of his reason and therefore does not differ from the animals, see *C.G.* 31, *infra*, 104. – In *C.G.* 4 Athanasius had said that evil is non-being and that man is mistaken in regarding this as good. Now he says that man wrongly regards the bodily world as the only good. This does not mean that Athanasius thinks that the bodily world does not exist, but compared with God, who really is, it can in a sense be said that the phenomenal world is not, and is not good (although it is God's good creation, cp. Augustin, *Confessiones* 11, 4: *tu ergo, domine, fecisti ea, qui pulcher es: pulchra sunt enim, qui bonus es; bona sunt enim, qui es; sunt enim. nec ita pulchra sunt nec ita bona sunt nec ita sunt, sicut tu conditor eorum, quo comparato nec pulchra sunt nec bona sunt nec sunt*).

> "And having turned away and having forgotten that it is in the image of the good God it no longer contemplates with the power it has in itself God the Word, in whose image it was created."

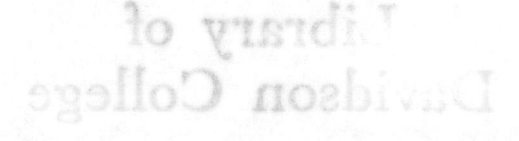

On the idea of "forgetting God or the original destination" see *C.G.* 3, *supra*, 21; on the power to contemplate God see *C.G.* 2, *supra*, 16 f.

> "But having left its identity it thinks of and shapes for itself that which is not."

It seems likely that ἔξω δὲ ἑαυτῆς γενομένη is the opposite of what is said in *C.G.* 2: τὴν ταὐτότητα σώζων and ὅλος ἐστὶν ἄνω ἑαυτῷ συνών. In its true identity the soul contemplates God, when it leaves its identity it imagines evil.

> "For having hidden in the muddle of fleshly desires the mirror it has as it were in itself and through which it could only contemplate the Image of the Father it no longer sees what the soul ought to see."

On the fleshly desires see *C.G.* 3, *supra*, 20 f.; on the mirror in the soul see *C.G.* 34, *infra*, 114.

> "But it carries itself around in all directions and sees only the things which affect its bodily senses."

On the wandering around of the soul which has lost its goal, i.e. ascetic life, see *C.G.* 5, *supra*, 28 f.

> "Hence, filled with all kinds of fleshly desire and confused by the impressions these give, it went on to shape the God whom it had forgotten in its mind in bodily and visible things, applying the name 'God' to what is visible and honouring only those things which it wants itself and sees as pleasurable. So the prime cause of idolatry is evil. For once men had learned to imagine for themselves evil which is not, they similarly shaped gods for themselves who are not."

Now it has been explained why evil in general is the cause of idolatry. In his desire man regards as being what is not, this manifests itself in particular in idolatry where man worships gods who are not. Pleasure in his fleshly desires is the primary sin. It could be said that sin in general is already idolatry, since in his sin man serves the bodily world, believing in and seeing nothing more than it. But although Athanasius does say that some gods are deified pleasures, see *C.G.* 9, *infra*, 45, he does not make the general statement that all sin is idolatry. Idolatry is caused by sin and it is the worst sin.

> "It is as when somebody, having descended into an abyss, no longer sees light and what can be seen in light, since his eyes look downwards and because water is poured over him, and perceiving only what is in the abyss, he believes that there is nothing more than those things and that what is visible to him is the true reality. Similarly also the foolish men of old, having descended to the desires and perceptions of flesh and having forgotten the knowledge and opinion about God, with an inadequate or rather irrational reasoning, shaped what is visible as gods, giving honour to the creation

instead of to the Creator, and deifying rather the works than their Cause and Creator, the Lord God."

This simile is briefly repeated in *De Inc.* 15. On the surface it looks like a far-fetched adaptation of Plato's famous simile of the cave (*Rep.* VII, 514 ff.), where it says that man wrongly regards the shadows of reality as reality itself. J. C. M. van Winden (in a review of the author's *Orthodoxy and Platonism in Athanasius. Synthesis of Antithesis?*, Leiden 1974², in the *Vigiliae Christianae* (23) 1975, pp. 317 f.) points out that there is no reason to suggest, as the author did, that Athanasius changed Plato's simile not only purposely but also clumsily. In fact, Athanasius develops the simile with some skill. What he wants to show is that man sank deeper and deeper in evil and in their idolatry degraded God more and more to lower things. In this they can be compared to somebody who under water keeps his eyes downwards and only dimly perceives reality, and the deeper he dives (as will be said in the next sentence) the more dimly he sees his objects. It appears that this is a logical adaptation of Plato's simile of the cave. - Interesting is Athanasius' remark that men in this situation obviously use their reason in an inadequate, or rather irrational, way: ἀμυδρῷ τῷ λογισμῷ, μᾶλλον δὲ ἀλογίᾳ χρησάμενοι. As has been shown by C. Andresen, *Logos und Nomos. Die Polemik des Kelsos wider das Christentum*, pp. 338 f. (cp. J. H. Waszink, Bemerkungen zu Justins Lehre vom Logos Spermatikos, *Mullus, Festschrift für Theodor Klauser*, Jahrbuch für Antike und Christentum, Ergänzungsband 1, Münster i.W. 1964, p. 386, J. Daniélou, *Message évangélique et culture hellénistique aux IIe et IIIe siècles*, Tournai 1961, p. 50), the word ἀμυδρός is a technical term in Middle-Platonism when used in connection with inadequate, but not completely false knowledge. (In this sense it appears e.g. in Albinus' explanation of Plato's simile of the cave: according to Albinus the people in the cave have only ἀμυδρὰς σκιάς of reality, *Epitome* 27, 4). It is especially used to indicate that man's religious knowledge is limited by the human capacity of understanding. In this sense the word ἀμυδρός appears a few times in the writings of Athanasius, see *Contra Arianos* 3, 32 (PG 26, 216B), 1, 29 (PG 26, 72B), 2, 17 (PG 26, 181D), *De Decr.* 12 (PG 25, 444D). The word obviously has this meaning here in *C.G.* 8, hence the correction ἀμυδρῷ τῷ λογισμῷ, μᾶλλον δὲ ἀλογίᾳ χρησάμενοι: for an attack on idolatry ἀμυδρός is not strong enough a word. - On the idea that men deify creation instead of worshipping the Creator see further *C.G.* 47, *infra*, 151.

"And as in the example just given those who descend into the abyss, the more they get downwards the more they move towards darker and deeper things, - the human race suffered something similar. For they not just got involved in idolatry and did not remain in the things with which they began, but as they spent their time in the first errors, so they invented for themselves new superstitions. And not satisfied with the first errors, they filled themselves with yet other evil things, making progress in the worst and extending their impiety even more. And Scripture, too, testifies to this when it says: *When the impious man comes to the depth of evil, he is disdainful* (*Prov.* 18:3)."

The fall of original man was a great evil, in the course of time evil errors of equal gravity were added to this. This means that the history of mankind was a constant fall. The 'first things' seem to be the planets which mankind adored at first, see *C.G.* 9. – On the idea that the development of idolatry is the road downwards see *C.G.* 7, *supra*, 37. The quotation from *Prov.* 18:3 is obviously caused by the fact that here the word βάθος occurs which seems to corroborate the simile of the βυθός, the word καταφρονεῖ is interpreted as the disreagard which man as a sinner has for God.

Chapter 9

Catalogue of the various forms of idolatry.

Translation and Commentary:

(9) "For once men's mind had taken a leap away from God and once men were following the road downwards in their thoughts and reasonings, they first attributed the honour of God to heaven, sun, moon and the stars, believing them not only to be gods, but also the causes of the other beings after them."

Since the road downwards begins with this kind of idolatry, it can be regarded as the least mistaken one. We regard it as the most likely that this "compliment" is paid to Plato, who says in a well known (see *infra*, 110 f.) passage in the *Timaeus* (41A/C) that the lower gods, i.e. the heavenly bodies, receive the commandment from the Demiurg to create as well: Θεοὶ θεῶν, ὧν ἐγὼ δημιουργὸς πατήρ τε ἔργων ... τρέπεσθε κατὰ φύσιν ὑμεῖς ἐπὶ τὴν τῶν ζώων δημιουργίαν, μιμούμενοι τὴν ἐμὴν δύναμιν περὶ τὴν ὑμετέραν γένεσιν. The first part of this section is quoted by Eusebius, *Praep. Evang.* 13, 18 (followed by a quotation from Philo, *De specialibus legibus* I 13: Τινὲς ἥλιον καὶ σελήνην καὶ τοὺς ἄλλους ἀστέρας ὑπέλαβον εἶναι θεοὺς αὐτοκράτορας, οἷς τὰς τῶν γινομένων ἁπάντων αἰτίας ἀνέθεσαν), cp. further Eusebius, *Demonstratio Evangelica* 3, 3; Origen, *Contra Celsum* 6, 10; Athenagoras, *Legatio* 6, 2. (On the deification of the heavenly bodies see further *infra*, 88 ff., *C.G.* 27 f.)

"Then, descending further in their darkened reasonings they called ether and air and what is in the air gods. And making progress in evil they further praised as gods the elements and the principles of the composition of the bodies, the warm and the cold and the dry and the wet substance."

For opposition against deification of the elements see further *C.G.* 27, *infra*, 90 f., cp. also *C.G.* 42, *infra*, 138 f.

"And as those who have fallen right down crawl on the earth like snails on the ground, similarly the most impious men having fallen and fallen away from the contemplation of God went on to deify men and images of men, some of them still alive, some after their death."

As has been observed (L. Leone, *op. cit.*, p. 15; R. W. Thomson, *op. cit.*, p. 23; P. Th. Camelot, *op. cit.*, p. 75) this is a reminiscence of Plato, *Timaeus* 92A, where it says that the most stupid men are made crawling beasts on the ground: τοῖς δ' ἀφρονεστάτοις αὐτῶν τούτων καὶ παντάπασιν πρὸς γῆν πᾶν τὸ σῶμα κατατενομένοις ὡς οὐδὲν ἔτι ποδῶν χρείας οὔσης, ἄποδα αὐτὰ καὶ ἰλυσπώμενα ἐπὶ γῆς ἐγέννησαν. Athanasius says: ὡς δὲ οἱ τέλεον πεσόντες, this indicates that he refers to a well known category, *viz.*, to those about whom Plato speaks in the *Timaeus*. This does not, of course, mean that Athanasius agrees with the doctrine of the transmigration of the souls. Just as he adopts the terminology of 'forgetting' from Plato's doctrine of the pre-existence of the souls whilst rejecting this doctrine itself, he adopts here terminology from Plato's doctrine of the transmigration of the souls whilst rejecting this doctrine itself. - The veneration of living men obviously refers to the cult of the Roman emperor which is Euhemerism: the gods are men who have been deified after their death. This is the major objection Athanasius makes against the Pagan gods, see especially *C.G.* 10 f., 16 ff.

"And deliberating and considering even worse things they transferred the divine and transcendent name of God even to stones, wood, reptiles (both in the sea and on the ground) and to irrational wild beasts, attributing to them every honour of God, thus turning away from the true and really being God, the Father of Christ."

For opposition against the adoration of stones and wood see *C.G.* 13, *infra*, 56 f. Men who do this forsake to use their reasonable soul (see *C.G.* 31, *infra*, 102), and degrade themselves to the level of animals, so they adore what they are themselves when they worship animals (cp. the previous sentence). Apologists link worship of animals especially with the Egyptians, see Aristides, *Apol.* 12, Athenagoras, *Leg.* 1, Clement of Alexandria, *Protreptikos* 2, 79, Eusebius, *Praep. Evang.* 2, 1, cp. J. Geffcken, *Zwei griechische Apologeten*, Leipzig und Berlin 1907, p. 73.

"And if only the audacity of the foolish men had stopped here, and if only they had not, going further, defiled themselves with impieties."

This ironic wish that idolators should have remained more reasonable is also expressed in *C.G.* 10 (in connection with the deification of not only men but also women) and *C.G.* 15 (in connection with the insensibility of the idols).

> "For some have fallen in their mind so far and have been darkened in their reason to such a degree that they imagined for themselves and even deified what does not exist at all. For having mixed up the rational with the irrational and having linked what is dissimilar in nature they venerate them as gods, as the Egyptians have dog-headed, serpent-headed and ass-headed gods and as the Libyans have the ram-headed god Ammon."

For the refutation of this kind of Gods of a mixed nature, see *C.G.* 22, *infra*, 77.

> "And others, having separated the parts of the bodies: head, shoulder, hand and foot, deified each and gave it divine worship, as if they were not satisfied with the fact that their object of worship consisted of a body as a whole."

L. Leone, *op. cit.*, p. 16 refers to Philo, *De Decal.* 16, 79 as a parallel. This worship is even worse than the worship of the whole bodies of animals. The reason may be that Athanasius later on insists that parts are in need of each other's help (see *C.G.* 27 f., *infra*, 90 f.), so parts of animals are even more impotent than whole animals and therefore even less suitable for being deified.

> "And others, extending their impiety, having deified the reason of the invention of these things and of their wickedness, *viz.*, their pleasure and desire, worship these, as they have Eros and Aphrodite of Paphos."

Since delight in pleasure and desire is sin, see *C.G.* 3, *supra*, 20 f., this is in fact the deification of sin. On the deification of Love etc. see further Clement of Alexandria, *Protrept.* 2, 26, 1; 3, 44, 2; 10, 102, 3; Eusebius, *Praep. Evang.* 5, 3; 7, 2.

> "Others, so to speak contending in the worse, had the audacity to deify their rulers or also the sons of their rulers either because they wanted to honour their rulers or because they were afraid of their tyranny, as there is their famous Zeus in Crete, Hermes in Arcadia, Dionysus in India, Isis in Egypt, Osiris, Horus and now Antinous, lover of the Roman emperor Hadrian whom they worship out of fear of him who gave the decree although they know that he is a man and not even an honourable man, but full of licentiousness, for when Hadrian visited the land of the Egyptians he ordered after the death of Antinous, the slave of his lust, that he be worshipped, himself loving the young man even after death, yet providing a refutation of himself and a proof against all idolatry that it was invented by men for no other reason than because of the desire of those who shaped it; as also the wisdom of God testifies beforehand when it says: The imagination of idols is the beginning of fornication (*Sap. Sal.* 14:12)."

Those who "contend in the worse" are probably the artists, who with their ambitions will seduce the masses to worship idols of kings, see *C.G.* 11, *infra*, 50, where *Sap. Sal.* 14:18-20 is quoted as a proof (cp. also *C.G.* 10, *infra*, 48 f.), cp. Clement of Alexandria, *Protrept.* 4, 51. - It is a popular theme in Christian apologists to point out (as Euhemer had done) that gods are not more than deified men, see e.g. Theophilus, *Ad Aut.* 2, 2; Clement of Alexandria, *Protrept.* 4, 54 ff.; Lactance, *Epit.* 6, Eusebius, *Praep. Evang.* 2, 6. Apologists also liked to attack the worship of Antinous, see J. Geffcken, *op. cit.*, p. 227 (to the list can be added Eusebius, *Praep. Evang.* 2, 6, who quotes Clement of Alexandria, *Protrept.* 4, 49, 1). To Athanasius the deification of Antinous is a further proof that idolatry is *inter alia* the deification of pleasure and desire. On the motive that Scripture testifies to this *beforehand* cp. *C.G.* 11, *infra*, 50 (for the use of *Sap. Sal.* 14:12 in this context see also Eusebius, *Praep. Evang.* 1, 9, 18; 7, 2, 6, cp. B. Gärtner, *The Areopagus Speech and Natural Revelation*, Uppsala 1955, p. 129). On the deification of Antinous and the theme of apotheosis by drowning see also W. den Boer, Συγγράμματα. *Studies in Graeco-Roman History*, Leiden 1979, pp. 207 ff.

> "And do not be surprised and do not think that what is being said is unreliable, since also not long ago and perhaps even until now the Roman senate decrees that those who were ever since the beginning ruling kings, either all or those whom they want to and about whom they decide in this way, belong to the gods, and (it) puts down as written law that they be worshipped."

It seems to us that this remark gives no indication about the date at which the apologetic treatises were written, as R. W. Thomson, *op. cit.*, p. XXII, believes, referring to the fact that in 337 Constantine was deified by the Roman senate. Athanasius says rather cautiously that this happened *perhaps* (τάχα) until 'now', and the word 'now' is rather vague, since he also applied it to the deification of Antinous (which was at the time of Athanasius two centuries ago).

> "For those whom they hate, of them they admit that they are enemies by nature and call them men. But those whom they regard as pleasant, of them they decree that they be worshipped because of their virtue, as if they had the power to deify, whilst they are men themselves and do not deny being mortal."

The objection is that gods are dependent on human arbitrariness, in the sense that men deify only those whom they like, - similarly Tertullian argues in *Apol.* 5, 1: *facit et hoc ad causam nostram, quod apud vos de humano arbitratu divinitas pensitatur. Nisi homini deus placuerit, deus non erit; homo iam deo propitius esse debebit.*

"But people who deify ought rather to be gods themselves. For that which makes must be more than what is made, and he who passes the judgement must necessarily dominate that on which the judgement is passed, and the giver certainly bestows what is in his possession. As surely also every king bestows what he possesses and is more and greater than those who receive. So if they decree to be gods whom they want to be gods, they first ought to be gods themselves."

Athanasius says repeatedly that the cause is more than what is caused, see *C. G.* 1: ὡς γὰρ καλὸν τὸ φῶς, καὶ καλλίων ὁ τοῦ φωτὸς ἀρχηγὸς ἥλιος, cp. *C.G.* 13. This is a well known philosophical tenet, see e.g. Cicero, *De nat. deor.* 2, 33, 86: *ea quae efferant aliquid ex sese perfectiores habere naturas quam ea quae efferantur* (cp. W. Theiler, *Porphyrius und Augustin, Forschungen zum Neuplatonismus*, Berlin 1966, p. 174; E. R. Dodds, *Proclus, The Elements of Theology*, Oxford 1963², p. 194) which was adopted by Christian writers, see Aristides, *Apol.* 1, 2; Theophilus, *Ad Aut.* 2, 3; Irenaeus, *Adv. Haer.* 4, 62; 2, 37, 3; 2, 56, 1; 3, 8, 3; Tertullian, *Adv. Marc.* 1, 13, 2; 2, 9, 7; *Adv. Herm.* 18, 5; Hilary, *De Trinitate* 1, 7; Gregory Nazianzen, *Oratio Theol.* III 15, IV 7, V 14; *Oratio* 20, 7; 20, 10; 25, 15; 40, 23; Augustin, *Conf.* 13, 20, 28; 13, 31, 46; *De vera rel.* 18, 35; *De Gen. c. M.* 1, 2, 4; *De civ.* 12, 1, 3; *En. in Ps.* 26, 8 (II); 39, 8; *Sermo* 96, 4, 4; 158, 7; *De div. quaest.* LXXXIII 28. – According to Athanasius the giver is κρείττων καὶ μείζων than the receiver. There is obviously no difference between these two words in this context. Athanasius does draw a clear distinction between these two words in his polemics against the Arians, there he says that κρείττων applies to what differs in substance, μείζων to what is of the same substance but differs quantitatively, see E. P. Meijering, *Orthodoxy and Platonism in Athanasius*, pp. 94 ff.

"But this is surprising that by dying themselves as men they prove their decree about those who have been deified by them to be a lie."

When the deifyers ought to be more than those deified, then it is impossible that the deifying men die, but the deified men as gods are immortal. This shows that the whole deification is a fraud.

CHAPTER 10

Further attack on the deification of men.

Translation and Commentary:

(10) "This custom is not new and did not begin with the Roman senate but it arose long before and was practised before in the invention of idols. For also the famous Greek gods of old, Zeus, Poseidon, Apollo, Hephaistos, and Hermes, and amongst the goddesses Hera, Demeter, Athena, and

> Artemis, about them the judgement was passed by the decrees of Theseus, about whom the Greek historians speak, that they had to be called gods."

This is the appeal to antiquity which must give credence to Athanasius' polemics: he is not merely attacking recent examples of idolatry but he is attacking what has existed for a long time, as Greek historians testify (cp. G. C. Stead, Rhetorical Method in Athanasius, p. 123). The historians mentioned are, of course, Plutarch and Apollodorus Mythographus.

> "And those who have passed the decree are mourned when they die as men, but those on whom they passed the decree, these are worshipped as gods. What a tremendous contradiction and madness! Although they know the one who passed the decree they give more honour to those upon whom he passed the decree."

This takes up the argument that the cause must be superior to what is caused (see *supra*, 47) and that therefore the deifying man cannot be mortal whilst the deified man becomes an immortal god (see *supra*, 46 f.).

> "And if only their foolish idolatry had stopped with men and if only they had not transferred the name of God to women. For even women, who cannot be safely consulted on public matters, are worshipped and venerated with the honour of God, as those on whom the decree was passed by Theseus, as we said above, and among the Egyptians Isis, Kore and Neotera, and among others Aphrodite."

On the motive of the ironic wish "If only they had not ..." see *supra*, 44 f. – These remarks should not be regarded as indicative of Athanasius' personal esteem of women, they merely reflect the fact that in antiquity women were subjected to men and had no political rights. – Kore and Neotera were titles of Isis, see P. Th. Camelot, *op. cit.*, p. 82 n. 1. For opposition against Aphrodite see *infra*, 54, *C.G.* 12.

> "For I believe it would be blasphemy even to name the others, since they are completely ridiculous."

This seems to be a renewed reference to the deification of human pleasures, see *C.G.* 9, *supra*, 45.

> "For many not only in times of old but also in our times, having lost their dearest ones, brothers, relatives and wives, and also many women having lost their husbands, all of whom nature proved to be mortal men, these men and these women they painted because of the deep sorrow about them and offered sacrifices to them and set them up, and later generations worshipped them as gods because of their shape and the ambitious skill of the artist, and hereby something unnatural happened to them. For those about whom their parents mourned as not being gods (for they would not have mourned about their loss if they had known them to be gods, for this is the reason that they – not only not believing them to be gods, but not to exist at all – represented

them in pictures in order to be consoled about their non-being by seeing the
likeness in their picture) to these foolish men pray as to gods and bestow
them the honour of the true God."

As appears from *C.G.* 11 this argument is taken from *Sapientia Sal.* 14,
see *infra*, 50, for further examples in Christian and Pagan writers see P.
Th. Camelot, *op. cit.*, p. 82 f. n. 2; interesting is the quotation R. W.
Thomson gives from Clement of Alexandria, *Protrept.* 2, 24, 3 who quotes
Xenophanes: εἰ θεοὺς νομίζετε, μὴ θρηνεῖτε αὐτοὺς μηδὲ κόπτεσθε· εἰ δὲ
πενθεῖτε αὐτούς, μηκέτι τούτους ἡγεῖσθε εἶναι θεούς, see also Tertullian, *Apol.*
10, 10: ... *ita rudes adhuc homines agebant, ut cuiuslibet novi viri adspectu quasi
divino commoverentur, cum hodie iam politi, quos ante paucos dies luctu publico
mortuos sint confessi, in deos consecrent.*

"For in Egypt even until now mourning rites are celebrated because of
the loss of Osiris, Horus and Typhon and the other gods."

The especially objectionable aspect of these rites are that gods are
mourned who killed each other, see Aristides, *Apol.* 12, 2, cp. J.
Geffcken, *op. cit.*, p. 74.

"And the brazen gongs in Dodona and the Corybantes in Crete prove
Zeus not to be a god, but a man, yea a man born from a cannibal father."

The worship of Zeus at Dodona is mentioned in *De Inc.* 47 as one of the
examples of how Pagan idolatry was abandoned after people believed in
the risen Christ. For opposition in general against gods whose graves are
known see e.g. Tertullian, *Apol.* 10, 4, and against the worship of Zeus in
Crete in particular cp. Minucius Felix, *Oct.* 21, 8; Theophilus *Ad Aut.* 1,
10; Athenagoras, *Leg.* 30, 3; Origen, *Contra Celsum* 3, 43; Clement of
Alexandria, *Protrept.* 2, 37, 4; Lactantius, *Div. Inst.* 1, 11, 45 ff.;
Eusebius, *Praep. Evang.* 3, 10, 21; cp. J. Geffcken, *op. cit.*, pp. 227 f.

"And this is amazing that even the great philosopher of the Greeks who
boasted he had deep thoughts about God, Plato, went with Socrates down to
Piraeus in order to worship Artemis who was shaped by man's skill."

This is a reference to Plato, *Rep.* I 327a, with this difference that
according to Plato it was Socrates who went together with Glaucon in
order to worship the goddess. We regard it as very likely that Athanasius'
alteration was caused by Origen, *Contra Celsum* 6, 3-4 (a passage which
also seems to have influenced Eusebius, *Praep. Evang.* 13, 14), where
Origen first refers to the fact that Celsus quotes Plato as saying (*Epist.*
VII 341C) that the highest good cannot be expressed in words, and then
goes on to criticize the fact that those who wrote such passages as this
about the highest good go down to Piraeus to pray to Artemis as a
goddess: καὶ δὴ καὶ Πλάτων ... τὰ περὶ τοῦ πρώτου ἀγαθοῦ διασημαινέτω ἕν

τινι τῶν ἐπιστολῶν καὶ φασκέτω μηδαμῶς ''ῥητὸν'' τὸ πρῶτον ἀγαθόν ... 'Αλλ' οἱ τοιαῦτα περὶ τοῦ πρώτου ἀγαθοῦ γράψαντες καταβαίνουσιν ''εἰς Πειραιέα'', προσευξόμενοι ὡς θεῷ τῇ 'Αρτεμίδι ...

Chapter 11

Refutation of deification from Scripture. Attack on the ways of life of the Greek gods.

Translation and Commentary:

(11) "Long ago Scripture taught about these and similar inventions of mad idolatry saying:"

For the motive of Biblical prediction of idolatry (implying that God cannot have been taken by surprise by evil and idolatry, since He foresaw it) cp. *C.G.* 14, *infra*, 58, *De Inc.* 3 (similarly Scripture refutes and predicts heresies beforehand, see e.g. *Contra Arianos* 3, 8, cp. Tertullian, *Adv. Marc.* 2, 2, 4; Hilary of Poitiers, *De Trin.* 3, 8).

"The imagination of idols is the beginning of fornification and their invention the corruption of life. For it has not existed from the beginning and will not exist forever" (*Sap. Sal.* 14:12-13).

For the important thought that idolatry did not exist from the beginning see *C.G.* 2, *supra*, 15 ff.

"For it entered the world through the vanity of men and therefore their prompt end was thought of. For when a father was exhausted by untimely sorrow he made an image of his son who had suddenly been taken away and honoured as now living a man who was at that time dead and handed on to his servants mysteries and rites, and then this impious custom was strengthened in time and was observed as a law" (*Sap. Sal.* 14:14-16a).

See for this thought further *C.G.* 10, *supra*, 48 f.

"And by the decrees of the rulers the carved images of those were worshipped whom men could not honour in their presence because they lived far away, having represented a picture of him who was at a distance, they honoured a visible image of the king in order to flatter with their zeal as present him who was absent. And the ambitious skill of the artist drove the ignorant to pay divine tribute. For the former, perhaps wanting to please the ruler, forced with his skill the likeness to be as good as possible. But the mass of the people, attracted by the pleasance of the work, now thought that he was the object of the worship who was shortly before honoured as man. And this became an obstruction to human life, for serving either misfortune or a tyrant, they ascribed the incommunicable name to stones and wood" (*Sap. Sal.* 16:6-21).

For this thought see also *supra*, 46 f., *C.G.* 9, and *supra*, 48, *C.G.* 10.

"So when on the testimony of Scripture the invention of idols had begun and taken its shape among men in this way it is now time to display to you the refutation of it, taking our arguments not so much from outside as from their own thoughts about these matters."

A refutation from outside seems to be the refutation from Scripture, a refutation from inside will show that on account of the Pagans' own thoughts the Pagan worship of gods is unreasonable.

"For if anybody took the actions of their so-called gods, in order to begin with them here below, he will find that they are not only not gods but even the basest of men."

The stories about the gods which the Pagans tell show that these are no gods. This can indeed be called a refutation 'from inside', since Stoics, Epicureans and Sceptics attacked the way of life of the gods as well, see J. Geffcken, *op. cit.*, pp. XVII ff.

"For it is possible indeed to see in their poets the love affairs of Zeus and his licentiousness."

This will be discussed extensively in *C.G.* 12, *infra*, 53 ff.

"It is possible to hear the story how he raped Ganymede and committed secret adulteries, and how he was afraid and feared lest against his will walls of Troy would be destroyed."

For further examples of Christian polemics against the story of Ganymede's rape see F. Geffcken, *op. cit.*, p. 67. For the secret adulteries of Zeus see *infra*, 53, *C.G.* 12. – When Zeus is afraid lest Troy would fall against his will, this implies that Zeus is subjected to fate, an idea which the Christians liked to attack, see *e.g.* Irenaeus, *Adv. Haer.* 2, 4, 4: *Et si necessitati serviens erit Pater universorum, et sub fatum cadet moleste gerens in his quae fiunt, praeter necessitatem autem et fatum nihil agere possit: similiter atque Homericus Jupiter qui per necessitatem dicit: Et ego enim tibi dedi velut volens, nolente animo* (in *Adv. Haer.* 2, 18, 4 he attacks the Stoic doctrine that God is subjected to fate); Tertullian, *Apol.* 25, 8: *Misera illa coniunx Iovis et soror adversus fata non valuit! plane "fato stat Iuppiter ipse"*. (In his polemics against the Arians Athanasius also opposes the idea that God is subjected to necessity, see especially 3, 62 (PG 26, 453 f.): The Son is not created by God's free will, since God does not have an ambiguous free will, cp. *supra*, 24, but God does not have a Son by necessity either. The Son is generated out of God's essence, similarly God is good by nature and not out of free will or by necessity: Εἰ δὲ διὰ τὸ ἐκ τούτων ἄτοπον οὐκ ἐκ βουλήσεως ἀγαθὸς καὶ οἰκτίρμων ἐστίν, ἀκουσάτωσαν ἄπερ ἐφήκασιν αὐτοί· οὐκοῦν ἀνάγκῃ καὶ μὴ θέλων ἐστὶν ἀγαθός· καὶ τίς ὁ ἀνάγκην ἐπιβαλὼν αὐτῷ; Εἰ δὲ ἄτοπόν ἐστιν λέγειν ἐπὶ θεοῦ ἀνάγκην, καὶ διὰ τοῦτο φύσει ἀγαθός ἐστιν).

A god who is subjected to fate is a powerless god, as appears from the following:

> "It is possible to see him grieved at the death of his son Sarpedon and (to see that) he wanted to help him but was unable to;"

Christians liked to attack this story, see e.g. Ps.-Justin, *Coh.* 2, Athenagoras, *Leg.* 21, Tertullian, *Apol.* 14, 3, *Ad Nat.* 1, 10, 39 (cp. J. Geffcken, *op. cit.*, p. 203).

> "and that he was plotted against by the other so-called gods, I mean Athena, Hera and Poseidon, but helped by a woman, Thetis, and the hundredhanded Aigaion;"

Gods who ask for and need each other's help are no gods, see *C.G.* 28, *infra*, 93, so *a fortiori* a god who is helped by human beings is no god.

> "and that he was overcome by his pleasures and served women and that he, because of them, took the risk of appearing in irrational animals, beasts and birds;"

When Zeus is overcome by his pleasures it happens to him what happened to original man when he became a sinner, see *C.G.* 3, *supra*, 20. On Zeus' appearances in animals when he approached women see also Aristides, *Apol.* 9, 6: Δεύτερος παρεισάγεται ὁ Ζεύς, ὅν φασι βασιλεῦσαι τῶν θεῶν αὐτῶν καὶ μεταμορφοῦσθαι εἰς ζῷα, ὅπως μοιχεύσῃ θνητὰς γυναῖκας, cp. Tertullian, *Apol.* 21, 8: ... deum ... squamatum aut cornutum aut plumatum, amatorem in auro conversum Danaes (see also J. Geffcken, *op. cit.*, p. 65).

> "and again that he went into hiding because of the plot of his father, but that Cronos was bound by him and that he castrated his father."

A similar attack on Kronos and Zeus is provided by Aristides, *Apol.* 9, 3-4, cp. J. Geffcken, *op. cit.*, pp. 64 f.

> "Now is it worthy to suppose him to be a god who has committed such great crimes and has been accused of things which are not even allowed by the common laws of the Romans to ordinary men?"

Laws are given to men as reasonable beings, so that they turn to good and avoid evil, animals which have no reason cannot consider and judge evil, see *C.G.* 32, *infra*, 107. So the behaviour of Zeus is below the level of men who obey laws, he belongs indeed to "the basest of men" (*supra*, 51). On the motive that the Pagan gods violate laws see also *C.G.* 12, 26 and Aristides, *Apol.* 13, 7: εἰ γὰρ οἱ νόμοι δίκαιοί εἰσιν, ἄδικοι πάντως οἱ θεοὶ αὐτῶν εἰσι παράνομα ποιήσαντες ἀλληλοκτονίας καὶ φαρμακείας καὶ μοιχείας καὶ κλοπὰς καὶ ἀρσενοκοιτίας (cp. J. Geffcken, *op. cit.*, p. 80).

CHAPTER 12

Further attack on the Pagan gods' way of life.

Translation and Commentary:

(12) "In order to mention only a few examples out of many (because there is a great number) who, having seen his unlawful behaviour against and destruction of Semele, Leda, Alcmene, Artemis, Leto, Maia, Europa, Danaë, and Antiope, or who having seen his attack on and effrontery against his own sister by having the same person as sister and wife would not ridicule him and sentence him to death?"

On brevity see *supra*, 3. – The attack on Zeus' adulterous behaviour is a commonplace in Christian apologists, see *e.g.* Aristides, *Apol.* 9, 6-7, Ps-Justin, *Coh.* 2, Athenagoras, *Leg.* 20, 3 (in 32, 1 Athenagoras refers to the fact that Zeus had his own sister as wife), Theophilus, *Ad Aut.* 1, 9; 3, 3; 3, 8, Clement of Alexandria, *Protrept.* 2, 27, Origen, *Contra Celsum* 1, 17; 4, 48, Eusebius, *Praep. Evang.* 2, 4, Tertullian, *Apol.* 21, 7 f., Lactance, *Div. Inst.* 1, 10 (cp. J. Geffcken, *op. cit.*, pp. 67 f., P. Th. Camelot, *op. cit.*, pp. 88 f. n. 1). – Athanasius says explicitly that human beings deserve the death penalty for such actions. He had argued that the Pagan gods are no more than mortal deified men, he now suggests that they are men who ought not to have been deified, but sentenced to death, i.e. exterminated. This is an argument which is also produced by Pagan philosophy (see J. Geffcken, *op. cit.*, p. XIX, p. 80), and *e.g.* by Aristides, *Apol.* 13, 7: παράνομοι ἄρα οἱ θεοὶ αὐτῶν καὶ ἔνοχοι πάντες θανάτου καὶ ἀσεβεῖς οἱ τοιούτους παρεισάγοντες), on the Roman laws cp. L. Leone, *op. cit.*, p. 25.

"For he not only committed adultery, but also deified the children who were born to him out of adultery, providing the delusion of deification as a cover for his unlawful behaviour, among whom are Dionysus, Heracles, the Dioscuri, Hermes, Perseus, and Soteira."

Soteira seems to be a title, not a name, and since a daughter of Zeus is referred to, it could be Artemis, cp. P. Th. Camelot, *op. cit.*, pp. 90 f. n. 1. – The idea behind this could be that nothing good can be expected from gods who are themselves the product of adultery.

"Who, having seen the implacable strife of the so-called gods against each other because of the Greeks and Trojans, will not condemn their weakness, for because of their mutual quarrel they also incited men."

Gods who need the help of men (in order to win a war) are no gods, cp. *supra*, 52, and *infra*, 93 ff., *C.G.* 28. Whilst Pagan gods incite men to go to war against each other, Christ teaches men to stop wars, see *De Inc.* 51: Ἕλληνες καὶ βάρβαροι κατ' ἀλλήλων ἐπολέμουν, καὶ ὠμοὶ πρὸς τοὺς συγγενεῖς ἐτύγχανον ... ὅτε δὲ εἰς τὴν Χριστοῦ διδασκαλίαν μεταβεβήκασι, τότε δὴ ... τὴν μὲν ὠμότητα τῶν φόνων ἀπέθεντο, καὶ οὐκ ἔτι πολέμια φρονοῦσι, πάντα δὲ αὐτοῖς εἰρηναῖα καὶ τὰ πρὸς φιλίαν καταθύμια λοιπόν ἐστι. The gods' role in the Trojan war is also ridiculed by Tertullian, *Apol.* 14, 2: *deos inter se propter Troianos et Achivos ut gladiatorum paria congressos depugnasse*, cp. Lactance, *Div. Inst.* 1, 3. Aristides makes the general observation that men imitate the gods' belligerent behaviour, *Apol.* 8, 4-6 (on the motive of men's imitation of the gods see *infra*, 87, *C.G.* 26). Pagan philosophy, too, was embarrassed by these myths, see *e.g.* Plato, *Rep.* 2, 378B/C: Οὐδέ γε, ἦν δ' ἐγώ, παράπαν ὡς θεοὶ θεοῖς πολεμοῦσί τε καὶ ἐπιβουλεύουσι καὶ μάχονται – οὐδὲ γὰρ ἀληθῆ – κτλ., – the Stoic Luculius Balbus in Cicero's *De natura deorum* 2, 28, 70: *nec vero ut fabulae ferunt bellis proeliisque caruerunt, nec solum ut apud Homerum cum duo exercitus contrarios alii dei ex alia parte defenderent ... Haec et dicuntur et creduntur stultissime et plena sunt futtilitatis summaeque levitatis.*

> "Who, having seen Ares and Aphrodite wounded by Diomedes, and Hera by Heracles and whom they call the god of the underworld, Aidoneus, and Dionysus by Perseus, Athena by Arcas, and Hephaistos thrown down and made lame, will not condemn their nature and withdraw from saying any more that they are gods and, hearing that they are transient and passible will not understand that they are nothing but men and weak men at that, and would not admire those who wounded more than those who were wounded?"

Beings which can be wounded are passible and therefore cannot be gods. For further examples of polemics against the fact that gods are wounded see J. Geffcken, *op. cit.*, p. 204, for Athanasius' opposition against the passibility of God see also *Contra Arianos* 1, 16 (PG 26, 45B), 2, 34 (PG 26, 220A); *Ep. ad ep. Aeg. et Lib.* 16 (PG 25, 576A) (on God's impassibility see further G.-L. Prestige, *God in Patristic Thought*, London 1959, pp. 6 ff.). – With the exception of Dionysus these are gods who are wounded by semi-gods, i.e. sons of Zeus and mortal women; this fact explains why Athanaisus adds that one should rather admire those who wound, i.e. the semi-gods, than those who are wounded (cp. his statement that those who deify are more than those who are deified, *supra*, 47).

> "Or who, having seen the adultery committed by Ares with Aphrodite and the trick played on both of them by Hephaistos, and how the other so called gods were invited by Hephaistos to witness the adultery, and how they came and saw their licentiousness, would not laugh and will not condemn their wickedness?"

For further examples of the apologists' attack on this story see J. Geffcken, *op. cit.*, p. 204.

"Or who would not laugh when he sees Heracles' mad behaviour and concupiscence towards Omphele out of drunkenness?"

Cp. Aristides, *Apol.* 10, 9: Τὸν δὲ Ἡρακλῆν παρεισάγουσι μεθυσθῆναι καὶ μανῆναι ... Πῶς δ' ἂν εἴη θεὸς μέθυσος ...;

"For it is not necessary to refute seriously their sensual acts and their unreasonable love affairs, their divine images in gold and silver, bronze and iron, stone and wood, since these things are in themselves a pollution and display by themselves the knowledge of their error."

He who is overcome by pleasure (of the moment) no longer uses his reason which distinguishes between good and evil, therefore these love affairs ought to be called 'unreasonable' (not, as R. W. Thomson translates, 'ridiculous', *op. cit.*, p. 35), cp. *supra*, 20 ff. and *De Inc.* 12: οἱ ἄνθρωποι, νικώμενοι ταῖς παραυτίκα ἡδοναῖς καὶ ταῖς παρὰ δαιμόνων φαντασίαις καὶ ἀπάταις, οὐκ ἀνένευσαν πρὸς τὴν ἀλήθειαν· ἀλλ' ἑαυτοὺς πλείοσι κακοῖς καὶ ἁμαρτήμασιν ἐνεφόρησαν, ὡς μηκέτι δοκεῖν αὐτοὺς λογικούς, ἀλλὰ ἀλόγους ἐκ τῶν τρόπων νομίζεσθαι. – As it was said that instruction about the true God is unnecessary since God reveals Himself (see *supra*, 9), it now says that a refutation of idolatry is unnecessary since it refutes itself.

"Because of this one should really pity those who are misled in this. For whilst they hate him who approaches their own wife as an adulterer they are not ashamed to deify those who teach adultery. And whilst they themselves have no intercourse with their sisters they adore those who do this. And whilst they admit that the corruption of boys is evil they venerate those who are accused of this. And what the laws do not even allow in men they do not blush to attribute this to their so-called gods."

Since obviously men know better there is no excuse for their idolatry, cp. *supra*, 40 ff. – In the *Vita Antonii* the unreasonable behaviour of the gods is used as an argument against the Greeks who question the rationality of the cross, see ch. 74 (PG 26, 945B): καὶ ἀπαιτούντων αὐτὸν λόγον περὶ τῆς καθ' ἡμᾶς ἐν Χριστῷ πίστεως· ἐπιχειρούντων δὲ συλλογίζεσθαι περὶ τοῦ κηρύγματος τοῦ θείου σταυροῦ καὶ βουλομένων χλευάζειν ... ὁ Ἀντώνιος ... ἔλεγε ... Τί κάλλιόν ἐστι, σταυρὸν ὁμολογεῖν, ἢ μοιχείας καὶ παιδοφθορίας προσάπτειν τοῖς παρ' ὑμῖν λεγομένοις θεοῖς; Τὰ μὲν γὰρ παρ' ἡμῶν λεγόμενα ἀνδρίας ἐστὶ τεκμήριον, καὶ καταφρονήσεως θανάτου γνώρισμα· τὰ δὲ ὑμέτερα ἀσελγείας ἐστὶ πάθη. This is the well known argument *tu quoque*, cp. G. C. Stead, Rhetorical Method in Athanasius, p. 126. – The gods teach the things they do themselves, see on this *C.G.* 25 f., *infra*, 85 ff.

CHAPTER 13

Attack on the images of gods.

Translation and Commentary:

(13) "Furthermore, when they adore pieces of stone and wood they do not see that they walk with their feet on and burn similar things, but call parts of these gods. And what they used a short time ago, this they adore having sculpted it in their folly."

In the same way the *Epistula ad Diognetum* 2, 2 and Lactance, *Div. Inst.* 2, 2, 23 f. argue against the images (cp. J. Geffcken, *op. cit.*, p. 273 n. 3). After the Pagans have become Christians the situation is according to Athanasius reversed again, see *De Inc.* 53: ... ὥστε τοὺς μὲν τὰ εἴδωλα προσκυνοῦντας λοιπὸν αὐτὰ καταπατεῖν ... -, with, of course, this difference that now the material out of which idols were made is consciously trodden upon.

> "They do not see and do not consider at all that they do not adore gods but the skill of the sculptor. For as long as the stone is unpolished and the matter unworked they tread on them and often use them for their own services, even the less honorary ones. But once the artist has put on them the measures of his own skill and has given matter the shape of a man or woman, then, having expressed their gratitude to the artist, they adore them further as gods, having bought them for a certain price from the sculptor."

In a similar way Justin argues on *Apol.* 1, 9, 2: Τί γὰρ δεῖ εἰδόσιν ὑμῖν λέγειν, ἃ τὴν ὕλην οἱ τεχνῖται διατιθέασι ξέοντες καὶ τέμνοντες καὶ χωνεύοντες καὶ τύπτοντες· Καὶ ἐξ ἀτίμων πολλάκις σκευῶν διὰ τέχνης τὸ σχῆμα μόνον ἀλλάξαντες καὶ μορφοποιήσαντες θεοὺς ἐπονομάζουσιν. - By buying an image people show that they are impressed by its beauty, which means that the beauty beguiles men and allures them to deify the artist's work, a thought which is expressed *disertis verbis* by Clement of Alexandria, *Protrept.* 4, 57, 5: ὑμᾶς δὲ ἄλλη γοητείᾳ ἀπατᾷ ἡ τέχνη, εἰ καὶ μὴ ἐπὶ τὸ ἐρᾶν προσάγουσα, ἀλλ' ἐπὶ τὸ τιμᾶν καὶ προσκυνεῖν τά τε ἀγάλματα καὶ τὰς γραφάς.

> "And often the maker himself of the idol, as if he had forgotten what he had made himself prays to his own works. And what a short time before he polished and sculpted, having applied his skills to these he called them gods."

Since Athanasius says "as if he had forgotten ..." (hereby suggesting that he did not really forget) he obviously here attacks the vanity of the artist who is so impressed by the beauty of his own work that he deifies it (on the artist's vanity see also *C.G.* 39, *infra*, 127).

> "But if one had to admire them one would have to acknowledge the skill of the artist's knowledge and not to give more honour to what has been made by him than to the maker. For matter did not adorn and deify skill, but skill matter. So it would be much more just that they adore the artist than what has been made by him, because he existed before the gods who

are the products of his skill and because they came into being according to his will."

Athenagoras argues in a similar way, see *Leg.* 15, 3: ὡς δὲ οὐ τὸν κέραμον προτιμότερον τοῦ ἐργασαμένου αὐτὸν ἔχομεν οὐδὲ τὰς φιάλας καὶ χρυσίδας τοῦ χαλκεύσαντος, ἀλλ' εἴ τι περὶ ἐκείνας δεξιὸν κατὰ τὴν τέχνην, τὸν τεχνίτην ἐπαινοῦμεν καὶ οὗτός ἐστιν ὁ τὴν ἐπὶ τοῖς σκεύεσιν δόξαν καρπούμενος. The Christians knew that Pagan philosophers made the same objections against worship of idols, see Origen, *Contra Celsum* 7, 62 (cp. 1, 5 and 3, 76), who quotes Celsus as saying that it is ludicrous wisdom which everybody except an utter infant can have that an image of stone or wood or bronze or gold which a man has wrought cannot be a god: εἰ μὲν ὅτι λίθος ἢ ξύλον ἢ χαλκὸς ἢ χρυσός, ὃν ὁ δεῖνα ἢ ὁ δεῖνα εἰργάσατο, οὐκ ἂν εἴη θεός, γελοία ἡ σοφία. Τίς γὰρ καὶ ἄλλος εἰ μὴ πάντη νήπιος ταῦτα ἡγεῖται θεούς ..., and Lactance who quotes Seneca as saying, *Div. Inst.* 2, 2, 14: *Et cum haec* (sc. *simulacra*) *tanto opere suspicant, fabros qui illa fecere contemnunt.* – When Athanasius says that the artist made the image as he wanted to he again stresses the arbitrariness of the creation of evil (cp. *C.G.* 7, *supra*, 28). In *C.G.* 47 Athanasius extends this argument to God and the world; people who venerate creation instead of the Creator are like people who admire the works of an artist more than the artist himself (see *infra*, 151), cp. Athenagoras, *Leg.* 15, 3: ... καὶ ἐπὶ τῆς ὕλης καὶ τοῦ θεοῦ τῆς διαθέσεως τῶν κεχοσμημένων οὐχ ἡ ὕλη τὴν δόξαν καὶ τὴν τιμὴν δικαίαν ἔχει, ἀλλ' ὁ δημιουργὸς αὐτῆς θεός.

> "But now, having elbowed out what is just and having dishonoured the knowledge and skill they adore what has been made with knowledge and skill. And when the man who had made it dies they honour as immortal what was made by him."

The general theme that one should not regard as immortal gods those who have been deified by mortal men (since the cause is more than what is caused, see *supra*, 47) is here applied to mortal artists of images of immortal gods.

> "If these things do not receive daily care, they certainly disappear in time because of their nature."

In *C.G.* 22 this will be said more extensively: images have to be renewed and reshaped because they are threatened in their existence by time and rain, see *infra*, 79.

> "And now would one not pity them also in this respect that seeing themselves they worship those who do not see and hearing themselves those who do not hear."

See on this further *C.G.* 15, *infra*, 60 f.

"And being by their nature men with soul and reason, they call gods those who do not move at all and have no soul."

This is also a traditional argument in Greek philosophy, see the quotation from Xenophanes given by Celsus and reproduced by Origen, *Contra Celsum* 1, 5 (cp. 7, 26): ὅμοια, ὡς εἴ τις τοῖς δόμοις λεσχηνεύοιτο, ποιεῖν τοὺς προσιόντας ὡς θεοῖς τοῖς ἀψύχοις, further examples in B. Gärtner, *op. cit.*, pp. 225 f.

"And this is amazing, that those whom they guard having them in their power, that they serve them as their masters."

For this argument see also *C.G.* 22, *infra*, 79.

"And do not think that I just say this or that I lie against them. For the proof of these things catches the eyes and all those who want to can see such things."

The refutation of gods and idols has so far been given 'from outside' (see *supra*, 51), i.e. with reasonable arguments which everyone can think of and which had been used by others before, so nobody can think that these are subjective opinions on the part of Athanasius (see also *Isaiah* 44:20: ἴδετε καὶ οὐκ ἐρεῖτε, ὅτι ψεῦδος ἐν δεξιᾷ μου, quoted in *C.G.* 14, *infra*, 59).

CHAPTER 14

Scriptural proof against the worship of idols.

Translation and Commentary:

(14) "But a stronger testimony about these things can be found in divine Scripture which taught long ago: "The idols of the Gentiles are silver and gold, the works of men's hands. They have eyes and will not see, they have a mouth and will not speak, they have ears and will not hear, they have noses and will not smell, they have hands and will not touch, they have feet and will not walk, they will not speak with their throat. But all those who make them become like them" (*Psalm* 113:12-16 (LXX)). Nor is there lack of prophetic condemnation of these things, but also in the prophets there is refutation of them when the Spirit says: "Those who make a god and all sculptors of vain things will be ashamed. And all were dried up from whence they came. And let the deaf among men all come and stand together and let them fear and be ashamed together. Because a workman sharpened the iron and worked it with an axe and shaped it with a hammer and set it up with the arm of his strength; and it will hunger and be weak and not drink water. For the workman chose wood, set it up in proportion and arranged it with glue and made it in the shape of a man and in the beauty of human being, he set it up in a house, the piece of wood which he cut from the forest, which the Lord had planted and the rain made increase, that it may provide fire to men and that man taking from it may be warmed. And having set it on fire

they baked bread on it and the rest they made into gods and adored them of which they burned half with fire. And having roasted meat on half of it, he ate and was filled. And having warmed himself he said: 'It is pleasant for me that I have warmed myself and saw fire.' And he adored the rest, saying: 'Deliver me, for Thou art my god.' They did not know how to consider that they had been deprived of sight so that they could not see with their eyes and know with their heart. And he did not consider in his heart and did not consider in his soul and did not understand in his mind that he burned half of it with fire and cooked breads on its charcoal, and that having cooked the meat he ate and the rest of it he made into an abomination, and they adore it. Know that their heart is ashes and they go astray, and nobody can deliver their soul. Look and you will not say that there is a lie in my right hand" (*Isaiah* 44:10-20).

The Scriptural refutation is called a better one than the refutation based on reason, but it contains the same argument as the latter one: the idols are lifeless and the products of men and it is absurd that man expects salvation from and pays divine honour to his own products. Athanasius had first given reasonable proofs against idolatry which show similarity with the Scriptural one. He obviously believes that reason confirms what Scripture says. Similarly he says in *C.G.* 6 that he intends to refute the heretics from Scripture and reason and in his refutation reasonable and Scriptural arguments are interwoven (see *supra*, 32), in *C.G.* 2 he quotes *Matth.* 5:8 after his description of the contemplation of the Divine (which is given largely in Platonic terminology), in *C.G.* 5 *Phil.* 3:14 is quoted after the image derived from Plato concerning the human soul, in *C.G.* 30 *Deuteronomy* 30:14 and *Luke* 17:21 are quoted in his expositions of mysticism which betray Platonic influence (see *infra*, 99 f.), in *C.G.* 35 *Rom.* 1:20 and *Acts* 14:15-17 are quoted after his Stoic-Platonic theory about the harmony of the universe which reveals God (see *infra*, 118).

> "And how should not be judged as atheists in the eyes of all men those who are accused of impiety by divine Scripture, too? Or how should not be possessed by an evil spirit those who are so clearly proven to be venerating what is lifeless instead of truth? What kind of hope do they have or what pardon could there be for them who put their trust on what is irrational and immovable which they venerate instead of the true God?"

One might expect that the reasonable refutation of idolatry would convince all men, and not the Scriptural one, since only Christians accept the authority of Scripture. This, too, shows that the apologetic treatises are primarily meant for Christians: when they see that Scripture refutes idolatry in a way which is congruous with reason, then they must come to the conclusion that all men should be convinced by this. - When people who have a reason and a soul which is in constant movement (see *supra*,

24), when such people venerate what is irrational and immovable, this is the apex of absurd behaviour.

Chapter 15

Recapitulation of the attack on idolatry given so far.

Translation and Commentary:

> (15) "And if only, if only the artist had fashioned the gods for them without forms, lest they have the clear proof of the insensibility. For they would have deceived the minds of the simple as if the idols could perceive if they did not have the symbols of the senses, such as eyes and noses and ears and hands and a mouth – immobile to use their senses and to perceive sensible things."

As it would have been in the Pagans' interest not to degrade themselves to the worship of female gods (*C.G.* 9, *supra*, 48), it would have been in their interest to present their idols in such a way as to be able to mislead the simple, i.e. the majority of people, as will appear in the second half of this chapter. Simple people might still believe that formless idols can somehow perceive what is sensible. But by giving them the symbols of senses they provide a clear proof that they cannot perceive and are completely immobile, i.e. a proof which can also be understood by simple people.

> "But now they have them and do not have them, they stand and do not stand, they sit and do not sit. For they do not have the activity of these organs but as the maker wanted in that position they remain. They do not provide any characteristic of God, but are completely lifeless and appear to have been set down merely by the skill of a man."

The senses which are lifeless are a clear proof against their divinity, as was made clear in *C.G.* 14 with a quotation of *Psalm* 113:12-16 (LXX). – In *De Inc.* 31 the living Christ will be put in contrast with these lifeless idols: τίνα ἄν τις εἴποι νεκρόν; τὸν τοσαῦτα ἐργαζόμενον Χριστόν; ἀλλ' οὐκ ἴδιον νεκροῦ τὸ ἐργάζεσθαι· ἢ τὸν μηδ' ὅλως ἐργοῦντα, ἀλλ' ὡς ἄψυχον κείμενον, ὅπερ ἴδιον τῶν δαιμόνων καὶ εἰδώλων ὡς νεκρῶν ὑπάρχει; ὁ μὲν γὰρ τοῦ θεοῦ Υἱὸς ζῶν καὶ ἐνεργὴς ὢν καθ' ἡμέραν ἐργάζεται, καὶ ἐνεργεῖ τὴν πάντων σωτηρίαν. (Prof. W. den Boer, Leyden, draws our attention to the fact that Julian accuses the Christians of abandoning the eternal gods and adoring the dead Christ, see K. J. Neumann, *Scriptorum Graecorum qui Christianam impugnaverunt religionem quae supersunt fasc. 3*, Leipzig 1880, 196, 16, cf. W. den Boer, *Scriptorum Paganorum I-II saec. de Christianis testimonia*, Leiden 1965, p. 42. For chronological reasons Athanasius cannot, of course, here answer the charge made by Julian.) On the insensibility of idols see also Clement of Alexandria, *Protrept.* 4, 51: τὰ δὲ ἀγάλματα ἀργά, ἄπρακτα, ἀναίσθητα ... ἔστιν γὰρ ὡς ἀληθῶς τὸ ἄγαλμα ὕλη νεκρὰ τεχνίτου χειρὶ μεμορφωμένη.

> "And if only the heralds and prophets of such false gods, I mean the poets and prose writers, had simply written that they are gods and had not written down their actions as well, as a proof of their non-divinity and shameful behaviour. For they could have cheated the truth with the mere title of divinity, or rather lead away the mass of the people from the truth, but now, relating the love affairs and licentiousness of Zeus, and the acts of corruption of boys by others and their rivalries for the pleasures of women, their fears and anxieties and other vices they refute themselves, that they do not only do not relate about gods, but not even about respectable men, but that they tell mythological stories about evil beings far from the good."

As the sculptor could have misled the simple people by not giving special forms to the idols, so the poets could have misled the mass of the people by not telling special stories about the acts of the gods. (Since both arguments are parallel, this implies that the simple people are the mass of the people.) On the unacceptable acts of the gods see *C.G.* 11-12, *supra*, 50 ff. Athanasius uses the word μυθολογεῖν in the literal sense of "telling human stories about gods"; here he accuses the Pagans of doing this, he will accuse the Arians of the same, see *Contra Arianos* 3, 65 (PG 26, 460B). Ever since Xenophanes (Diels, FVS B 23 ff.) and Plato (see especially *Rep.* 376 ff.) the myths about the gods were criticised as immoral and harmful. Athanasius has so far taken these myths literally. In itself this seems incompatible with his view that the gods do not exist: one can not tell true stories about beings which do not exist. What Athanasius means to say is: if these stories are true, then the beings about which they are told cannot be gods. These unacceptable stories show that the gods are no more than deified vile human beings. – In the next chapter Athanasius will discuss the opposite view that these stories are false, but that the gods about whom they are told do exist.

CHAPTER 16

Attack on attempts made by some Pagans to explain the myths away.

Translation and Commentary:

(16) "But perhaps the impious will in this matter take refuge in the distinctive nature of the poets, saying that it belongs to the specific character of the poets to invent what is not and to compose untrue myths in order to please the audience, and will say that this is the reason why they composed the stories about the gods as well."

The view that the poet writes not true things, but writes in order to please is *e.g.* expressed by Plato, *Leges* 667D/E: Οὐκοῦν ἡδονῇ κρίνοιτ' ἂν μόνον ἐκεῖνο ὀρθῶς, ὃ μήτε τινὰ ὠφελίαν μήτε ἀλήθειαν μήτε ὁμοιότητα ἀπεργαζόμενον παρέχεται, μηδ' αὖ γε βλάβην, ἀλλ' αὐτοῦ τούτου μόνον ἕνεκα γίγνοιτο τοῦ συμπαρεπομένου τοῖς ἄλλοις, τῆς χάριτος, ἣν δὴ κάλλιστά τις ὀνομάσαι ἂν ἡδονήν, ὅταν μηδὲν αὐτῇ τούτων ἐπακολουθῇ. This was attacked in connection with the myths by Christians, see Ps.-Justin, *Coh.* 3 and Clement of Alexandria, *Protrept.*, 7, 73 ff., cp. 4, 52 f.

"But it will be shown that this is even the stalest excuse of all on account of their own views about these matters and of their own expositions. For if what is found in the poets is fictitious and false, then the names themselves are false given to Zeus, Kronos, Hera and Ares, and the others. For similarly, as they say themselves, the names, too, have been invented and there is no Zeus, Kronos or Ares at all, but the poets invent them as existing in order to deceive the audience. But when the poets invent what is not, how do they worship them as being?"

This could either be part of a rhetorical play, *viz.*, the argument by elimination (see on this argument in Athanasius: G. C. Stead, Rethorical Method in Athanasius, p. 127 and pp. 129 ff.). In that case he first discusses the possibility that the poets lie about the names and the acts of the gods, and then goes on to discuss the possibility that they tell the truth about the names but lie about the acts. Then he would oppose a view which might be held but of which no defenders can be traced. But it could also be that Athanasius here has in mind the well-known method of allegory which was applied in various ways by ancient writers (see on this subject: J. C. Joosen and J. H. Waszink, Allegorese, *RACT*, pp. 283 ff., J. Pépin, *Mythe et allégorie. Les origines grecques et les contestations judéo-chrétiennes*, Paris 1976[2]). But the argument has to be strained in order to be applied to certain people. The Sceptics cannot be envisaged here, since they did reject the existence of gods on account of the myths told about them (see *e.g.* J. Geffcken, *op. cit.* pp. XIX f.), but they cannot be accused of inconsistency, *viz.*, of venerating those whose existence they deny, and this is what Athanasius claims they do. Perhaps Athanasius has the Stoics in mind. As appears from *Vita Antonii* (PG 26, 949A/B) he knows about the physical interpretation given by the Stoics to the gods of mythology, in the sense that they stand for elements of the world or planets: 'Ἐὰν δέ, ὡς ἀκούω, θέλησητε λέγειν μυθικῶς λέγεσθαι ταῦτα παρ' ὑμῖν; καὶ ἀλληγορεῖτε ἁρπαγὴν κόρης εἰς τὴν γῆν, καὶ Ἡφαίστου χωλότητα εἰς τὸ πῦρ, καὶ Ἥραν εἰς τὸν ἀέρα, καὶ Ἀπόλλωνα μὲν εἰς τὸν ἥλιον, καὶ Ἄρτεμιν μὲν εἰς τὴν σελήνην, τὸν δὲ Ποσειδῶνα εἰς τὴν θάλασσαν (see on this *e.g.* Athenagoras, *Leg.* 22, Cicero, *De nat. deor.* 2, 24, 63 f., Minucius Felix, *Oct.* 19, 10, cp. J. Pépin, *op. cit.*, p. 98). If the Stoics are meant here, then those who say that the names are false do not differ from those who will be attacked instantly, *viz.*, those who say that the names are true but the actions applied to them false. What the Stoics say is that the legends about these gods and the persons of these gods have a deeper meaning. If it is this theory which is attacked by Athanasius, then he forces it into the rhetorical alternative: either one admits that both the names and the acts are false (which is the only way out), or one tries to argue in a more subtle way that the names are right but the acts false, or *vice versa*, but this will prove to be no way out:

> "Or perhaps they will say again that the names are not invented but that they lie about their acts? But this is nevertheless not a safe excuse for them either, for if they lied about their acts, they certainly lied about the names of those of whom they related the acts to be. Or if they tell the truth about the names, they necessarily also tell the truth about the acts. Furthermore, those who told the myths about the existence of these gods surely also know what gods ought to do and certainly would never attribute human ideas to gods, as one would not attribute the activity of fire to water, for the one burns and the other one has a cold substance. So if the actions are worthy of gods, then also those who perform the acts will be gods. But if to commit adultery and the acts mentioned above are characteristic of men and of evil men at that, then those who performed them would be men and not gods. For the acts must be in accordance with the natures, in order that he who acts is known from his action, and the act can be known from the nature."

The key to this argument is the last sentence: names and acts must be in accordance with each other. Then true acts cannot be attributed to false names, but only true acts to true names and false acts to false names. It is possible that again Athanasius has the advocates of allegory in mind here. In both cases they can be refuted. If true acts are attributed to true names, then the rejectable acts of the gods show that the Pagan 'gods' are evil beings, and evil beings are no gods. If false acts are attributed to false names then this shows that the gods do not exist at all. (This is again the rhetorical argument by elimination: Athanasius leaves no room for the possibility that the acts and names are false on the surface, but have a true and deeper meaning.) The argument that names and acts must be in accordance with each other could have been taken from those who allegorize the myths: with the help of etymologies of the names of the gods they describe the real activities of the various gods (see *e.g.* Cicero, *De nat. deor.* 2, 24, 64 ff. cp. J. Pépin, *op. cit.*, p. 126). With these allegories they want to get rid of the embarrassing stories about their gods, Athanasius then wants to show that they should be consistent and not only get rid of the stories but also of those about whom they are told: the gods.

> "For example, if somebody discusses water and fire and makes statements about their activities, he would not say that water burns and fire is cold. Nor, if somebody talked about the sun and earth, would he say that the earth gives light and that the sun is sown with plants and fruits, but if he did, he would surpass all madness."

The background of this argument could be the physical interpretation given by the Stoics of the gods as elements of the world or as planets (see *supra*, 62). If one tells mythological stories about gods who are elements or planets, this is as mad as if one says that water burns etc. If Athanasius has this theory in mind here, then he hereby wants to show that he is not convinced at all by these allegories (cp. the Sceptic Cotta in Cicero, *De nat. deor.* 3, 24, 62).

> "Similarly their prose writers and most of all their most outstanding poet, if they had known that Zeus and the others were gods, would not have attributed such actions to them which show that they are not gods, but men and intemperate men at that."

If the prose writers and Homer are to be taken seriously they must show with their myths that the 'gods' they speak about are not gods but men. This assumes that they tell the truth in telling these stories: the acts did happen, but they are not the acts of god, but of men. There is also the other possibility that as poets and writers they do not tell the truth:

> "Or if as poets they told false things and you tell false stories about the gods, why did they not also lie about the manliness of the heroes and invent weakness instead of manliness and manliness instead of weakness."

The 'you' who tells false stories about the gods in the Pagan who claims that it is the task of the poets to do just this (see *supra*, 61). But this immediately leads to the question whether the poets only lied about the acts of the gods and not about the acts of the heroes as well, so that everything they say is fictitious and false.

> "For as with Zeus and Hera, they should also have lied about cowardice of Achilles and they should have admired strength of Thersites, and they should have attacked stupidity of Odysseus and invented madness of Nestor, and they should have told stories about effeminate acts of Diomedes and Hector and about manliness of Hecabe. For with all, as they say themselves, the poets should invent and lie."

As they tell stories about gods which do not fit in with the nature of gods, so they should have told stories about their heroes which are incompatible with the character of these heroes. Athanasius here either deploys the rhetorical *reductio ad absurdum*, whereby he suggests that everybody knows that Achilles was a hero and Thersites a coward, but that nevertheless the poets should have falsely portrayed Achilles as a coward and

Thersites as a hero. Then Athanasius leaves unanswered the question how everybody can know that Achilles is a hero if the poets portray him as a coward, since the source of knowledge about Achilles are the poets. So it could also be possible that Athanasius here demands that they should have told stories about Achilles' manliness *and* his cowardice, thereby making it clear that they are telling fictitious and contradictory stories. Athanasius would then here take the line of the Sceptic who prove that the truth cannot be known by proving opposite things about the same matter (cp. C. J. de Vogel, Greek, *Philosophy. A Collection of Texts with Notes and Explanations*, Volume III, Leiden 1969, pp. 202 f.).

> "But now with respect to men they guarded the truth, but they did not shrink from accusing falsely the so-called gods."

This is not Athanasius' view, but obviously the view of those who allegorize the stories about the gods, but regard the stories about the Homeric heroes as true. Athanasius wants these people to be consistent and regard all stories as fictitious. This fictitiousness can appear from the fact that contradictory stories are told about the heroes, but also about the gods. This leads to a discussion of the following defence of the gods of mythology which somebody might produce:

> "For one of them might also say that they lie in respect of their licentious acts, but in their words of praise, when they call Zeus the Father of gods, the Supreme, the Olympian and Ruler in heaven, they do not invent but tell the truth. But not only I but anybody could prove this argument to be against them. For the truth will again be against them according to the proofs given above. For the acts prove them to be men, but the praise is beyond the nature of men. But each of these two is inconsistent, for neither is it characteristic for those in heaven to do such things, nor can anybody suppose to be gods who do such things."

If one says that the negative things are untrue but the positive things true, then the negative things apply to the *acts* of the gods, the positive things to the *nature* of the gods, but it had been shown that statements about the nature and the acts of the gods must not be inconsistent, and it is inconsistent to ascribe to any beings the acts of men and the nature of gods. The consistent application of the statement quoted in the beginning of this chapter, *viz.*, that the poets tell fictitious stories in order to please the audience, is that *all* they say about gods' and men's nature and acts is fictitious, thereby themselves proving the non-existence of the gods.

CHAPTER 17

The myths show that the so-called gods are in fact mortal men.

Translation and Commentary:

In the previous chapter Athanasius had shown that the claim that poets merely want to please the audience is no way out for the Pagans, since a consistent application of this claim and method implies that all the poets say is fictitious. Now Athanasius makes it clear that he does not regard this refutation as sufficient, since an even more embarrassing one for the Pagans can be produced.

> (17) "What then is left to think save that their praise is false and meant to please, but that the acts speak out the truth against them?"

In the previous chapter it had been made clear that the words of praise about the gods' nature cannot be wrong whilst the stories about their acts are true, but this was shown on the basis of a consistent application of allegory. Now he reveals his disbelief in this method, and this will make things worse for the Pagans.

> "And one can recognize this to be true form a customary habit. For nobody, when he wants to praise someone, also condemns his behaviour."

Here the honest wish to praise somebody is envisaged: if one intends to do this, one does not pick out people whose conduct one condemns.

> "But they rather extol with praise those whose acts are bad and who are therefore criticized in order to hide their unlawful behaviour, having misled the audience with excessive praise."

Here a dishonest, misleading praise is envisaged which is expressed in hyperboles. This is a very venomous remark, since only bad orators do this, – manuals in fact warn against going so far in using hyperboles, since the audience may refuse to believe them, see *e.g.* Quintilian, *Inst. Or.* 8, 6, 73 f.: *Quamvis est enim omnis hyperbole ultra fidem, non tamen esse debet ultra modum, nec alia via magis in* κακοζηλίαν *itur ... Quo magis intuendum est, quousque deceat extollere quod nobis non creditur.*

> "So it is as when somebody, wanting to praise somebody else, does not find in his conduct and virtue of the soul a reason for his praise, since these are shameful, then extols them in a different way by granting them what is beyond them. Similarly their admired poets, ashamed of the mean acts of their so-called gods, attributed to them a superhuman name, not realizing that they will not overshadow their human behaviour with superhuman fancies, but will rather prove with their human defects that the notion of God does not fit them."

If one hears this one may wonder how it is possible that the Greek poets behave like bad orators. This will now be explained:

> "And I believe that the gods' passions and their actions have been told by the poets even against their purpose. For since they strove to attribute the,

as Scripture says, incommunicable name and honour of God to those who are not gods but mortal men, what they attempted in their evil courage was both a great and an impious thing, and for this reason they were forced by truth against their purpose to expound their passions, in order that to all later generations their passions as contained in the writings about them would be the proof that these are not gods."

The claim that poets merely want to please the audience and allegory may, if consistently applied, prove the non-existence of the gods, but it could be an excuse for the poets. But in reality no such excuse is available to them: what they attempted was impious (on the τόλμα of idolatry see *supra*, 44), viz., to transfer the incommunicable name of God (*Sap. Sal.* 14:21, quoted in *C.G.* 11, *supra*, 50) to idols. In order to prevent them from misleading later generations, the divine truth forces them to behave like bad orators and hereby makes them look foolish: they ascribe human acts to divine beings, proving these beings not to be divine but human. So the gods are nothing but fancifully deified evil men. This is indeed much worse than allegory which implies that fictitious stories are told about fictitious divine beings in order to please the audience.

Chapter 18

Continuation of the refutation of the euhemeristic interpretation of gods.

Translation and Commentary:

(18) "So what defence and what proof of their being gods have those who falsely venerate them? For from what has been said shortly before our reasonable argument has shown that they are men and dishonourable men at that."

This is a reference to the arguments given in *C.G.* 11-17.

"But perhaps they will turn to this defence and take pride in the useful things for life invented by them, saying that for this reason they are also regarded as gods, because they have been useful to men. For Zeus is said to have exercised the art of sculpture, Poseidon that of steersman, Hephaistos smithery, Athena weaving, Apollo music, Artemis hunting, Hera equipment, Demeter farming and others other arts, as the historians have related about them."

Athanasius here again refers to the well known euhemeristic theory that the gods are deified men, see *e.g.* Eusebius, *Praep. Evang.* 2, 2, Lactance, *Div. Inst.* 1,18, Cicero, *De nat. deor.* 2, 23, 60 (for further examples see L. Leone, *op. cit.*, p. 34). Christians, of course, rejected this theory as Athanasius does in the present chapter. But he also uses it in a rhetorical way for his own purpose: the Greeks deified Asclepius because he practised healing, then they should not oppose the worship of the Lord who wrought many miracles, see *De Inc.* 49. (Tertullian uses the theory against the god of Marcion. The god of Marcion should at least have produced one small chickpea in order to be preached as some new Triptolemus, see *Adv. Marc.* 1, 11, 5.)

> "But men should not have attributed these and similar skills only to them, but to the common human nature, looking at this men invent the arts. For most people say that art is an imitation of nature. So if they became skilful about the arts which they practised, it is not necessary to regard them because of this also as gods, but rather as men. Because the arts do not stem from them, but they themselves imitated nature in these arts. For being men who can by nature (as the definition given about them states) receive knowledge, it is not amazing at all if they themselves with their human mind looking at their nature, and having received its knowledge, invented the arts."

The definition of art as an imitation of nature goes back to Aristotle, *Phys.* II 2 194 a 21: εἰ δὲ ἡ τέχνη μιμεῖται τὴν φύσιν (cp. Plato, *Rep.* X 597 and *Leges* X 888e ff.; for further similar statements in Aristotle see I. Düring, *Aristoteles. Darstellung und Interpretation seines Denkens*, p. 242 n. 398). Athanasius' remark that "most people" say this seems to be justified by the fact that this statement appears in popular Hellenistic literature, see *e.g.* Cicero, *De nat. deor.* 2, 22, 57-58, Ps-Aristotle, *De mundo* 396 B 11 f. For the definition that man can by nature receive knowledge see Aristotle, *Top.* 5, 4, 5 (132 b 1 ff.): ἐπεὶ τὸ ζῷον ἐπιστήμης δεκτικὸν κατὰ παντὸς ἀνθρώπου ἀληθεύεται καὶ ᾗ ἄνθρωπος, εἴη ἂν ἀνθρώπου ἴδιον τὸ ζῷον ἐπιστήμης δεκτικόν. – What Athanasius wants to show with these generally accepted views on art is that the invention of arts is nothing special which justifies deification, since by his nature every man in principle has the ability to invent an art. He proves this by specifying nature which is imitated as human nature. This is not implied in the well known definition of art as an imitation of nature (in general), but Athanasius needs this specification in order to show that (in the hypothetical case that any deification is acceptable) the artist deserves more to be deified than his product: the product is merely an imitation of the artist's nature.

> "Or if they say that they deserve to be called gods because of the invention of arts, then it is time to call gods also the inventors of other arts according to the argument with which also the former ones have been judged worthy of such a name. For the Phoenicians invented the alphabet, Homer heroic poetry, Zeno the Eleatic dialectic, Korax of Syracuse rhetoric, Aristaios bee culture, Triptolemus the sowing of food, and Lycurgus of Sparta and Solon of Athens laws. Palamedes invented the composition of letters, numbers, measures and weights. And others

proclaimed other and different things useful for the life of men according to the testimony of the historians. So if skills deify and because of these gods have been sculpted, then necessarily later inventors than these of other arts are according to them gods as well."

Having refuted the theory that invention deserves deification, he now shows that if one grants the theory to be right one still can prove that it has been applied with arbitrary limitations: many more inventors ought to have been deified. This is a typically Sceptic way of arguing, *viz.*, the argument of the *sorites*; Cicero, *De nat. deor.* 3, 17, 43 ff. quotes Carneades as giving it in a refutation of Stoic theology. – Athanasius provides a list of inventors of various arts about which he holds different views. His view on the heroic art of Homer is negative (see *C.G.* 16-17, *supra*, 61 ff.), on the laws positive (see *infra*, 107), the importance of (the composition of) letters is put into perspective in *Vita Antonii* 73 (PG 26, 945A): when the Greeks ridicule Antony for being unable to write, Antony says that mind is the cause of letters and not *vice versa*, therefore he who has a sound mind needs no letters. (Clement of Alexandria gives a long list of inventors in *Strom.* 1, 16, 74 ff. – a section quoted by Eusebius, *Praep. Evang.* 10, 6 – with which he wants to show that not the Greeks but the Barbarians invented useful things and that the Greeks borrowed them from the Barbarians, the Hebrews amongst them.)

> "Or if they do not regard these worthy of the honour of God, but acknowledge them to be men, then it follows that also Zeus and Hera and the other ones should not be called gods, but should also be believed to have been men, and above all that they were not even respectable men, as they also prove them to be nothing but men from the sculpting of their images."

As he likes to do (cp. *supra*, 31) Athanasius confronts his opponents with a crude alternative: either the invention of arts deserves deification, but then all and not only some inventors ought to be deified, or it does not deserve deification, but then no inventor ought to be deified. In both cases the deification of some inventors (as is found in Pagan idolatry) is absurd.

CHAPTER 19

Attack on the images of the gods and on attempts to justify them.

Translation and Commentary:

(19) "For when they sculpt them what other form do they apply to them than the one of men and women and of even lower beings than these which are of an irrational nature, all sorts of birds, tame and wild quadrupeds and all sorts of reptiles which the earth, see and all the nature of the water produces?"

The subdivision of chapters artificially breaks the argument. As the word γάρ indicates this first sentence explains what was said in the last sentence of the previous chapter. There Athanasius had said that by sculpting idols the Pagans prove that their gods are in fact men and not respectable men at that. This will now be explained:

> "For men having fallen into the irrationality of passions and pleasures and seeing nothing more than pleasures and desires of the flesh, since they had their minds fixed on these irrational things, they also shaped the Divine in irrational things according to the variance of their own passions and having sculpted an equal number of gods. For they have pictures of quadrupeds, reptiles and birds as also the interpreter of the divine and true piety says: "They became vain in their reasonings and their stupid heart was darkened. Professing to be wise they became fools, and they exchanged the glory of the incorruptible God for the likeness of an image of a corruptible man, and of birds, quadrupeds and reptiles. Therefore God handed them over to passions of dishonour" (*Rom.* 1:21-24). For previously having been affected in their souls by irrational pleasures, as I said above, they fell into the fashioning of such gods. And having fallen they further roll along in these things as people who have been abandoned because they have turned away from God, and they model God the Father of the Word in irrational things."

Man's fall means that he forgets being created in God's image as a rational being and turns to physical pleasures and is ruled by these, thus becoming an irrational being. As irrational beings men fashioned irrational gods. So whilst rational man is the true image of the true God, irrational men shape irrational gods in their own image. This proves the claim made at the end of the previous chapter that it appears from the sculpting of idols of gods that the gods are men and not respectable men at that. – The idolators roll along, this is the opposite of what he should do: walk on the road which leads to knowledge of the true God, see *supra*, 29, *C.G.* 5 and *infra*, 100, *C.G.* 30.

> "When the so-called philosophers and wise men of the Greeks are confronted with a refutation of these matters they do not deny that their apparent gods are the forms and models of men and irrational beings. But in defence they say that they have them for this reason that the Divine may respond and appear to them, for the Invisible Himself could only be known through such statues and rites."

Not only Christians, but also Greek philosophers attacked the images of gods, and some philosophers defended the images in the way Athanasius quotes here (and in which Athenagoras quotes the defence in *Leg.* 18, 1, see J. Geffcken, *op. cit.*, pp. XXI f., who refers to the Stoic Dion of Prusa who explains the images as a kind of comfort to men because of the absence of the gods themselves, and a similar interpretation given by the Platonist Maximus).

"And those who are even greater philosophers than these and think that they say more profound things say that these things were made and modelled for the invocation and appearance of divine messengers and powers for this reason that appearing through these they would provide them with knowledge about God. And that these are so to speak letters for men, and in reading them they can receive knowledge about God from the appearance through them of divine messengers."

Those who hold this view are complimented in a guarded way: they *are* greater philosophers and *think* that they say more profound things, - in *C.G.* 21 (see *infra*, 74) it says that the view *is* more profound and in *C.G.* 10 that Plato *boasted* he had deep thoughts about God (see *supra*, 49). These remarks reflect the fact that Athanasius' view on Platonism was less unfavourable than his view on other philosophical systems (this applies to the majority of early Christian writers). Athanasius here refers to a theory which is found in the Neo-Platonists (cp. L. Leone, *op. cit.*, p. 37 and A. H. Armstrong, Some Comments on the Development of the Theology of Images, *Studia Patristica* IX, Berlin 1966, pp. 117 ff.). The closest comes Porphyry, Περὶ ἀγαλμάτων, *Orph. Fragm.* 6, 1, quoted by Eusebius: Σοφίας θεολόγου νοήματα δεικνύς, οἷς τὸν θεὸν καὶ τοῦ θεοῦ τὰς δυνάμεις διὰ εἰκόνων συμφύλων αἰσθήσει ἐμύνησαν ἄνδρες τὰ ἀφανῆ φανεροῖς ὑποτυπώσαντες πλάσμασι τοῖς καθάπερ ἐκ βίβλων τῶν ἀγαλμάτων ἀναλέγειν τὰ περὶ θεῶν μεμαθηκόοσι γράμματα (cp. also Plotinus, *Enn.* 4, 3, 11). See on this matter also W. den Boer, Συγγράματα, p. 161.

"Such is their mythology, for it is no theology. Far from it! But if somebody examined the argument carefully he will find that their view is not less false than those that were shown to be false above."

Mythology is human stories about gods that are false (see *supra*, 61 ff.), theology is the right way of speaking about the true God. The refutation promised here will be given in *C.G.* 21, see *infra*, 74 ff.

CHAPTER 20

Refutation of the first defence of images given by Greek philosophers.

Translation and Commentary:

(20) "For somebody could say to them, coming forward to the bar of truth:"

This remark justifies the attempt to apply the rules of rhetoric to the interpretation of Athanasius' arguments: Athanasius says himself that he speaks as it were in court with truth as judge; cp. *De Inc.* 29: ... δῆλον ἂν εἴη παρὰ ἀληθείᾳ δικαζούσῃ ... and Origen, *Contra Celsum* 1, 1.

> "How does God respond or is He known through these images? Through the matter of which they are made or through the form in them?

This is again the rhetorical argument by elimination which Athanasius likes to use, see G. C. Stead, Rhetorical Method in Athanasius, p. 127 and pp. 129 ff.

> "For if it is through matter what is the need of form and why does God not simply appear through all matter before it was shaped? In vain they also erected walls around their temples, enclosing one stone or piece of wood or bit of gold since the whole earth is full of this stuff."

The form confines the all-embracing God to a certain quantity of matter whilst in reality God is present in all matter. The same confinement of God takes place if the opposite is true:

> "But if the form imposed becomes the reason of the divine appearance, what is the need of matter, gold and other stuff and why does God not rather appear through natural living beings of which the statues are the forms? For the opinion about God would according to the same argument have become better, if He appeared through living beings both rational and irrational and was not sought in lifeless and umnoving objects."

The idea behind this could also be (apart from the reason given in the next sentence) that in this case God appears through forms which He has imposed Himself, since He is the Creator of the animals. Now man degrades God by making Him appear in a form which is a human imitation of forms imposed by God.

> "Because of this they particularly commit impiety against themselves. For although they abominate and turn away from natural beings, quadrupeds, birds and reptiles, either because of their wildness, or because of their filth, nevertheless they sculpt models of them in stone, wood and gold and then deify them. But they ought rather to adore the living beings themselves than to worship their models in these images."

This says from a different angle what was suggested repeatedly before: by adoring irrational beings man adores what is below and not what is above him. He cannot try to excuse himself that he does not realize this, since he apparently abominates these beings and turns away from them, and instead of adoring the living animals (which is already completely unacceptable) he adores something even lower than they are, *viz.*, their lifeless models. (Clement of Alexandria, *Protrept.* 4, 51 f. argues that whilst statues have no sense moles and field-mice have.)

> "Or perhaps none of these, neither the form nor matter is the reason of God's presence, but only the art with skill evokes the Divine, since it is itself an imitation of nature. But if God enters the statues because of skill, what then is the need of matter, since the skill is in men? For if in general God

appears through the art and this is the reason that the statues are worshipped as gods, then men as the originators of art ought to be adored and worshipped, because they are both rational beings and have the skill in themselves."

This argument is rather strained; it clearly is developed *ad hoc*. The definition already given of art, *viz.*, that it is an imitation of nature (see *C.G.* 18, *supra*, 68) makes it possible to deny that outward matter or outward form are the cause of God's appearance, since a third possibility arises: the inward skill of the artist; this could be the cause of God's appearance. It is illogical to ask in this context again why matter was necessary, as was asked when form was called the cause of God's appearance. Athanasius must know that an artist needs matter in order to express his skill. But he argues in the way he does in order to find the cause of God's appearance not in outward statues but in man himself. Then man should be deified as the originator of art. This only means that as the adoration of living animals is less unacceptable than the adoration of images of animals, so the adoration of men is less unacceptable than the adoration of animals (cp. *C.G.* 9, *supra*, 44), but it still remains rejectable. In *C.G.* 18 Athanasius had argued that since art is an imitation of nature invention is *no* reason for deification, he now twists the argument in order to show that since man's skill of art is an imitation of nature, it shows that there is at least more reason to deify men than (images of) animals. But rather uncautiously (and *ad hoc*) he calls men the originators of art. This he explicitly denied in *C.G.* 18, calling nature the originator of its imitation, art, and this he will deny in *De Decr.* 11 where he says that man receives his skill as an artist from God (PG 25, 441C): οἱ δὲ ἄνθρωποι τὴν ὑποκειμένην ὕλην ἐργάζονται, εὐξάμενοι πρότερον, καὶ τὴν ἐπιστήμην τοῦ ποιεῖν λαβόντες παρὰ τοῦ πάντα δημιουργήσαντος θεοῦ διὰ τοῦ Λόγου. Rather interestingly this remark shows some similarity with Plotinus' views on arts. Athanasius says that man receives his skill to create (out of substance) from God who creates (out of nothing) through His Logos. This implies that human skill or art has some resemblance with God's Logos, – Plotinus says something similar when he explains that products of art are not just imitation of nature, but in the end an imitation of the ideas in the intelligible world which are the cause of nature, see e.g. *Enneads* 5, 8, 1, 35-36: οὐχ ἁπλῶς τὸ ὁρώμενον μιμοῦνται (sc. αἱ τέχναι), ἀλλ' ἀνατρέχουσιν ἐπὶ τοὺς λόγους, ἐξ ὧν ἡ φύσις (cp. Augustin, *De div. quaest.* LXXXIII 78: *Ars illa summa omnipotentis Dei, per quam ex nihilo facta sunt omnia ... ipsa operatur etiam per artifices, ut pulchra atque congruentia faciant; quamvis non de nihilo, sed de aliqua materia operentur*, see on this subject A. H. Armstrong, Plotinus. Man and Reality, *The Cambridge History*, pp. 233 f., and K. Flasch, Ars imitatur naturam.

Platonischer Naturbegriff und mittelalterliche Philosophie der Kunst, *Parusia. Studien zur Philosophie Platons und zur Problemgeschichte des Platonismus*. Festgabe für Johannes Hirschberger herausgegeben von Kurt Flasch, Frankfurt/M. 1965, pp. 270 ff.).

CHAPTER 21

Attack on the Neo Platonic defence of images of the Divine.

Translation and Commentary:

(21) "Regarding their second and as they pretend more profound defence, somebody could consistently say the following as well: If, o Greeks, these images have not been made by you because of the manifestation of God, but because of the presence of messengers in them, why do you make the statues through which you invoke the powers greater and above the very powers you invoke through them?"

The Platonists claim that not God, but only divine messengers appear in the images. Athanasius will show that the images are given the title of God and are therefore more than the messengers they are supposed to invoke. – What is attacked here is the theory that angels can be invoked through images, a theory which is found in the *Corpus Hermeticum*, *Asclepius* 37, and in which it says that this invocation of demons and angels gives life to the statues: ... *proavi nostri ... invenerunt artem qua efficerent deos. cui inventae adiunxerunt virtutem de mundi natura convenientem eamque miscentes, quoniam animas facere non poterant, evocantes animas daemonum vel angelorum eas indiderunt imaginibus sanctis divinisque mysteriis, per quas idola et bene faciendi et male vires habere potuissent*. Something similar appears in Plotinus, *Enn.* 4, 3, 11, 1-6, who says that the ancient sages wanted to secure the presence of divine beings through the erection of shrines, these sages realized that the divine Soul is present everywhere, but that its presence can be secured more readily when an appropriate receptacle is elaborated, through which some portion of It can be received: καί μοι δοκοῦσιν οἱ πάλαι σοφοί, ὅσοι ἐβουλήθησαν θεοὺς αὐτοῖς παρεῖναι ἱερὰ καὶ ἀγάλματα ποιησάμενοι, εἰς τὴν τοῦ παντὸς φύσιν ἀπιδόντες, ἐν νῷ λαβεῖν ὡς πανταχοῦ μὲν εὐάγωγον ψυχῆς φύσις, δέξασθαί γε μὴν ῥᾷστον ἂν εἴη ἁπάντων, εἴ τις προσπαθές τι τεκτήναιτο ὑποδέξασθαι δυνάμενον μοῖράν τινα αὐτῆς (see A. H. Armstrong's review of the author's *Orthodoxy and Platonism in Athanasius* in the *Journal of Theological Studies* (1970), p. 190). – Athanasius says that he wants to refute this argument consistently (ἀκολούθως), it will indeed appear that he takes the same line of argument as he has taken so far in his refutation of the idols, which is that he shows that more honour is given to what is lower than to what ranks higher:

"For whilst you carve the forms because of the comprehension of God, as you say, you ascribe the honour and title of God Himself to just these statues, hereby becoming guilty of sacrilege. For whilst you confess that the power of God transcends the smallness of the statues and therefore dare not invoke God through them, but only the lower powers, you yourselves pass over these powers and give the title of just Him whose presence you fear to express to stones and pieces of wood and call them gods instead of stones and human arts and adore them."

The key to this argument lies in the observation made by Athanasius that the Pagans in fact ignore these lower divine powers and call the statues 'god', hereby applying to them the name of God whilst they fear to say that God Himself appears in these statues. In the quotation from Plotinus *Enneads* 4, 3, 11 given above Plotinus does speak about the presence of gods in the statues. Just as in his polemics against the Arians Athanasius here assumes that the word 'God' can only be applied to the being which is fully and supremely divine and that there are no lower gods, lower gods are no gods at all, see e.g. *Contra Arianos* 3, 8, 16 (PG 26, 337, 356), *Ep. ad episc. Aeg. et Lib.* 4 (PG 25, 545). (The Platonists apply the title 'god' much more easily to beings lower than the Supreme God, this is in fact a very important difference between Platonic and orthodox Christian thought, cp. the following observation made by A. H. Armstrong, Man in the Cosmos, *Plotinian and Christian Studies*, London 1979. ch. XXII, p. 6 = *Romanitas et Christianitas, Studia J. H. Waszink... oblata*, Amsterdam-Oxford 1973, p. 6: "It is a contrast between a monotheism which sees the One God, the unique, unchallengeably and unchangingly transcendent, source of all reality and goodness, communicating divinity to all beings whom his spontaneous creativity brings into existence according to their capacity to receive it, and the monotheism of the 'jealous god', separated by an unbridgeable gulf from his creation, guarding his divinity as an unique prerogative which it is blasphemy and idolatry to attribute to any other being.") Having got rid of the lower divine beings Athanasius can now attack this Neo Platonic defence of images with the same arguments with which he refuted the defence of images in the previous chapter:

"For if these are to you, as you falsely claim, as letters for the contemplation of God, then it is not just to give more honour to what signifies than to what is signified."

On the idols as letters see *C. G.* 19, *supra*, 71. – It is clear that the object of signification causes the act of signification and is therefore more than it, cp. *De Inc.* 40: ἐλθόντος γὰρ τοῦ σημαινομένου, τίς ἔτι χρεία τῶν σημαινόντων ἦν; καὶ παρούσης τῆς ἀληθείας, τίς ἔτι χρεία τῆς σκιᾶς ἦν;

(Things are, of course, different when τὸ ποιοῦν and τὸ ποιούμενον are put in contrast to each other, see *C.G.* 9, *supra*, 47.)

> "For also if somebody writes the name of a king he would not without danger give more honour to the letter than to the king. But such a person would receive death as penalty, and the letter is shaped by the skill of the writer. In the same way you, too, if you had a strong reasoning, would not transfer such an important characteristic of divinity to matter, and you would not have given more honour to the statue than to the man who made it. For if like letters they signify at all the appearance of God and because of this as signifying God are worthy of deification, then so much more he who sculpted and shaped these, I mean again the artist, ought to be deified as much more powerful and divine than these, since these were carved and formed according to his will."

For the idea that the letter is shaped by the skill of the writer see the quotation given *supra*, 69, from *Vita Antonii* 73, where it says that the mind is prior to letters. Having established a clear parallel between the letters and matter he can refute the images by saying that *if* matter as signifying God is worthy of deification, then the artist is even more worthy of deification, since he applies his skill to matter, cp. *C.G.* 13, *supra*, 56 f.. (R. W. Thomson's translation, *op. cit.*, p. 59 is incorrect: "For if like letters they really indicate the manifestation of God, on that account as signs of God they are worthy of deification." This suggests that Athanasius agrees with deification of images, but Athanasius only hypothetically agrees with this in order to be able to show that the artist has more right to be deified than the product of his skill, – but in reality neither the artist nor his product are worthy of deification). The claim by the Platonists that the images are like letters makes Athanasius compare the writer with the artist. Since writing is a skill Athanasius can argue against the theory that the pieces of writing are worthy of deification as he argued against the deification of the works of the artist.

> "So if the letters are worthy of admiration, much more the writer excels in admiration because of the art and the skill of his soul. So if it is not right to regard them as gods for this reason, one might again ask them about the madness of idols wanting to learn from them the reason for such a form."

The skill of the artist deserves more to be deified than the product (if anything deserves deification at all). In the previous chapter it was asked why matter is necessary if the skill makes the Divine appear (see *supra*, 72 f.), now the question is asked why a specific form is deified if the skill of the artist is more than the form.

It is almost needless to say that this attack on the Neo Platonic interpretation of images is purely rhetorical and falls far short of any serious refutation of it. The Neo Platonists did not want to adore stones and idols, they wanted to be reminded by the idols (which they could see) of the incorporeal and invisible powers, cp. A. H. Armstrong, The Development of the Theology of Images, pp. 124 f.

CHAPTER 22

Attack on the various forms of the images of the Divine.

Translation and Commentary:

(22) "For if it is because the Divine has a human form that the statue is modelled in such a way, why do they also apply to it the form of animals? But if its form is that of irrational living beings, why do they also apply to it the figures of rational beings? But if it is both together, and if they comprehend God in both ways, because He has the figure of irrational and rational beings, why do they divide what is a unity and make a difference between the figure of irrational beings and of men, and why do they not always sculpt them in both ways such as the figures in the myths, Scylla and Charybdis, the Hippocentaur and the dog-headed Anoubis of the Egyptians? For they either ought to picture them only in such a way with two natures, or if they have only one form the other form should not be added to them."

The argument is again the one by elimination and runs in the same way as when the question was discussed of whether the Divine appears through form or matter of the statues: Either the Divine has a human form, but then only statues of human forms should be made (which is not the case), or it has the form of animals, then only statues of these forms should be made (which is not the case either), or it has a mixed nature (like the beings talked about in the myths, then only such statues should be made. This latter possibility (of the gods having two natures) is again subdivided: either they have two natures and then they should be modelled in such a way, or they have not two but only one nature, but then they should not be modelled with two natures. – These are to Athanasius only rhetorical and not real alternatives, the veneration of images of animals has been described as a worse form of idolatry than the veneration of human images (*C.G.* 9 and 20, *supra*, 44 and 72), and in *C.G.* 9 it said that beings of mixed nature do not exist at all (*supra*, 45), a claim which is indirectly repeated in the present chapter when it says that these beings appear in the myths, and myths lie about the nature of the so called divine beings, see *C.G.* 16-17, *supra*, 61 ff. – The same argument by elimination is now applied in discussing the question of whether the Divine has a male or a female form:

"And again if the forms of these gods are male, why do they also apply to them female forms? And if they have female forms, why do they also falsely speak about their male forms? And if again they are both at the same time, they ought not to be divided but both be put together and become such as the so called hermaphrodites in order that their superstition should provide to those who look at it not only impiety and misrepresentation but also reasons for laughter."

Female gods are a form of even worse idolatry than male gods, see C.G. 10, *supra*, 48, – these images in fact provide the refutation of Pagan idolatry from inside, see C.G. 11, *supra*, 51.

"And in general, if they suppose the Divine to have a body, so that they imagine and picture a stomach and hands and feet, and also neck an breast and further the organs which generate men, look into what an impiety and godlessness their mind has fallen that they imagine such things about the Divine. For then it follows that it certainly suffers also the other bodily experiences, so that it is also cut and divided and again perishes completely. But these and similar things are not characteristic of God, but rather of the bodies on earth. For God is incorporeal, imperishable and immortal, not in need of anything for any purpose."

In rejecting anthropomorphous images of the Divine or God Athanasius reproduces a commonplace (cp. for the following: J. Geffcken, *op. cit.*, p. 39). Especially the Sceptics attacked anthropomorphism (see e.g. Cicero, *De nat. deor.* 1, 25, 71 ff.), *inter alia* the idea that there should be male and female gods with sexual organs (see Cicero, *De nat. deor.* 1, 33, 92: ... *quaeque procreationis causa natura corpori adfinxit ea frustra habebit deus*. Philo, too, explicitly says against the Epicureans and against Egyptian mythology that God has no limbs and no sexual organs, and he says this in words which show great similarity with what Athanasius says here, see *De post. Caini* 3-4: πρόσωπον μὲν γὰρ ζῴου τμῆμά ἐστιν, ὁ δὲ θεὸς ὅλον, οὐ μέρος· ὥστ' ἀνάγκη καὶ τὰ ἄλλα προσαναπλάττειν, αὐχένα καὶ στέρνα καὶ χεῖρας <καὶ> βάσεις, ἔτι δ' αὖ γαστέρα καὶ τὰ γεννητικὰ καὶ τὸ ἄλλο τῶν ἐντός τε καὶ ἐκτὸς ἀνάριθμον πλῆθος· ἀκολουθεῖ δ' ἐξ ἀνάγκης τῷ ἀνθρωπωμόρφῳ τὸ ἀνθρωποπαθές, ἐπεὶ καὶ ταῦτα οὐ περιττὰ καὶ παρέλκοντα, τῆς δὲ τῶν ἐχόντων ἐπίκουρα ἀσθενείας ἡ φύσις ἀπειργάζετο τὰ ὅσα πρὸς οἰκείας χρείας τε καὶ ὑπηρεσίας ἀκολούθως ἐφαρμόττουσα. τὸ δὲ ὂν οὐδενὸς χρεῖον, ὥστ' εἰ μηδὲ τῆς τῶν μερῶν ὠφελείας, οὐδ' ἂν ἔχοι μέρη τὸ παράπαν. Christians insisted on the incorporeality as well, see e.g. Origen, *De Princ.* I Praef. 8 ff.; 1, 1, Athenagoras, *Suppl.* 8, 2, Irenaeus, *Adv. Haer.* 2, 15, 3, cp. 2, 16, 4; 2, 42, 2. The rejection of corporeality in God plays an important part in Athanasius' polemics against the Arians: Because God does not consist of parts He cannot be affected in the way men are affected, especially He is not affected in the act of generating the Son see e.g. *Contra Arianos* 1, 16, 28 (PG 26, 45, 69); 2, 34 (PG 26, 220), *Ep. ad episc. Aeg. et Lib.* 16 (PG 25, 573), *De Decr.* 11 (PG 25, 444A). On the thought that God is not in need of anything see C.G. 28, *infra*, 94 f.

"But these statues are perishable and have the forms of bodies and they need the care of men, as has also been said before. For we often see that those who have become old are renewed and that those whom time or rain or further one or other of the living beings on earth threatened to make disappear are reshaped again."

See on this *C.G.* 13, *supra*, 57, on the perishable nature of the idols see also Lactance, *Div. Inst.* 2, 4.

"Therefore one should accuse them of folly, because of what they themselves are the makers, these they call gods."

See on this *C.G.* 9, *supra*, 47.

"And because what they themselves take care of with their arts in order to prevent them from perishing, from these they themselves ask salvation. And because of whom they know very well that they need their care, by them they regard it as just that their own needs are fulfilled."

See on this *C.G.* 13, *supra*, 57.

"And because those whom they enclose in small alcoves, they are not ashamed to call lords of heaven and the whole earth."

The true God embraces all things as the Lord of heaven and earth, see *C.G.* 6, *supra*, 32 f., the idols are enclosed in alcoves and as such called the lords of heaven and earth, the apex of absurdity, cp. Aristides, *Apol.* 3, 2: ... καὶ συγκλείσαντες ναοῖς προσκυνοῦσι θεοὺς καλοῦντες ..., cp. J. Geffcken, *op. cit.*, p. 50.

Hereby the attack on the images of gods has been ended and the attack on the gods themselves will now be resumed again.

CHAPTER 23

Attack on the variety of the gods of the Pagans.

Translation and Commentary:

(23) "One could not only learn from these things their godlessness, but also from the fact that their opinions about the idols themselves are in disagreement. For if these are gods, as they say and argue about them, to which of these should one adhere and which kind of them should one regard as more powerful in order either to adore God confidently or, as they say, not to doubt that one knows the Divine in these. For not the same ones are called gods with all people, but for the most part as many nations as there are, such is the number of invented gods as well."

(The word εἴδωλον here has the meaning of 'idol', 'false god', as is often the case. When Athanasius wants to make it clear that he means the image of a false god and not the false god himself, then he uses the words ἄγαλμα, γλύμμα, εἰκών, see especially *C.G.* 19-21.) It is strange that Athanasius first asks in general to which one of the many gods one should adhere, - this is the typically Sceptic argument against the existence of gods and God: the variety of gods speaks against it (see e.g. Cicero, *De nat. deor.* 1, 1, 2; 1, 6, 14), the Sceptics use this argument against belief in any gods, Athanasius adopts it as an argument against Pagan polytheism. But having asked to which one of the gods one should adhere Athanasius goes on to argue in a more subtle way: Which kind of gods are more powerful so that they are rightly adored (see *C.G.* 6, where it says that if there are two gods the more powerful one must be the true God, see *supra*, 33 f.), - but this implies that the adoration of a plurality of gods is possible, an idea to which Athanasius is, of course, opposed. This plurality of most powerful gods could perhaps refer to a special kind of gods who are found everywhere. They would together so to speak represent the one Supreme God. Then Athanasius goes on to quote the theory that one knows the Divine (the Supreme God) in all these gods. He could here have in mind a theory as e.g. put forward by a typical representative of popular philosophy, the Platonist Maximus of Tyre, *viz.*, that there is one God in whom Greeks and Barbarians, people on the mainland and in the sea, wise and unwise believe, and that there are many subordinate gods, sons of God (the idea behind this is then that the various gods are manifestations of the one God and that the various people in the end all believe in one and the same God), see Maximus, XI 5a-b (ed. Hobein): Ἐν τοσούτῳ δὴ πολέμῳ καὶ στάσει καὶ διαφωνίᾳ ἕνα ἴδοις ἂν ἐν πάσῃ γῇ ὁμόφωνον νόμον καὶ λόγον, ὅτι θεὸς εἷς πάντων βασιλεὺς καὶ πατὴρ καὶ θεοὶ πολλοί, θεοῦ παῖδες, συνάρχοντες θεοῦ. Ταῦτα καὶ ὁ Ἕλλην λέγει, καὶ ὁ βάρβαρος λέγει, καὶ ὁ ἠπειρώτης, καὶ ὁ θαλάττιος καὶ <ὁ σοφὸς καὶ ὁ> ἄσοφος, cp. Celsus in Origen, *C.C.* 1, 23 f.; 8, 2. Athanasius would then, if it is this theory which he is here referring to, prove that the many different gods cannot be manifestations of one and the same Supreme God. (For further examples of criticism by Pagan and Christian writers of the contradictory religions see P. Th. Camelot, *op. cit.*, pp. 124 f., to which can be added Athenagoras, *Leg.* 1; 14, Tertullian, *Apol.* 24, 7 f., Eusebius, *Praep. Evang.* 1, 4, Hilary of Poitiers, *De Trin.* 1, 4.)

"And there are even places where one region and one city is internally divided concerning the worship of idols: The Phoenicians do not recognize the so called gods of the Egyptians, neither do the Egyptians worship the same idols as the Phoenicians. And the Scythians do not accept the gods of the Persians, nor the Persians those of the Phoenicians. But also the Pelasgians reject the Thracian gods, and the Thracians do not recognize those of the Thebans. With respect of the idols the Indians differ from the Arabs, and the Arabs from the Ethiopians and the Ethiopians from them. And the Syrians do not worship the idols of the Cilicians, and the people of

Cappadocia again call others than these ones gods. The Bithynians imagined for themselves other and the Armenians again other gods. And why should I need to name many? Those on the mainland adore other gods than those in the islands, and the islanders worship other gods than those on the mainland. And in general every city and village, not recognizing the gods of the neighbours, prefers its own gods and believes only them to be gods. For it is unnecessary to speak about the abominations in Egypt, for everybody can see with his own eyes that the cities have opposite and conflicting objects of worship, and the neighbours always strive to worship the opposite of the neighbours. So the crocodile which is adored as god by some, he is regarded as an abomination by the neighbours; and the lion, who is venerated as god by some, him the neighbours do not only not venerate, but having found him they even kill him as a wild beast. And the fish which is deified by some, it is caught as food by others. Hence we find with them wars and factions and every pretext for murder and every pleasure of passions."

It is interesting that Athanasius only provides examples of cities and countries which are in conflict with each other about their gods, he does not give examples of one city which is internally divided about gods, but this is what he mentions first. He could allude to this when he later on compares the harmony of the universe with the harmony of a city under one ruler, see *infra*, 124, 141. – In the *De Incarnatione Verbi* it will be an important theme that the risen Christ puts an end to these factions and this diversity of cults, see *De Inc.* 46: καὶ τό γε θαυμαστόν, διαφόρων ὄντων καὶ μυρίων σεβασμάτων, καὶ ἑκάστου τόπου τὸ ἴδιον ἔχοντος εἴδωλον, καὶ μὴ ἰσχύοντος τοῦ παρ' αὐτοῖς λεγομένου θεοῦ τὸν πλησίον ὑπερβῆναι τόπον, ὥστε καὶ τοὺς ἐκ γειτόνων πεῖσαι σέβειν αὐτόν, ἀλλὰ μόλις καὶ ἐν τοῖς ἰδίοις θρησκευομένου – οὐδεὶς γὰρ ἄλλος τὸν τοῦ γείτονος ἐσέβετο θεόν, ἀλλ' ἕκαστος τὸ ἴδιον ἐφύλαττεν εἴδωλον, νομίζων τῶν πάντων αὐτὸ κύριον εἶναι – μόνος ὁ Χριστὸς παρὰ πᾶσιν εἷς καὶ πανταχοῦ ὁ αὐτὸς προσκυνεῖται, cp. 51, see also Eusebius, *Praep. Evang.* 1, 4: ... ἅμα δὲ τῇ τοῦ σωτῆρος ἡμῶν εὐσεβεστάτῃ καὶ εἰρηνικωτάτῃ διδασκαλίᾳ τῆς μὲν πολυθέου πλάνης καθαίρεσις ἀπετελεῖτο, τὰ δὲ τῆς τῶν ἐθνῶν διαστάσεως παῦλαν αὐτίκα παλαιῶν κακῶν ἀπελάμβανεν; ὃ καὶ μάλιστα μέγιστον ἡγοῦμαι τεκμήριον τυγχάνειν τῆς ἐνθέου καὶ ἀφορήτου δυνάμεως τοῦ σωτῆρος ἡμῶν.

"And this is amazing that, as the historians relate, the Pelasgians having learned from the Egyptians the names of the gods they do not recognize the Egyptian gods, but worship other ones than those."

Herodotus, *Historiae*, I, is, of course, of great importance as background of this theory. Eusebius, *Praep. Evang.* 1, 9 and 2, 1 quotes the historian Diodorus' *World History* who says that the Greeks learned about the gods from the Egyptians (religion having started in Egypt) and gave to these gods other names; according to Athenagoras the names of the gods came from the Egyptians to the Greeks, *Leg.* 28, 3: παρὰ δὲ τούτων (sc. τῶν Αἰγυπτίων) εἰς Ἕλληνας ἦλθε τὰ ὀνόματα τῶν θεῶν. In Eusebius this is meant as a proof that the Greeks are in their wisdom dependent on the Barbarians, a theory with which Athanasius does not work.

> "And in general of all people who have gone mad in idolatry the opinion and worship is at variance, and the same people do not have the same idols."

This is a summary of the whole argument given in this chapter: the various nations have various gods and even within one and the same nation different gods are worshipped.

> "And this understandably happens to them. For having fallen from the contemplation of the one God, they fell into the many and different things. And having turned away from the true Word of the Father, Christ, the Saviour of all, their mind is rightly distracted towards many things."

Athanasius here evokes the words with which he described Adam's fall (*C.G.* 3, *supra*, 22), hereby suggesting that what applies to sin in general applies to the worst form of sin, idolatry, in particular.

> "And as those who have turned away from the sun and have found themselves in dark places circle around in many impassable roads and do not see those who are present and imagine those who are not there as present and 'seeing do not see' (*Matth.* 13:13), in the same way those who have turned away from God and have become dark in their souls have a wandering mind and like drunken men and blind men imagine what is not."

The simile with which the invention of evil was compared in *C.G.* 7 (*supra*, 36) is here used again for the invention of idols. The walking around in impassable circles may be contrasted with the walking on the way which leads to the right knowledge of God, see *supra*, 29, *C.G.* 5, and *C.G.* 30, *infra*, 99 f. – It is important to notice that these people are not senseless, but that they use their senses in the wrong way, which implies that there is no excuse for their idolatry.

Chapter 24

Attack on the fact that the sacrifices offered to the gods are deified themselves.

Translation and Commentary:

> **(24)** "These observations are no mean proof of their true godlessness. Since there is a plurality of different gods according to city and country, and since one destroys the god of the other, all are destroyed by all."

In his attack on the two gods of Marcion Athanasius had already made the claim that these two gods are mutually destructive (*C.G.* 7, *supra*, 35 f.). This is now said of the many gods of the Pagans as well by proving that the very beings which are regarded as gods by some people are offered as sacrifices to other gods:

> "For on the one hand gods of some become the sacrifices and libations of the so called gods of others, and on the other hand the sacrifices of some are the gods of others. The Egyptians venerate the ox and Apis who is a calf, and others sacrifice these to Zeus. For even if they do not sacrifice exactly those whom they have deified, by sacrificing similar ones they seem to offer the same. The Libyans hold as god a sheep which they call Ammon, and it is slaughtered as a sacrifice to many gods by others. The Indians worship Dionysus, calling him symbolically wine, and others use him for libations to other gods. Others give honour to rivers and springs and above all the Egyptians to water and call these gods. And nevertheless others and the Egyptians themselves who worship these, wash away with water the dirt of others and of themselves and throw away with contempt what is left. And almost all the idols which the Egyptians made are used by other people as sacrifices to gods, so that the Egyptians could be ridiculed by others that they do not deify gods but what are for others and even themselves propitiatory offerings and sacrifices."

For places where these forms of worship are mentioned see L. Leone, *op. cit.*, pp. 45 f. and P. Th. Camelot, *op. cit.*, pp. 126 ff. The ridicule which the Egyptians deserve from other people is not put forward as a reality "so that the Egyptians are ridiculed" as R. W. Thomson translates, *op. cit.*, p. 67 (cp. P. Th. Camelot, *op. cit.*, p. 129), but as a possibility (expressed by the word ἄν together with χλευάζεσθαι), and this way of putting it is even more venomous: the other people could ridicule the Egyptians, but they are so stupid and blinded by their own idolatry that they do not do so. – It should be noticed that this is not a general attack on sacrifices (as is found in e.g. Clement of Alexandria, *Strom.* 7, 6, 31 ff., Eusebius, *Praep. Evang.* 4, 8 ff., Lactance, *Div. Inst.* 6, 25, *Epit.* 18), since such vital questions as of whether God needs sacrifices or needs to be propitiated by them and the Pagan defence of sacrifices are not at all discussed. The only thing Athanasius wants to show in this chapter is that various sacrifices are deified by various people, which is a further proof of Athanasius' claim that men deify what is below them. (On the true way of purifying oneself see *C.G.* 34, *infra*, 113 f.).

CHAPTER 25

Attack on human sacrifices.

Translation and Commentary:

> **(25)** "And further some have been carried away to such impiety and madness that they slaughter and sacrifice to their false gods the very men of whom they are images and forms. And these possessed people do not see that what is slaughtered as sacrifice are the models of the gods who are shaped and adored by them and to whom they offer men. For they offer almost like to like or rather better to worse. For they offer living beings to lifeless ones and rational beings to immobile ones."

Since men have made these images of anthropomorphous gods, and since the product is less than the producer, the images of the so called gods are below men and then in human sacrifices human beings are offered to what is below men. Men not only adore what is below them but offer their lives to these beings. On the fact that the idols lack life and movement see *supra*, 60 ff.

> "For the Scythians called Taurians offer to their so called virgin the victims from shipwreck and all the Greeks they capture, acting to such a degree in a godless way against their fellow men, thereby proving the cruelty of their own gods. For those whom Providence has saved from the dangers of the sea, these they themselves slaughter, almost frustrating Providence, for they try to conceal with their beastly soul the well doing of Providence. Others when they come home from war as victors, then divide their prisoners into hundreds, take one from each hundred and slaughter these to Ares, as many as they choose one per hundred."

They prove the cruelty of their gods with these human sacrifices. This will be made clear towards the end of this chapter where it says that men imitate the behaviour of their gods. – Whilst Providence, i.e. the true God, saves men from the dangers of the sea, the Taurians spoil the well doing of Providence by killing what Providence has saved. – Athanasius here makes a difference between the victims of shipwreck and prisoners of war, Clement of Alexandria only mentions men who have been shipwrecked and then captured as strangers by the Taurians, see *Protrept.* 3, 42, 3: Ταῦροι δὲ τὸ ἔθνος ... οὓς ἂν τῶν ξένων παρ' αὐτοῖς ἕλωσι, τούτων δὴ τῶν κατὰ θάλατταν ἐπταικότων, αὐτίκα μάλα τῇ Ταυρικῇ καταθύουσιν Ἀρτέμιδι. Origen briefly mentions the offering of strangers by the Taurians, see *De Princ.* 2, 9, 5, *Contra Celsum* 5, 27. Clement of Alexandria draws attention to the fact that Euripides speaks about this in his tragedies, *Protrept.* 3, 42, and Tertullian briefly dismisses these as stories which belong to the stage, *Apol.* 9, 5: *remitto fabulas Tauricas theatris suis*.

> "And not only the Scythians practise such abominable things because of their inborn barbarous character, but this practise is typical of the evil of idols and demons."

On the proverbial barbarity of the Sythians cp. Origen, *Contra Celsum*

1, 1: οὕτως παρ' ἀληθείᾳ δικαζούσῃ οἱ νόμοι τῶν ἐθνῶν οἱ περὶ ἀγαλμάτων καὶ τῆς ἀθέου πολυθεότητος, νόμοι εἰσὶ Σκυθῶν καὶ εἴ τι Σκυθῶν ἀσεβέστερον.

"For also the Egyptians formerly used to offer such bloody sacrifices to Hera. Phoenicians and Cretians sought to propitiate Kronos with the sacrifice of their own children. And formerly the Romans worshipped the so called Jupiter Latiaris with human sacrifices. And absolutely all polluted and were polluted, some in this others in another way. They were polluted themselves by committing murder and they polluted their own temples by the smoke of such sacrifices."

Athanasius only claims that the Scythians still offer human beings, these other examples are given as examples of what happened in the past. In this he differs from Clement of Alexandria who presents the human sacrifices as still happening, *Protrept.* 3, 43. Tertullian presents some as of the past, others as still happening (the sacrifices to Jupiter Latiaris belonging to the latter category, cp. J. Geffcken, *op. cit.*, p. 66). – Porphyry explicitly denies that human offerings still happen, see *De Abstin.* 2, 54 f., quoted by Eusebius, *Praep. Evang.* 4, 16. – On the claim that the offering of human beings is in fact committing murder see also Clement of Alexandria, *Protrept.* 3, 42, 9: οὐ γὰρ οὖν παρὰ τὸν τόπον ἱερεῖον γίνεται ὁ φόνος ..., ἀλλὰ φόνος ἐστὶ καὶ ἀνδροκτασία ἡ τοιαύτη θυσία.

"From these practices evil spread amongst men into multiplicity. For seeing their demons take pleasure in these things, they, too, immediately imitated their gods in such evil acts, believing that the imitation of superior beings (as they think) is a typically right thing. Hence men were overcome by the murder of men, sacrifices of children and all kinds of licentiousness."

Athanasius here makes no difference between demons and gods: the demons take pleasure in these sacrifices and men imitate their gods by committing murder. If he knows about the claim made by Porphyry that sacrifices are not offered to gods but to demons, then he ignores it, see *De Abstin.* 2, 36: Οἶδε δὲ ὁ τῆς εὐσεβείας φροντίζων ὡς θεοῖς μὲν οὐ θύεται ἔμψυχον οὐδέν, δαίμοσι δέ, ἀλλ' ἤτοι ἀγαθοῖς ἢ καὶ φαύλοις, and *De Abstin.* 2, 58: Ὅτι δὲ οὐ θεοῖς, ἀλλὰ δαίμοσι τὰς θυσίας τὰς διὰ τῶν αἱμάτων προσῆγον οἱ τὰς ἐν τῷ παντὶ δυνάμεις καταμαθόντες ... (both quotations are given by Eusebius, *Praep. Evang.* 4, 15). – On the imitation of gods see *C.G.* 26, *infra*, 87.

"For almost every city has become full of every licentiousness because of the imitation of the manners of their gods. And in the eyes of the idols only he is wise who receives from them a testimony of licentiousness."

The worst religious rites, human sacrifices, lead to the worst behaviour. All this is caused by the idols who (as Athanasius says ironically) can only regard as wise him who acts like them, *viz.*, in licentiousness. (Christians had a special interest in attacking human sacrifices since they themselves were accused of offering their children, see e.g. Tertullian, *Apol.* 7-8, hence the opening sentence of Tertullian's description of Pagan man slaughter, *Apol.* 9, 1: *Haec quoque magis refutaverim, a vobis fieri refutaverim partim in aperto partim in occulto, per quod forsitan et de nobis credidistis.*)

CHAPTER 26

Attack on the sexual practices associated with idolatry and on the bad examples of behaviour which the gods set.

Translation and Commentary:

(26) "Formerly women were sitting out in public in idol temples in Phoenicia offering the price of their bodies to the local gods, believing that they conciliated their goddess by prostitution, and that they could incur her goodwill through these practices. And men, denying their nature and not wanting to be men any more forge the nature of women as if with these they pleased and gave honour to the mother of their so called gods. And they all live together with the lewdest beings and rival with each other in what is even worse. And as the holy servant of Christ, Paul said: 'For their women have turned natural intercourse to an unnatural one. And likewise the men, having abandoned the natural intercourse with women, burned with desire for each other, men performing obscene acts with men' " (*Rom.* 1:26-27).

Three practices are attacked here: sacred prostitution, self-castration in honour of Cybele (those who do this want to assimilate themselves to the goddess, hence the remark that they assume female nature), and finally homosexuality. P. Th. Camelot, *op. cit.*, p. 133, wrongly interprets self castration as homosexuality and pederasty. Homosexuality is here referred to (without being named) in the third place and described as even worse than self castration and sacred prostitution. Similarly in *De Inc.* 5 homosexuality is referred to without being named as the last one of a catalogue of sins (whereby it is suggested that this is the worst of all sins), and there, too, this is followed with the quotation of *Rom.* 1:26-27: οὐκ ἦν δὲ τούτων μακρὰν οὐδὲ τὰ παρὰ φύσιν, ἀλλ' ὡς εἶπεν ὁ τοῦ Χριστοῦ μάρτυς Ἀπόστολος· κτλ (cp. *C.G.* 9, *supra*, 45, where after a reference to the cult of Antinous instituted by his lover Hadrianus *Sap. Sal.* 14:12 is quoted: The devising of idols is the beginning of fornification). - It is interesting that Celsus, too, is very critical of the cult of Cybele and says that her priests take advantage of the lack of education of gullible people and lead them wherever they wish, - and claims that this happens also among the Christians who believe without reason, see Origen, *Contra Celsum* 1, 9. Athanasius (like the other Christians, see the examples listed by L.

Leone, *op. cit.*, p. 49) obviously strongly dissociates Christian faith from these sexual practices and says that it is typical of Paganism.

> "By doing these and similar things they confess and prove that their so called gods have led such lives. For from Zeus they learned pederasty and adultery, from Aphrodite fornication, from Rhea licentiousness, from Ares murder, from others other such things which the laws punish and every decent man turns away from."

When Athanasius says that the gods taught the men evil things (cp. *C.G.* 12, *supra*, 55) and that men imitated their gods (cp. *C.G.* 25, *supra*, 85), this is a venomous remark: The gods are below men, they are perverted images of men, as Athanasius has cogently argued so far, so man imitates what is a perversion of himself. What man, of course, should do is imitate the true God, see e.g. *Contra Arianos* 3, 19 (PG 26, 361B/C), *De Decr.* 20 (PG 25, 452B) where he speaks about τὴν ἐν ἡμῖν λεγομένην μίμησιν ἣν ἐξ ἀρετῆς διὰ τὴν τῶν ἐντολῶν τήρησιν ἡμεῖς προσλαμβάνομεν, cp. Justin Martyr, *Apol.* II 13 (Plato uses μίμησις in order to express the relation between the intelligible and the sensible world, cp. W. Windelband, *Geschichte der Philosophie* 1928[12], p. 100). – On what men learned from Zeus and Aphrodite, see *C.G.* 12, *supra*, 53 ff., Rhea has so far not been mentioned, Ares was criticized because of adultery and the fact that he was wounded was taken that he is no god. When Athanasius here in *C.G.* 26 claims that men learned murder from Ares this is obviously caused by the fact that Ares was the wargod. (On further examples of criticism of these gods by early Christian writers see L. Leone, *op. cit.*, pp. 49 f.) On the gods and the laws see *supra*, 55, and *infra*, 107. – The claim that Pagans followed the bad examples set by their gods was a popular theme with Christian apologists, see e.g. Aristides, *Apol.* 11, 5: ὅθεν λαμβάνοντες οἱ ἄνθρωποι ἀφορμὴν ἀπὸ τῶν θεῶν αὐτῶν ἔπραττον πᾶσαν ἀνομίαν καὶ ἀσέλγειαν καὶ ἀσέβειαν, Tertullian, *Apol.* 9, 16: *Proinde incesti qui magis quam quos ipse Iuppiter docuit*, Lactance, *Div. Inst.* 1, 21, Minucius Felix, *Oct.* 30, cp. J. Geffcken, *op. cit.*, p. 66.

> "So is it just still to believe these to be gods who do such things, and not rather to regard these because of the licentiousness of their manners as more irrational than irrational beings? Is it just to regard the worshippers themselves as men and not rather to pity them as more irrational than irrational beings and more lifeless than what is lifeless? For if they consulted the mind of their soul, they would not have fallen headlong into these errors, and they would not deny the true God, the Father of Christ."

The claim that the gods and their imitators, men, are more irrational than irrational beings is either purely rhetorical, or Athanasius wants to suggest that those who have a soul and a mind, but do not use these in the right way so that they refrain from doing evil, are even worse than those beings who have no soul and mind and therefore cannot distinguish between good and evil, cp. *C.G.* 31-32, *infra*, 102 ff.

The worst forms of idolatry have now been detected and refuted, Athanasius will now turn to what seem less objectionable forms of idolatry.

CHAPTER 27

Attack on the deification of parts of the universe.

Translation and Commentary:

(27) "But perhaps those who have risen above these things and are stunned by creation, will, convinced by the refutations of these abominations, not deny themselves that these things can easily be refuted and condemned by all men. But they will think that this view of theirs is safe and their worship of the universe and parts of the universe irrefutable. For they will take pride in revering and worshipping not just stones and woods and forms of men and animals, birds, serpents and quadrupeds, but the sun and the moon, and all the heavenly cosmos, and on the other hand the earth and all the nature of the moist. And they will say that nobody can prove that these are no gods by their nature, since it is obvious to all that they are not lifeless and irrational, but that they transcend even the nature of men, since these live in heaven and men on earth. It is right to consider and examine this as well. For in these things, too, reason will certainly find the refutation to be just."

Those who deify parts of the cosmos stand on a higher level than the worshippers of idols. In *C.G.* 9 something similar was said when the desciption of the road downwards of the various forms of idolatry began with those who adore heavenly bodies (see *supra*, 43). Eusebius, *Praep. Evang.* 1, 6 quotes the theory that the Phoenicians were the first to declare the heavenly bodies to be gods: Φοίνικας τοιγαροῦν καὶ Αἰγυπτίους πρώτους ἁπάντων ἀνθρώπων κατέχει λόγος ἥλιον καὶ σελήνην καὶ ἀστέρας θεοὺς ἀποφῆναι, μόνους τε εἶναι τῆς τῶν ὅλων γενέσεως καὶ φθορᾶς αἰτίους (cp. Clement of Alexandria, *Protrept.* 5, 66, 1 ff., see L. Leone, *op. cit.*, p. 50). But it seems as if Athanasius here primarily thinks of Plato and his followers. In a well known passage of the *Cratylus*, *viz.*, 397C it says that the first inhabitants of Greece, just like the barbarians, regarded the heavenly bodies as gods: φαίνονταί μοι οἱ πρῶτοι τῶν ἀνθρώπων τῶν περὶ τὴν Ἑλλάδα τούτους μόνους ἡγεῖσθαι οὕσπερ νῦν πολλοὶ τῶν βαρβάρων, ἥλιον καὶ σελήνην καὶ γῆν καὶ ἄστρα καὶ οὐρανόν (quoted by Eusebius, *Praep. Evang.* 1, 9). Plato also regards the heavenly bodies as living beings with a body and a soul, see *Leges* X 896E-899B. - The Platonist Celsus attacks the Jews that whilst they worship the heavens and the angels in it, they reject its most sacred and powerful parts, the sun, moon and stars and he claims that if the whole is God, then the parts ought to be gods as well, see *Contra Celsum* 5, 6: Πρῶτον οὖν τῶν Ἰουδαίων θαυμάζειν ἄξιον, εἰ τὸν μὲν οὐρανὸν καὶ τοὺς ἐν τῷδε ἀγγέλους σέβουσι, τὰ σεμνότατα δὲ αὐτοῦ μέρη καὶ δυνατώτατα, ἥλιον καὶ σελήνην καὶ τοὺς ἄλλους ἀστέρας ἀπλανεῖς τε καὶ πλανήτας, ταῦτα παραπέμπουσιν· ὡς ἐνδεχόμενον τὸ μὲν ὅλον εἶναι θεόν, τὰ δὲ μέρη αὐτοῦ μὴ θεῖα. To Plotinus, too, the heavenly bodies are divine, see e.g. *Enneads* 2, 9, 9, 30 ff.: ἄστρα δὲ τά τε ἐν ταῖς ὑποκάτω σφαίραις τά τε ἐν τῷ ἀνωτάτω διὰ τί οὐ θεοὶ ἐν τάξει φερόμενα καὶ κόσμῳ περιιόντα. Origen rejects the view that the stars are divine, but not the view that they have a soul. According to Origen they do have a soul, since they can obey God, see *De Princ.* 1, 7, 3: *Putamus ergo posse ea per hoc animantia designari, quod et mandata dicuntur accipere a deo, quod utique non nisi rationabilibus animantibus fieri solet* (cp. H. Chadwick, *Origen, Contra Celsum*, p. 271 note 6, and his paper, Origen, in: *The Cambridge History of Later Greek and Early Medieval Philosophy*, p. 189). Athanasius will not only refute the divinity of the heavenly bodies, but he also seems not to share Origen's view that the stars have a soul, since he says that he will refute the whole theory about the divine heavenly bodies (which includes the claim that they have a soul and a reason, - cp. also Lactance, *Div. Inst.* 2, 5, 14, who says that the movements of the stars are not voluntary, but necessary, i.e. instituted by God).

> "But before we look at this and begin our proof, it is enough that creation itself almost cries out against them and shows its Maker and Creator, God, who is also the King of it and of the universe, the Father of our Lord Jesus Christ."

As it said in the beginning of the whole treatise, the 'crying out' of creation in itself is enough to learn about the Creator, any further proofs can add nothing to this revelation (see *supra*, 9).

> "The so called wise men turn away from Him, but adore and deify the creation made by Him, although the creation, too, adores and confesses the Lord, whom they deny by adoring it."

The Pagans, i.e. here the Platonists, adore creation whilst creation does not want to be adored, - this is the most stupid thing men can do, cp. *C.G.* 47, *infra*, 151 f.

> "For when they gape in this way in admiration at the parts of this creation and believe these to be gods, then the fact that the parts are in need of each other could easily refute them."

Christian apologists like to claim that Pagans are stunned by creation and therefore deify it (hereby showing that they do not think things out, otherwise they would have found the Creator behind creation), see e.g.

Origen, *Contra Celsum* 5, 10: οὐ τοίνυν ἦν εὔλογον ... καταπλαγῆναι τὸ αἰσθητὸν ἡλίου καὶ σελήνης καὶ ἄστρων φῶς ἐπὶ τοσοῦτον, ὥστε διὰ τὸ αἰσθητὸν φῶς ἐκείνων νομίσαι ἑαυτοὺς κάτω πού εἶναι ... κἀκείνοις προσκυνῆσαι, Lactance, *Div. Inst.* 2, 5, 5: ... *earum rerum admiratione opstupefacti et ipsius artificis obliti, quem videre non poterant, opera eius venerari et colere coeperunt nec umquam intellegere quiverunt, quanto maior quantoque mirabilior sit qui illa fecit ex nihilo.* – What is in need of anything cannot be God, see *C.G.* 28, *infra*, 93.

"For they reveal and signify Him who is also their Lord and Maker, the Father of the Word, with the irreproachable order of obedience to Him, as also the divine law says: 'The heavens declare the glory of God, and the firmament proclaims the work of His hands' " (*Psalm* 19:2).

What obeys is less than what commands, when the heavenly bodies obey a commandment, then they cannot be divine, cp. what Aristides says of the elements of the world, *Apol.* 3, 3: εἰ δὲ τὰ στοιχεῖα φθαρτά ἐστι καὶ ὑποτασσόμενα κατὰ ἀνάγκην, πῶς εἰσι θεοί;

"The proof of these things is not obscure but even very clear for those whose mental eye is not completely blind."

This proof will be given by showing that the parts of creation can only function together. Athanasius will make use of doxographical material in order to make this clear to everybody by coming forward with popular explanations of natural laws. In *C.G.* 35-36 (see *infra*, 116 ff.) he will say that these laws have been instituted by the Creator. So here the natural laws function as a proof that God is the Creator of the world and that parts of the world are not divine. Christians can also follow the opposite line and express scepticism about the explanations given to events in nature in order to leave room for God's power over the world, see e.g. Irenaeus, *Adv. Haer.* 2, 41, 2: ... *etiam eorum quae ante pedes sunt (dico autem quae sunt in hac creatura, quae et contrectantur a nobis, et videntur, et sunt nobiscum) multa fugerunt nostram scientiam, et Deo haec committimus. Oportet enim eum prae omnibus praecellere*, Lactance, *Div. Inst.* 3, 8, 29: *si ad causas rerum naturalium* (sc. *scientia referenda est*), *quae beatitudo mihi erit proposita, si sciero unde Nilus oriatur vel quidquid de caelo physici delirant.* Eusebius, *Praep. Evang.* 7, 3 claims that the Hebrews were the first to discover the physical laws of the universe and to discover that the bodily nature is irrational and lifeless, and caused by a living and creative Principle, i.e. God, cp. Clement of Alexandria, *Strom.* 5, 32-38.

"For if somebody takes the parts of creation by themselves and considers them separately, e.g. the sun alone, the moon separately, and on the other side separated from their mutual connection the earth and the air, the warm, cold, dry, and wet substance, then he will find that absolutely nothing is self-sufficient, but that they are all in need of each others' help and that they subsist through each others' support."

What is not self-sufficient is not God (see *infra*, 93), this will now be shown with the help of what is generally regarded as natural laws:

"For the sun revolves together with the whole heaven and is encompassed by it and could never get outside heaven's rotation."

See for this the description Athenagoras gives of Aristotle's doctrine, *Leg.* 6, 3: ὁ δὲ 'Αριστοτέλης καὶ οἱ ἀπ' αὐτοῦ ... σῶμα μὲν αὐτοῦ τὸ αἰθέριον νομίζοντες τούς τε πλανωμένους ἀστέρας καὶ τὴν σφαῖραν τῶν ἀπλανῶν κινούμενα κυκλοφορητικῶς, and Eusebius, *Praep. Evang.* 14, 16, 8 (cp. H. Diels, *Doxographi Graeci*, Berlin 1879, p. 305).

"The moon and the other stars testify to the help they receive from the sun."

This is probably a reference to the theory of Thales that the moon is lightened by the sun, see the quotation given by Eusebius, *Praep. Evang.* 15, 29: Θαλῆς καὶ οἱ ἀπ' αὐτοῦ ἀπὸ τοῦ ἡλίου φωτίζεσθαι τὴν σελήνην (see H. Diels, *op. cit.*, p. 358), and Hippolytus, *Philos.* 8, 8 (H. Diels, *op. cit.*, p. 562), and the theory of Metrodorus that the stars are lightened by the sun, see the quotation given from Plutarch by Eusebius, *Praep. Evang.* 15, 48: Μητρόδωρος ἅπαντας τοὺς ἀπλανεῖς ἀστέρας ὑπὸ τοῦ ἡλίου καταλάμπεσθαι (see H. Diels, *op. cit.*, p. 346).

"And it also appears that the earth does not give fruits without rain. And rain could not come down to earth without the help of clouds."

Cp. for this Chrysippus' definition: ὑετὸν δὲ φορὰν ὕδατος ἐκ νεφῶν, see H. Diels, *op. cit.*, p. 468.

"But also clouds could not appear and subsist by themselves without air."

Behind this may lie Anaximanes' definition that the clouds are thickened air: 'Αναξιμένης νέφη μὲν γίνεσθαι παχυνθέντος ἐπὶ πλεῖον τοῦ ἀέρος, see H. Diels, *op. cit.*, p. 370.

"And the air is not made hot by itself, but by the ether and only gives light when it is illuminated by the sun. And springs and rivers will never subsist without the earth. And the earth is not supported by itself, but rests on the substance of the waters, and it, too, is enclosed being put together in the centre of the universe."

As the moon and the stars receive their light from the sun, so does the air. On the fact that the earth rests on the water cp. the quotation Aristotle gives from Thales that the earth floats like a piece of wood on the water, *De caelo* 294 a 29, on the earth as placed in the centre of the universe see Aristotle *De caelo* 296 a 24 ff., cp. I. Düring, *op. cit.*, p. 369, - Athanasius will use this fact as an indication of God's omnipotence, see *C.G.* 36, *infra*, 121.

> "The sea and the great ocean which flows around the whole earth is moved by the winds and is driven in the direction in which the power of the winds impels it."

According to Aristotle and Posidonius high and low tide are caused by winds, see the quotations given by H. Diels, *op. cit.*, pp. 382 f.

> "And the winds themselves do not subsist by themselves, but according to those who have spoken about these things subsist because the air is warmed by the ether and because of the warmth in the air itself, and blow everywhere through the air."

Cp. for this the explanation Metrodorus gives of winds: Μητρόδωρος ὑδατώδους ἀναθυμιάσεως διὰ τὴν ἡλιακὴν ἔκκαυσιν γίνεσθαι ὁρμὴν πνευμάτων, see H. Diels, *op. cit.*, p. 375 (Aristotle, too, says that winds are caused by the sun, see H. Diels, *op. cit.*, p. 382). - About several of these natural laws referred to by Athanasius Irenaeus expresses scepticism, at least concerning their usefulness, see *Adv. Haer.* 2, 41, 2: *Quid autem possumus exponere de Oceani accessu et recessu, cum constet esse certam causam ... Vel quid dicere possumus quomodo pluviae ... et collectiones nubium, et nebulae, et ventorum emissiones et similia his efficiuntur ... quae haec autem nubium praeparatio, aut qui status nebulae ... In his omnibus nos quidem loquaces erimus, requirentes causas eorum: qui autem ea facit solus Deus veridicus est.* Hilary of Poitiers expresses similar scepticism in order to safeguard faith in God as the omnipotent Creator, see *De Trin.* 12, 53, *En. in Ps.* CXXIX 1.

> "For regarding the four elements of which the nature of the bodies consists, I mean warm and cold, dry and wet, who is so deflected from a sound mind as not to know that these things subsist if they are put together, but when they are separated and put on their own, they even destroy each other according to the power of what is strongest in them; for warm is destroyed by the cold when it is stronger, and again the cold disappears through the power of the warm. And again the dry is wettened by what is wet, and the latter is dried by the former."

What can be destroyed by something else cannot be divine. In *C.G.* 37 (see *infra*, 121 ff.) Athanasius will argue that God ordered those mutually destructive elements to be in harmony and prevented the strongest element from destroying all the other ones. - For opposition against deification of elements of the earth see also Aristides, *Apol.* 3 ff. and the many further examples listed by J. Geffcken, *op. cit.*, p. 50. - Athanasius' insistence on the natural laws shows some similarity with the Epicureans' insistence on them. Both Athanasius and the Epicureans hereby want to exclude the possibility that the elements are divine. But then, of course, they diverge: the Epicureans want to show that there is no need to interpret natural events as divine acts (see e.g. Lucrece, *De rer. nat.* 6, 43 ff.), Athanasius wants to make it clear that nature is God's creation and subjected to God's will.

CHAPTER 28

Parts of the universe are not divine and the universe as a whole is not divine.

Translation and Commentary:

(28) "So how could these be gods when they need each others' help? Or how could it be right to ask for their help, when they themselves, too, ask for each others' help?"

In the previous chapter it had been established that the various parts of the cosmos can only function together, in this sense they need each others' help in order to function. This will again be interpreted as a proof that these parts are not divine:

"For if it is true to say about God that He is not in need of anything, but that He is self-sufficient and full of Himself, and that all things subsist in Him and that it is rather He who gives to all; how is it right to call gods the sun and the moon and the other parts of creation which are not such, but even need each others' help?"

Any doubt about God's self-sufficiency is rejected by Athanasius in the strongest possible terms, see *C.G.* 39: ἐν θεῷ δὲ λέγειν εἶναί τι ἐλλιπές, ἀσεβὲς οὐ μόνον, ἀλλὰ καὶ πέρα τῶν ἀθεμίτων ἐστί. In his polemics against the Arians Athanasius stresses that the Son exists from all eternity, if He did not, there would be a growth in God's being, and such a growth is incompatible with God's perfection which is not wanting of anything, see *Contra Arianos* 1, 17-18 (PG 26, 45 ff.); God's self-sufficiency excludes the Arian doctrine that God needed the Son as a tool creation, see *Contra Arianos* 2, 41 (PG 26, 233A/B). God's self-sufficiency is, of course, a commonplace in Christian and Pagan writers, see e.g. Aristides, *Apol.* 1, 2; 10, 2, Justin Martyr, *Apol.* I 10, 1; 13, 1, Theophilus, *Ad Aut.* 2, 10, Irenaeus, *Adv. Haer.* 4, 25, 3; 4, 29; 4, 31-32; 4, 49, 2, Tertullian, *Adv. Marc.* 2, 18, 3, *Ad Scap.* 2, 8, *Adv. Jud.* 5, 3 ff., Origen, *Contra Celsum* 8, 21, Hilary of Poitiers, *De Trin.* 3, 7; 6, 19, *En. in Ps.* II 14, 15, cp. J. Geffcken, *op. cit.*, p. 38, E. Norden, *Agnostos Theos, Untersuchungen zur Formengeschichte religiöser Rede*, Stuttgart 1956[4], pp. 13 f., B. Gärtner, *op. cit.*, pp. 216 ff.

"But perhaps they, too, acknowledge that when the parts are separated and taken by themselves they are in need, since the proof is obvious. But putting them all together and constituting as it were a big body, they will say that the whole is God. For when the whole subsists, the elements will have no need from outside, but the whole will become self-sufficient and independent in all respects, the so called wise men will say, only in order to be refuted also from this angle."

What Athanasius seems to have here in mind is Plato's description of the world body in *Timaeus* 32D-34B, which is summarized by Albinus, *Epit.* 12, 3 in the following way: Τῷ δὲ μηδὲν ἔξωθεν ὑπολείπεσθαι καὶ μονογενῆ τὸν κόσμον ἐποίησε καὶ κατὰ τὸν ἀριθμὸν τῇ ἰδέᾳ εἰκασμένον μιᾷ οὔσῃ, πρός τε τούτοις ἄνοσον καὶ ἀγήρω, ἅτε αὐτῷ μηδενὸς προσιόντος τοῦ κεραίνειν πεφυκότος, αὐτάρκη τε καὶ οὐδενὸς ἔξωθεν δεόμενον.

"For this argument will show even more than the previous ones their impiety and moreover great lack of education. For if separate things put together complete the whole, and the whole is put together by the individual parts, then also the whole consists of parts and each is a part of the whole. But this is far removed from the ideas about God. For God is a whole and not parts and does not consist of different things, but is Himself the Maker of the composition of all things. Look what a great impiety they expound about the Divine in saying this. For if He consists of parts, He will certainly appear unlike Himself, since He also has His completeness from different things. For if He is sun, He is not moon, and if He is moon, He is not earth, and if He is earth, He would not be sea. And in this way taking each part separately, one will find the foolishness of such an argument of theirs."

The argument is that if God as a whole consists of different parts, there is a variety in God. But the one God stands in contrast to any variety, see *supra*, 22. To this Athanasius adds his favourite argument by elimination: if God consists of various things, He cannot be all these things at the same time, but only one of them, which is incompatible with the idea that God is the whole. This cannot be regarded as a refutation of Plato's statement that the world body is perfect because it consists of *perfect* parts, see *Timaeus* 32D: ... τάδε διανοηθείς (sc. ὁ δημιουργός), πρῶτον μὲν ἵνα ὅλον ὅτι μάλιστα ζῷον τέλεον ἐκ τελέων τῶν μερῶν εἴη ... (For further opposition against the idea that God consists of parts see *C.G.* 22, *supra*, 78).

"One could also condemn these statements by making this observation from the human body. For as the eye is not the ear and the ear not the hand, and the stomach not the chest, and again the neck is not the foot, but each of these has its own operation, and one body consists of these different parts, having its parts together according to need, but separated when the time comes when nature which has put them together separates them as God wishes in His commandment, – so (may our argument receive forgiveness from Him who is mightier) if they, putting together the parts of creation into one body, call this God, then He must by Himself be dissimilar to

Himself, as has been shown, and He will again be divided in the natural way in which parts are divided."

In creation the general rule holds true that what has been added can also be taken away, see e.g. *Contra Arianos* 1, 17 (PG 26, 48C): τὰ γὰρ προστιθέμενα, φανερὸν ὅτι καὶ ἀφαιρεῖσθαι δύναται (as in general what has a beginning of existence also has an end, see *infra*, 110 f.). This law has been instituted by the Creator, but it is blasphemy to subject the Creator to laws which He has given to His creation. Athanasius explicitly says that he mentions this only in a hypothetical way, his opponents in fact force him to mention it, since they state this as a reality. Likewise in his polemics against the Arians he sometimes says that he is forced by his opponents to say things for which he asks God's forgiveness, see *Contra Arianos* 1, 23 (PG 26, 60A); 3, 63 (PG 26, 456A), *Ad Ser.* 1, 16 (PG 26, 568C), cp. Irenaeus, *Adv. Haer.* 2, 46, 1, Hilary of Poitiers, *De Trin.* 2, 2; 5, 1; 6, 22; 8, 2. – In order to avoid the idea that God, like man, consists of parts, early Christian writers liked to say that God does what He does (e.g. seeing and hearing) in His totality, see e.g. Hilary of Poitiers, *En. in Ps.* CXXIX 3: *Deus autem, qui et ubique et in omnibus est, totus audit, totus videt, totus efficit, totus incedit*, cp. Irenaeus, *Adv. Haer.* 1, 6, 1; 2, 15, 3; 2, 16, 4; 2, 42, 2; 4, 21, 2, Novatian, *De Trin.* 6, 36, R. M. Grant traces this back to the famous line of Xenophanes, Diels, *F.V.S.* 1, 24: οὖλος ὁρᾷ οὖλος δὲ νοεῖ, οὖλος δέ τ' ἀκούει, see his paper, Early Christianity and Pre-Socratic Philosophy, *H. A. Wolfson Jubilee Volume*, American Academy for Jewish Research, Jerusalem 1965, pp. 376 ff.

CHAPTER 29

The conflicting parts of creation cannot be gods and cannot by themselves produce a harmony.

Translation and Commentary:

(29) "One could also refute their godlessness in another way by regarding the truth. For if God is by nature incorporeal and invisible and untouchable, how do they imagine God to be a body, and how do they worship with God's honour what can be seen with eyes and what we touch with our hand?"

This is in fact a repetition of the argument given in *C.G.* 22, amplified with the observation that if God is untouchable He should not be identified with objects which can be touched. It is a typically Epicurean tenet that what is corporeal can be touched, see Lucrece, *De rer. nat.* 1, 305: *tangere enim et tangi nisi corpus nulla potest res*, cp. Tertullian, *De anima* 5, 6,

Adv. Marc. 4, 8, 3, see J. H. Waszink's edition of the *De anima*, p. 46* and p. 130.

> "And again, if the reasonable argument about God holds true, that He is almighty and that nothing holds power over Him, but that He has power and rules over all, how do those who deify creation not see that it is outside such a definition about God? For when the sun is below the earth, the earth overshadows its light so that it cannot be seen, but in the daytime the sun hides the moon with the brightness of its light. And hail often damages the fruits of the earth. And the fire is extinguished when there is some flood of water. And spring makes winter disappear, summer does not let spring exceed its limits, and it is itself prevented by autumn from surpassing its own times. So if they were gods, they ought not to be overcome and hidden by each other, but always be together and exert their common operations."

On the definition of God as almighty see *supra*, 33, *C.G.* 6. – It had been shown in *C.G.* 27 and 28 that the various parts of creation can only function together and in this sense need each others' help, and that what needs help cannot be divine. Now this is described in a more negative way: the various parts of creation hinder each other in exerting each their full power. This means that one part is (at least for a while) more powerful than another part, and this is incompatible with the belief that parts of creation are divine, i.e. almighty. So what is limited by something else cannot be God and almighty, – in a similar way Irenaeus argues against the existence of more than one God, *Adv. Haer.* 2, 1, 4: *Oportet enim aut unum esse qui omnia continet, et in suis fecit unumquodque eorum quae facta sunt, quemadmodum ipse voluit, aut multos rursus et indeterminatos factores et deos, ab invicem quidem accipientes, ad invicem autem desinentes per omnem partem: et alios omnes a foris ab altero quodam maiore contineri, et velut inclusos et manentes in suis unumquemque eorum confiteri necessitas erit, neminem autem horum omnium esse Deum. Deerit enim unicuique eorum partem minutissimam habenti ad comparationem omnium reliquorum, et solvetur Omnipotentis appellatio*, cp. also Tertullian, *Adv. Marc.* 1, 4, 5-6. – What Athanasius now demands is not that they should function together (this is what they do according to Athanasius), but that they all exert all their powers at the same time and not some of their power at some of the time.

> "Day and night the sun and moon and the rest of the choir of the stars ought to have equal light together and this should shine to all and all should be illuminated by them. Summer, winter, spring and autumn ought to exist together unchangeably at the same time. The sea ought to mix with the springs and together provide drink to men. Calm and blowing of winds ought to happen at the same time. Fire and water ought together to give one and the same help to men. For also would nobody have received any damage from them, since they are according to them gods, and gods do nothing in order to damage, but rather everything in order to help. But if this cannot happen because of their mutual opposition, how is it still possible

to call those who are in mutual opposition and conflict and cannot stay together gods or worship them with the honours of God? But those who are unharmonious by nature, how can they give peace to others who ask for it and become arbiters of harmony for them?"

When there is a conflict among the gods, these gods cannot end the conflict among men by giving peace; elsewhere Athanasius states the general rule that the like cannot give help to the like, this applies here to the fact that conflicting gods cannot help conflicting men by giving peace (see *Contra Arianos* 2, 67 (PG 26, 289C): "Ἡ ποία βοήθεια παρὰ τῶν ὁμοίων τοῖς ὁμοίοις γένοιτ' ἄν, δεομένων καὶ αὐτῶν τῆς αὐτῆς βοηθείας;). Only the truly almighty God, who has bound together the conflicting parts of creation (see *C.G.* 36-37, *infra*, 119 ff.) and is Himself above such a conflict, can give harmony and peace (see *C.G.* 43, *infra*, 140 f.).

"So rightly neither the sun nor the moon nor any other part of creation, let alone the statues of stone, gold and other material, and not Zeus and Apollo and the other gods about whom the poets speak in their myths could truly be gods, as our argument has shown. But some of these are parts of creation, others are lifeless beings, others merely mortal men."

The statues are lifeless, see *C.G.* 14-15 (*supra*, 58 ff.), the gods of mythology are mortal men, see *C.G.* 10 ff. and 17 f. (*supra*, 47 ff., 65 ff.).

"Therefore also the worship and deification of these things is an instruction not of piety, but of godlessness and all impiety and a proof of a great deviation from the knowledge which has as its object the one and only true God, I mean the Father of Christ."

The refutation of idolatry, not only by Scripture, but also by the Pagans' own thoughts about their religion which was promised in *C.G.* 11 (*supra*, 51) has now been given: it is a deviation from the true God and Father of Christ who revealed Himself in the beginning by creating man in His image (see *C.G.* 2, *supra*, 16 ff.).

"So when this has been refuted in this way and when it has been shown that Greek idolatry is full of all godlessness and has not been brought into the life of men in order to help but to hinder, come on, as we promised in the beginning, let us, error having been refuted, further follow the way of truth, and let us contemplate the Ruler and Creator of the universe, the Word of the Father in order to know through Him God His Father and in order that the Greeks learn how far they have cut themselves off from the truth."

Idolatry hinders human life, since it causes a false way of life (see *supra*, 43 ff., 85, 87). Man should break with this way of life and return to his original destination, i.e. the contemplation of the Word of God and through Him of the Father (see *supra*, 16 ff.).

Part III

(30-34)

MAN HAS A SOUL AND A REASON

Introduction

In this part of the treatise Athanasius returns to the theme which was discussed in the beginning: Man's soul is created in the image of God and therefore man can contemplate God and His Word. Against unnamed Pagans and heretics who (seem to) deny that man has a soul or who in their idolatry behave as if they had no soul it is proved that man has a rational and immortal soul. Man differs from the animals (τὰ ἄλογα) in that he is rational. The primary function of human reason is to guide the body and to distinguish between good and evil. The various limbs and senses of the body have a natural inclination to do certain things. It is the task of the human reason to bridle these natural inclinations. Athanasius here argues with well known commonplaces, and he obviously does so on purpose. In this way he can convince everybody that those who adore lifeless beings and animals debase themselves to a level which man should despise and on which he forsakes the special gift which distinguishes man from other living beings: reason (31-32).

Having shown that man has a rational soul Athanasius goes on to prove that man has an immortal soul (33). The proof of immortality is given with the well known argument of Plato: the soul is in constant movement and therefore its life cannot come to an end. But Athanasius manages to give this proof without linking the immortality of the soul to its pre-existence. Like all orthodox Christians Athanasius is opposed to the doctrine of the pre-existence of the soul. By stressing that the soul has been created by God's will he is able to refer the soul's life after death also to an act of God's will. This does not mean that he teaches the immortality of the soul as a gift of God, whilst to Plato and his followers the immortality is a natural quality of the soul. The argument for the preservation of the soul by God's will is given with the help of a well known argument of Plato which Christians before Athanasius had already adopted. – Two more arguments for the immortality of the soul also have clear philosophical roots: The first one is derived from the activities of the soul during the sleep of the body, and the second one says that, since the soul can think about immortality it must itself be immortal. Behind this latter argument lies the commonplace in Greek philosophy that there is a similarity between the knowing subject and the known object.

Finally Athanasius exhorts his readers in typically Platonic language to purify their souls and to return to God and to the original destination of man: a life in contemplation (34). The Platonic language must show that man has no excuse when he fails to purify his soul and to return to God: The Platonists show in their writings that man should do just this, but they do not put their theory into practice, instead they take part in idolatry.

Chapter 30

In his soul man can find the way to the true God.

Translation and Commentary:

(30) "What has been said before has been shown to be nothing but error against human life. But the way of truth will lead to the God who really *is*."

The first sentence refers to all the forms of idolatry which have been discussed in the previous part of the treatise. – On the way which leads to the really being God and which sharply differs from the circling around in error see also *C.G.* 5, *supra*, 29.

"In order to receive a knowledge and unerring conception of this we are in need of nothing other than ourselves."

In *Vita Antonii* 20 (PG 26, 873A), a chapter which shows great similarity with the present one, it says explicitly that the learning which the Greeks seek by making long journeys is not needed, since man only needs himself, i.e. his own will to practise virtue: Ἕλληνες μὲν οὖν ἀποδημοῦσι, καὶ θάλατταν περῶσι, ἵνα γράμματα μάθωσιν· ἡμεῖς δὲ οὐ χρείαν ἔχομεν ἀποδημῆσαι διὰ τὴν βασιλείαν τῶν οὐρανῶν ... Οὐκοῦν ἡ ἀρετὴ τοῦ θέλειν ἡμῶν μόνον χρείαν ἔχει. This is in line with what is said here, since the way of the soul is the way in which man makes the right use of the soul and constrains the bodily impulses.

"And the way towards God is not, as God is Himself above all things, also far away from or outside us, but it is within us and we have the possibility to find its beginning, as also Moses taught by saying: '*The word of faith is inside your heart*' (*Deut.* 30:14). The Lord, too, meant this when He confirmed it by saying: '*The kingdom of God is within you*' (*Luke* 17:21)."

On God as above all things see *C.G.* 2, *supra*, 16. For the idea that Christ confirms what Moses said and its anti-Marcionite background see *C.G.* 6, *supra*, 32. *Luke* 17:21 is also quoted in the same context in *Vita Antonii* 20. – Similar thoughts can be found in Plotinus' treatise Περὶ τοῦ καλοῦ, which, being his first piece of writing, will largely reflect earlier Platonic tradition, see e.g. *Enn.* 1, 6, 8, 3 f.: ἴτω δὴ καὶ συνεπέσθω εἰς τὸ εἴσω ὁ δυνάμενος, and *Enn.* 1, 6, 9, 7: ἄναγε ἐπὶ σαυτὸν καὶ ἰδέ, cp. P. Courcelle, *Recherches sur les Confessions de Saint Augustin*, Paris 1968², pp. 107 ff. (cp. also *infra*, 113 f.).

> "For when we have the faith and the kingdom of God within ourselves, we can quickly contemplate and think of the King of the universe, the saving Word of the Father. And let the Greeks who worship idols not come forward with excuses. And let nobody else simply mislead himself, as if he did not have such a way, and as if he therefore found an excuse for his godlessness. For we have all embarked on it and have it, even if not all want to go it but deviating rather want to walk besides it, because the pleasures of life drag them from outside."

Because man's soul has been created in God's image, man can with his soul (the mind of this soul) contemplate God, see *C.G.* 2, *supra*, 16 ff. This applies to man in general, therefore no excuse for idolatry is possible. Those who do not want to life according to their original destination are misled by bodily pleasures, see *C.G.* 3, *supra*, 20. In this context *Luke* 17:21 and *Deut.* 30:14 confirm the idea that man can contemplate God because he is created in God's image and show that man has no excuse for not contemplating the true God. Origen uses these two Biblical texts (of which the second one is quoted in *Rom.* 10:8) in a similar way, see *De Princ.* 1, 3, 6: ... *participatio dei patris pervenit in omnes tam iustos quam peccatores et rationabiles atque irrationabiles et in omnia omnino quae sunt. Ostendit sane et apostolus Paulus .. dicens* (here a quotation from *Rom.* 10:6-8 is given) ... *Et hoc est quod dixit quia 'excusationem non habent homines pro peccato suo', ex quo eis divinus sermo vel ratio ostendere coeperit in corde discretionem boni ac mali, ut per hanc debeant refugere et cavere quod malum est ... Item quod omnes homines non sunt extra communionem dei, hoc modo evangelium docet, dicente salvatore ...* (here a quotation from *Luke* 17:20-21 is given).

> "And if somebody asked which it is, then I say that it is the soul of every man and the mind within it. Because only through it God can be contemplated and thought about."

L. Leone, *op. cit.*, p. 58, says that Athanasius may here vaguely refer to Plato's doctrine of the tripartition of the soul, P. Th. Camelot, *op. cit.*, pp. 134 f. note 2, following J. Roldanus, *Le Christ et l'homme dans la théologie d'Athanase d'Alexandrie*, Leiden 1968, pp. 53-55, regards this as unlikely. We regard it as likely that the doctrine of the tripartition of the soul is presupposed here: There is a clear reference to this doctrine in *Epistula ad Marcellinum* 27 (PG 27, 40A): ἐν τῇ ψυχῇ διάφορα κινήματα φαίνεται καὶ ἔστι ἐν αὐτῇ τὸ λογίζεσθαι, καὶ τὸ ἐπιθυμεῖν καὶ τὸ θυμοειδές. The λογίζεσθαι is there directed to τὰ βέλτιστα. Here in *C.G.* 30 it appears that the νοῦς is a special function of the soul and that the νοῦς knows God. Further on in this chapter it says that man not only has a soul, but a reasonable one (ψυχὴν λογικήν). So the soul can be called reasonable since it has a νοῦς. The implication of this is that the νοῦς is identical with τὸ λογίζεσθαι which is referred to in *Epist. ad Marcell.* 27. It should, however, be noted that these are to Athanasius not as to Plato separate parts of the soul, but different functions of the soul, and that Athanasius does not share Plato's view that only the highest part of the soul is immortal. Athanasius will prove that *the* soul (as a whole) is immortal (see especially *C.G.* 33, *infra*, 108 ff.). (On Plato's doctrine of the tripartition of the soul see Plato, *Rep.* IV 440E-441C, IX 580D, Albinus, *Epit.* 24, Origen, *De Princ.* 3, 4, 1).

> "Unless the impious will, as they denied God, in the same way also reject the idea that they have a soul, saying this with more right than other things. For it is typical of those who have no mind to deny its Maker and Creator, God."

To Athanasius God and the soul are of course closely connected, since it is man's soul which has been created in God's image. – The rejection of God and the soul has more right in itself than the other things the Pagans say. This is an extremely venomous remark: Those who deny this do what is typical of people who are out of their mind. When such people make other statements (e.g. about the justification of forms of idolatry) they say things which are wrong and to which they are not even entitled, – they are entitled to the denial of God's existence and of the existence of the soul, because they are out of their mind.

> "So that every man has a soul, and a rational one at that, this, too, must be demonstrated with a few words for the sake of the simple, especially since some of the heretics deny this, too, believing that man is nothing but the visible form of his body. In order that, when this has been shown, they can have by themselves a clearer refutation of idolatry."

P. Th. Camelot, *op. cit.*, pp. 152 f. note 2, suggests, that one should in this context rather think of materialist philosophers who deny that man has a soul than of Christian heretics. One might then think of the Epicureans. It is true that in *C.G.* 34 Athanasius obviously means Greek idolators when he attacks those who believe that man has no rational soul, see *infra*, 112. But we regard it as unlikely that Athanasius should call here in *C.G.* 30 Pagan philosophers 'heretics', – he clearly distinguishes between philosophers and heretics, partly in order to be able to claim that the heretics received their ideas from the philosophers (see *supra*, 29 ff.). It is not possible to identify these heretics with absolute certainty, but we would like to refer to the possibility that Athanasius may have in mind Jewish Christians, who claim that man's creation in God's image applies to his body and not to his soul, and that Athanasius draws from this the conclusion that they deny that man has a soul, especially a rational and immortal soul. This could be the reason why he wants to prove just this in the following chapters: man has a rational soul with which he can think things divine, and this soul is immortal. This double proof could well be meant *inter alia* to convince the reader that the Jewish Christians are wrong in denying the soul's immortality and in denying that the image of God becomes apparent in his rationality. See on this G. Quispel, Sein und Gestalt, *Gnostic Studies* II, Istanbul 1975, p. 145 and, Ezekiel 1:26 in Jewish Mysticism and Gnosis, *Vigiliae Christianae* (34) 1980, p. 9. Quispel refers especially to the *Pseudo-Clementine Homilies* 3, 7, 2: ὁ γὰρ ὄντως ὢν οὗτός ἐστιν, οὗ τὴν μορφὴν τὸ ἀνθρώπου βαστάζει σῶμα, cp. 17, 7. – When Athanasius says that the Pagans have a clearer refutation of idolatry by themselves he means to say that when they realize that they have a rational soul and an immortal soul, they also ought to realize that they ought not to adore lifeless and temporary idols.

Chapter 31

The fact that man can distinguish between good and evil shows that he has a rational soul.

Translation and Commentary:

> (31) "A first and not insignificant proof of the fact that the soul of men is rational stems from the fact that it differs from the irrational beings. For it is for this reason that we have the natural custom to call them irrational, since the human race is rational."

This is, of course, a commonplace in both Pagan and Christian literature, see the examples quoted by L. Leone, *op. cit.*, p. 59 (to which could be added Eusebius, *Praep. Evang.* 7, 18, 3). – The remark also has a rhetorical background, *viz.*, the argument from opposites: when animals are irrational, then men who differ from the animals must be rational, see G. C. Stead, Rhetorical Method in Athanasius, p. 126.

> "Furthermore perhaps this, too, would not be an unimportant proof, that only man considers what is outside him and thinks about what is not present and reconsiders it and with his judgement chooses the better one of the reasonings. For irrational beings only look at what is present and move only to what is in eyesight, also if they afterwards incur harm. But man does not only move towards what is visible, but also passes a judgement with his reasoning on what he sees with his eyes. So often having started to move he is held back by reasoning, and having thought he thinks again. And every-

body observes, if he is a friend of the truth, that the mind of men differs from bodily senses. And for this reason that mind is different, it becomes the judge of these very senses."

This is a description of man if he lives according to his original destination, sinners and idolators do not, of course, live in this way, see *supra*, 16 ff. The thoughts which Athanasius here expresses and the language with which he does it are to a large degree Platonic. Albinus says that the part of the soul which is called τὸ ἡγεμονικόν is situated in the head, and that we there also find τὸ λογιστικόν and τὸ κρῖνον, see *Epit*. 17, 4: ... οἱ θεοὶ ... τὸ ἡγεμονικὸν κατὰ λόγον περὶ τὴν κεφαλὴν καθίδρυσαν ... Ἐν τούτῳ καὶ τὸ λογιστικὸν καὶ τὸ κρῖνόν τε καὶ τὸ θεωροῦν. With this part of his soul man chooses virtue out of free will, see *Epit*. 31, 1. This part of the soul is distinguished from τὸ ὁρμητικόν (*Epit*. 25, 7), and for the spontaneous movement Albinus uses the word ὁρμᾶν (just as Athanasius does here in *C.G.* 31). It is a commonplace to say that man differs from the animals since only man has foresight and memory, see e.g. Cicero, *De off.* 1, 4, 11: *Sed inter hominem et beluam hoc maxime interest quod haec... ad id solum quod adest quodque praesens est, se accommodat, paulum admodum sentiens praeteritum et futurum. Homo autem, quod rationis est particeps... facile totius vitae cursum videt ad eamque degendam praeparat res necessarias*, Hilary of Poitiers, *De Trin.* 1, 2; 9, 59.

"And what these perceive, that the mind judges, and remembers it and shows what is better to the senses. For the eye can only see, the ears hear, the mouth taste, the nose smell, the hands touch. But to decide what one ought to see and to hear and to touch, to taste and to smell is no longer the task of the senses, but of the soul and its mind. Certainly, the hand can take a sword and the mouth can take poison. But it does not know that these things harm, if the mind makes no judgement."

The senses have no idea of good and evil, man's mind has, cp. *Vita Antonii* 20 (PG 26, 873B): Τὸ γὰρ εὐθεῖαν εἶναι τὴν ψυχήν, τοῦτό ἐστι τὸ κατὰ φύσιν νοερὸν αὐτῆς ὡς ἐκτίσθη ... ἐὰν γὰρ μείνωμεν ὡς γεγόναμεν, ἐν τῇ ἀρετῇ ἐσμεν· ἐὰν δὲ λογιζώμεθα τὰ φαῦλα, ὡς κακοὶ κρινόμεθα, and Origen, *De Princ.* 3, 1, 3: Τὸ μέντοι λογικὸν ζῷον καὶ λόγον ἔχει πρὸς τῇ φανταστικῇ φύσει, τὸν κρίνοντα τὰς φαντασίας καί τινας μὲν ἀποδοκιμάζοντα, τινὰς δὲ παραδεχόμενον, ἵνα ἄγηται τὸ ζῷον κατ' αὐτάς· ὅθεν ἐπεὶ ἐν τῇ φύσει τοῦ λόγου εἰσὶν ἀφορμαὶ τοῦ θεωρῆσαι τὸ καλὸν καὶ τὸ αἰσχρὸν αἷς ἑπόμενοι θεωρήσαντες τὸ καλὸν καὶ τὸ αἰσχρὸν αἱρούμεθα μὲν τὸ καλόν, ἐκκλίνομεν τὸ δὲ αἰσχρόν, ἐπαινετοὶ μέν ἐσμεν ἐπιδόντες ἑαυτοὺς τῇ πράξει τοῦ καλοῦ, ψεκτοὶ δὲ κατὰ τὸ ἐναντίον. Again the thoughts and the language used by Athanasius are to a certain degree Platonic. Albinus, too, says that when somebody moves towards what is evil it is because he thinks it is good. This is in line with what Athanasius says of the senses. But then Albinus goes on to say that nobody sins on purpose, if he does sin, it is by error, see *Epit.* 31, 1: εἰ δέ τις ἐπὶ κακίαν ὁρμᾷ, πρῶτον μὲν οὐχ ὡς ἐπὶ κακίαν αὐτὴν ὁρμήσει, ἀλλ᾽ ὡς ἐπ᾽ ἀγαθόν· εἰ δὲ καὶ παραγίνεταί τις ἐπὶ κακίαν πάντως ὁ τοιοῦτος ἐξηπάτηται, ὡς δι᾽ ἐλάττονός τινος κακοῦ ἀποκοινησόμενος μεῖζον ἀγαθόν, καὶ ταύτῃ ἀκουσίως ἐλεύσεται, ἀδύνατον γὰρ ὁρμᾶν τινα ἐπὶ κακὰ βουλόμενον ἔχειν αὐτά, οὔτε ἐλπίδι ἀγαθοῦ οὔτε φόβῳ μείζονος κακοῦ (cp. Plato, *Timaeus* 86D: κακὸς μὲν γὰρ ἑκὼν οὐδείς). With this latter statement Athanasius does not, of course, agree, since it is essential to his whole refutation of idolatry that man turns to evil out of free will. Albinus says that virtue happens because of free will, evil happens against free will (*Epit.* 31, 1: τῷ δὴ τὴν ἀρετὴν ἑκούσιον εἶναι ἕπεται τὸ τὴν κακίαν ἀκούσιον ὑπάρχειν), according to Athanasius both virtue and evil are caused by free will. - (On the example of the sword which man's hand can take see *C.G.* 4, *supra*, 23.)

> "And in order to look at this in a simile it is like a well tuned lyre and the musician who plays it with skill. For as the strings of the lyre each have their own sound, the one deep, another high, another medium, another very high, and another still different, and their harmony cannot be determined and their concord be known without the artist, - for then their harmony is shown and their concord is right, when he who holds the lyre strikes the strings and touches everything in a harmonious way, - in this way when also the senses of the body are put into harmony like a lyre when the understanding mind rules them, then the soul determines and knows what it makes and does."

As L. Leone rightly indicates (*op. cit.*, p. 60) this simile is derived from the well known passage Plato, *Phaedo* 86E ff. The simile is briefly repeated in *C.G.* 32, elsewhere the harmony of the universe, instituted by God, is compared with a lyre, see *C.G.* 35, 39, 42, 47.

> "But this is only characteristic of men, and this is the rational activity of the soul of men, through the use of which it differs from the irrational beings and shows that it is really different from the bodily appearance."

That man is no more than the visible body is claimed by some heretics (at least in the way Athanasius presents their views, see *C.G.* 30, *supra*, 101 f.), but this would imply that man does not differ from the animals, which he does, as was stated in the beginning of this chapter, see *supra*, 104.

> "For often when the body lies on the ground man looks at and contemplates what is in heaven, and often when the body is quiet and rests and sleeps, man inside is moving and contemplates what is outside himself, he traverses foreign lands and meets friends and through this often divines and knows beforehand his daily actions. What else could this be but a rational soul, in which man considers and thinks about what is beyond him."

Whilst the body sleeps man contemplates what is in heaven, this means that in his dream man returns to his original destination, since he was created in order to contemplate the Divine, see *C.G.* 2, *supra*, 16 ff. - The movement of the soul during the sleep of the body is taken as a proof of the soul's existence, a theory which appears already in the school of Aristotle, see F. Wehrli, *Die Schule des Aristoteles, Texte und Kommentar, Heft III, Klearchos*, Basel 1948, fr. 7 and pp. 47 ff., cp. Irenaeus, *Adv. Haer.* 2, 50 and 2, 52 (be it in a different context, *viz.*, a discussion of the pre-existence of the soul), Tertullian, *De anima* 45, 1. In his dreams man traverses foreign lands, says Athanasius, cp. Tertullian, *De anima* 43, 12: *probat se mobilem semper, terra mari peregrinatur*, for further parallels see J. H. Waszink's edition p. 472. - The mantic function of dreams was a commonplace: Aristotle seems to express scepticism about it, see I. Düring, *op. cit.*, p. 562, the Stoics asserted it, see *Stoicorum Veterum Fragmenta* 2, pp. 1197 f. (cp. Tertullian, *De anima* 46, 11), Philo, *De somniis* II 1: συνίσταται δὲ τὸ τρίτον εἶδος (sc. τῶν θεοπέμπτων ὀνείρων) ὁπόταν ἐν τοῖς ὕπνοις ἐξ ἑαυτῆς ἡ ψυχὴ κινουμένη καὶ ἀναδονοῦσα ἑαυτὴν κορυβαντιᾷ καὶ ἐνθουσιῶσα δυνάμει προγνωστικῇ τὰ μέλλοντα θεσπίζῃ (cp. Calcidius, *Timaeus translatus commentarioque instructus*, cap. CCLVI). Origen expresses approval of this doctrine which is held according to him by all who believe in providence, see *Contra Celsum* 1, 48: ... ὄναρ πεπίστευται πολλοὺς πεφαντασιῶσθαί τινα μὲν θειότερά τινα δὲ περὶ μελλόντων βιωτικῶν ἀναγγέλλοντα εἴτε σαφῶς εἴτε καὶ δι' αἰνιγμάτων, καὶ τοῦτ' ἐναργές ἐστι παρὰ πᾶσι τοῖς παραδεξαμένοις πρόνοιαν. - Man has a rational soul which differs from the body because man can think about what is above him, is Athanasius' final conclusion to this whole argument, - cp. to this Origen, *De Princ.* 1, 1, 7: *Si qui autem sunt qui mentem ipsam animamque corpus esse arbitrantur, velim mihi responderent, quomodo tantarum rerum tam difficilium tamque subtilium rationes assertionesque recipiat ... Unde certe incorporalium intellectus corpori inest? ... Unde etiam divina dogmata quae manifeste incorporea sunt, sentire atque intellegere potest?*

CHAPTER 32

Further proof that man has a rational soul.

Translation and Commentary:

(32) "This, too, could be an exact proof for those who are still turned towards the shamelessness of unreason."

These are the people who because they do not believe in the fact that man has a rational soul adore things which are lifeless, *i.e.* have no soul, and practise shameless acts, see especially *C.G.* 26, *supra*, 87.

"How, while the body is mortal by its nature, does man think about immortality and often defies death for the sake of virtue?"

Here the proof of the soul's rationality is combined with the proof of its immortality. We shall deal with the immortality in explaining *C.G.* 33, *infra*, 108 ff.

"Or how, since the body is temporal, does man see what is eternal so that he despises what is in front of him and fixes his desire on those things? The body itself will not have such thoughts about itself and cannot consider these things outside itself, for it is mortal and temporal. But what thinks about what is opposite and against the nature of the body must be something different. So again what could this be except a rational and immortal soul?"

The rationality of the soul appears from the fact that the soul can think what the body cannot think. – On the defiance of death for the sake of virtue see also *De Inc.* 27 ff. where the Christians' willingness to die is taken as a proof of Christ's resurrection (cp. *De Inc.* 47). – In *Vita Antonii* 16 (PG 26, 868A) the brevity of life is put into contrast with eternal life: Ὅλος γὰρ ὁ τῶν ἀνθρώπων βίος βραχύτατός ἐστι, μετρούμενος πρὸς τοὺς μέλλοντας αἰῶνας· ὥστε καὶ πάντα τὸν χρόνον ἡμῶν μηδὲν εἶναι πρὸς τὴν αἰώνιον ζωὴν, cp. *Contra Arianos* 2, 76 (PG 26, 309A), – the fragility and brevity of human life is a commonplace in early Christian and ancient Pagan literature, see e.g. Irenaeus, *Adv. Haer.* 2, 5, 1, Theophilus, *Ad Aut.* 2, 3, Lactance, *Div. Inst.* 3, 12, 4, 13, Hilary of Poitiers, *De Trin.* 3, 13, Cicero, *Tusc. Disp.* 1, 38, 91; 1, 39, 94 (see further *Ciceronis Tusculanarum disputationum libri V erklärt von* M. Pohlenz, Stuttgart 1957 (I-II), pp. 111 f.). Augustin puts the brevity of human life either in contrast with the whole time of the world (see e.g. *Sermo* 108, 3) or, just like Athanasius, with God's eternity (see e.g. *Sermo* 124, 4, *En. in Ps.* 91, 8 (I); 102, 22; 120, 10, cp. H. I. Marrou, *L'Ambivalence du Temps et de l'Histoire chez Saint Augustin*, Montréal/Paris 1950, pp. 43 ff., and M. Moreau, Mémoire et Durée, *Revue des Etudes Augustiniennes* (1) 1955, pp. 242 f.).

"For not from outside, but from inside it makes resound in the body what is better, as the musician in the lyre."

On the comparison of the soul and the body with the musician and the lyre see *C.G.* 31, *supra*, 104.

"And again if it is the nature of the eye to see and of the ear to hear, how do they turn away from this and choose that? For who is it that turns away the eye from seeing, or who is it that prevents the ear which hears by nature from hearing? Or who is it that often hinders taste, which tastes by nature, from exerting its natural impulse? And who is it that withholds the hand, which by nature is active, from touching something? Who is it that turns away smell, which is made for smelling, from perceiving it? Who is it that does these things against the natural impulse of the body?"

This is a repetition of the argument given in *C.G.* 31, see *supra*, 103, with this small difference that in *C.G.* 31 emphasis was laid on the fact that the soul makes a choice within the activities of the senses, here in *C.G.* 32 on the fact that it can block the activities of the senses.

> "Or how does the body, having turned away from its nature, turn towards the counsels of somebody else and drive according to the nod of that other being? All this shows nothing but a rational soul which governs the body. For it is not the body's nature to drive itself, but it is led and directed by another, as also a horse does not yoke itself, but is driven by its master."

The body does not govern itself, but the rational soul governs the body. On the comparison between the soul and the body and the driver and the horse see *C.G.* 5, *supra*, 28 f. The implication of what is said about the horse and its driver is that animals have no free will, but are, if they are not ruled by men ruled by their natural impulses, cp. *Contra Arianos* 3, 18-21 (PG 26, 360 ff.) where it says *inter alia* that the animals are set as examples to man, but only in the sense that man who is changeable should imitate what is unchangeable, in this sense he should imitate the animals which are unchangeable because they are below the level of free will and God who is above it, cp. further Irenaeus, *Adv. Haer.* 4, 61, 1: *irrationabilia sive inanimalia quae sua voluntate nihil possunt agere, sed cum necessitate et vi ad bonum trahuntur in quibus unus sensus et unus mos, inflexibiles et sine iudicio qui nihil aliud esse possunt praeterquam quod facti sunt,* Justin Martyr, *Apol.* I 43, 8: οὐ γὰρ ὥσπερ τὰ ἄλλα, οἷον δένδρα καὶ τετράποδα μηδὲν δυνάμενα προαιρέσει πράττειν, ἐποίησεν ὁ θεὸς τὸν ἄνθρωπον.

> "For this reason there are also laws for men to do good and to turn away from evil. But for irrational beings evil remains unconsidered and undetermined, since they are devoid of rationality and a rational thinking."

Laws are for beings who have a reason. The gods of the Pagans are irrational because they do not act according to the laws given to men, which means that they are in fact below the level of man who has in his soul been created in God's image, cp. *supra*, 51 ff., 85, 87. So the honour of man as a rational being is that he can obey laws, cp. Tertullian, *Adv. Marc.* 2, 4, 5: ... *ut solus homo gloriaretur quod solus dignus fuisset qui legem a Deo muneret,* Irenaeus, *Adv. Haer.* 4, 25, 1: *Haec enim gloria hominis perseverare ac permanere in Dei servitute.*

> "So I believe it has been shown with the preceding arguments that there is a rational soul in men."

As appears from the μέν in this sentence and the δέ of the first sentence of the next chapter, these two sentences are closely connected. In the first sentence the conclusion from the arguments given in *C.G.* 31-32 is drawn: man has a rational soul, in the latter sentence it is announced what will be proved in the next chapter: man has an immortal soul. Both arguments are closely connected: In the proof of the rationality of the soul its immortality was already referred to, in the proof of its immortality the rationality will also play a part.

CHAPTER 33

Proof of the soul's immortality.

Translation and Commentary:

> (*33*) "But that the soul is also made immortal, this too must be known in the ecclesiastical instruction in order to prove that idols must be put away with."

The link between the immortality of the human soul and the refutation of idolatry is that man who has an immortal soul not adore perishable idols, see *supra*, 57, 79.

> "Now knowledge about this could come nearer from the knowledge about the body and from the fact that it differs from the body. For if our argument has shown that it differs from the body, and the body is mortal by nature, then the soul must be immortal, since it is not like the body."

This is again the rhetorical argument from opposites, see *supra*, 31. That the soul differs from the body had been shown in *C.G.* 31-32, where primarily the rationality of the soul was discussed.

> "And again, if the soul moves the body, as has been shown, and is itself not moved by other things, then it follows that the soul is moved by itself and that after the burial of the body it is again moved by itself. For it is not the soul which dies, but because of its departure the body dies. So if this, too, were moved by the body, it would follow that when the mover departs it dies. But if the soul also moves the body, then it must rather move itself. But if it is moved by itself, then it must live also after the death of the body. For the movement of the soul is nothing other than its life, certainly as we also say that the body then lives when it moves and that its death occurs when it ceases to move."

That the soul moves the body was said in *C.G.* 4, *supra*, 24 f., and again argued extensively in *C.G.* 31-32, *supra*, 102 ff. As has been observed (see e.g. L. Leone, *op. cit.*, p. 63 and P. Th. Camelot, *op. cit.*, p. 161) an important background to this argument is Plato, *Phaedrus* 245C ff., a passage which was well known in later times, see e.g. Albinus, *Epit.* 5, 5, Numenius, *fragm.* 47 (ed. Des Places), Plutarch, *De an. procr.* 1013C and

1016A, Cicero, *De ant. deor.* 2, 32, Calcidius, *Commentarius*, cap. LVII, Ps.-Justin, *Coh.* 6, Tertullian, *De anima* 6, 1 ff. Plato's argument runs as follows: What is constantly in movement is immortal. What is moved by something else has finite movement and finite life. Only what moves itself does not stop moving, since it is itself the beginning of the movement which means that it is unoriginated (ἀγένητον) and what is unoriginated is imperishable. When one compares this with Athanasius' argument not only the similarities, but also the differences become apparent. Plato links the immortality of the soul to its pre-existence, Athanasius does not. In *Vita Antonii* 74 (PG 26, 948A) Athanasius in fact explicitly attacks the doctrine of the pre-existence of the souls and makes St. Antony tell the Greek philosophers: ὑμεῖς δὲ πλανᾶσθε, ὅτι περὶ ἀγεννήτου ψυχῆς ἐξηγεῖσθε. As a Christian (cp. J. H. Waszink in his edition of Tertullian's *De anima*, pp. 120 ff.) Athanasius believes that the soul was created by God, see *C.G.* 35: ... ὁ θεὸς ... κηδόμενος τῶν ὑπ' αὐτοῦ γενομένων ψυχῶν, and that the movement of the soul has been started by God, see *C.G.* 44: τῇ αὐτοῦ (sc. τοῦ θεοῦ Λόγου) προνοίᾳ καὶ σώματα μὲν αὔξει, ψυχὴ δὲ ἡ λογικὴ κινεῖται, καὶ τὸ λογίζεσθαι καὶ τὸ ζῆν ἔχει.

> "One could see this also more clearly from its various activities in the body. For if also when it has entered the body and is bound to it, it is not restricted to the measure of the smallness of the body, but often, whilst the body is lying on the bed and is not moving, but sleeping as in death, it is awake according to its own power and transcends the nature of the body; and as it were departing from it, yet remaining in the body, it places before its mind and contemplates what is above the earth, and often also meets the saints and angels who are outside the earthly bodies and goes towards them putting its confidence in the purity of its mind."

The soul's activity during the sleep of the body was already discussed in *C.G.* 31, *supra*, 104 f. To what was said there Athanasius now adds that in the sleep the soul, encouraged by its purity, meets saints and angels, this means that in sleep man does what original man did and what is the destination of man, see *C.G.* 2, *supra*, 17 f. According to Tertullian, *De anima* 9, 4, a Christian woman had in a state of ecstasy conversations with angels, see on this J. H. Waszink's edition p. 168, cp. also Clement of Alexandria, *Paed.* 2, 9, 82, 3, who stresses the activity of the soul during sleep and says that its special function is to wake up man and thereby make him equal to the grace of the angels by living eternally: ... ἀγγελικῇ τὸν ἄνθρωπον ἐξισάζει χάριτι, τῆς ζωῆς τὸ ἀΐδιον ἐκ τῆς ἐγρηγορέναι μελέτης προσλαμβάνουσα. – When Athanasius says that the body sleeps *as in death* this is already an indication that he wants to draw conclusions from the soul's activities during the sleep of the body about the soul's activities after the death of the body. Behind this lies the idea that there is a similarity between sleep and death, which is expressed by the metaphor that sleep is a mirror of death, see Tertullian, *De anima* 42, 3 and 50, 1, and the parallels quoted in J. H. Waszink's edition, p. 460.

> "So how much more will it not have a clearer knowledge of immortality, when it has been freed from the body at the moment when God who has bound it to the body wants it? For if even when it was bound to the body it lived the life outside the body, much more it will live also after the death of the body, and it will not stop living because of God who has made it so through His Word, our Lord Jesus Christ."

This is the rhetorical argument *a fortiori*, see on this argument G. C. Stead, Rhetorical Method in Athanasius, p. 126. In itself this argument is here not very convincing: Life of the soul after the body's death does not become clearer if there is life of the soul during the body's sleep, if the argument could be developed the other way round then it could rightly be said that if the soul lives after the body's death it *a fortiori* lives during the body's sleep. Athanasius develops the argument *a minore ad maius*, it would only be convincing if it were developed *a maiore ad minus*. – Important in this argument is that it appears from it that according to Athanasius the soul's movement in itself does not guarantee immortality. Immortality is not a quality of the soul, but it is God's gift to the soul: because God has made the soul in such a way that it can move after the death of the body, therefore the soul is immortal. This doctrine differs from Plato, *Phaedrus* 245C ff., but it is in line with what Plato says elsewhere, *viz.*, in *Timaeus* 41A ff. (a section Athanasius was probably familiar with, see *C.G.* 9, *supra*, 43): what has come into being is not immortal by itself, but will be saved from death by the will of the Demiurge. This is said there about the lower gods who are the planets and the earth and who together form the universe (cp. A. E. Taylor, *A Commentary on Plato's Timaeus*, Oxford 1928, pp. 248 ff.). In Middle Platonism one referred to this text when one wanted to counter the claim that the world cannot have been created, since in that case the world would have as end as well, see Atticus, *fragm.* 4 (ed. J. Baudry): Since the universe has been created by the will of God it can be preserved by the will of God. (On the Aristotelian background of the tenet that what has been generated is destructible see J. Pépin, *Théologie cosmique et théologie chrétienne*, Paris 1964, pp. 81 ff.). Justin Martyr applies this theory to the preservation of the souls of the righteous people, see *Dial.* 5, 1-6, 2 and J. C. M. van Winden, *An Early Christian Philosopher*, pp. 84 ff. Justin explicitly refers to Plato's *Timaeus* (*Dial.* 5, 4), Irenaeus argues in favour of the immortality of the souls of the Christians without an explicit reference to this passage in the *Timaeus*, but it is obvious that he has it in mind. In *Adv. Haer.* 2, 56, 1 he compares the preservation of the soul by

God's will with the preservation of the stars and the whole world by God's will: *Quemadmodum enim coelum quod est super nos, firmamentum, et sol, et luna, et reliquae stellae, et omnia ornamenta ipsorum, cum ante non essent, facta sunt, et multo tempore perseverant secundum voluntatem, sic et de animabus, et de spiritibus, et omnino de omnibus his quae facta sunt quis minime peccabit: quando omnia quae facta sunt initium quidem facturae suae habeant, perseverant autem quoadusque ea Deus et esse, et perseverare voluerit.* This comparison can easily be explained against the background of a Middle Platonic interpretation of *Timaeus* 41A/B in which the lower gods are understood to be the planets and the earth, i.e. the whole universe (cp. Origen, *De Princ.* 2, 3, 6: ... *dicunt quidam de hoc mundo, quoniam corruptibilis quidem est ex eo quod factus est, nec tamen corrumpitur quia corruptione fortior ac validior est voluntas Dei*). – What becomes clear from the present argument given by Athanasius is that he uses not only Plato, *Phaedrus* 245C ff. in order to prove the immortality of the soul, but also Plato, *Timaeus* 41A, and that he manages, by combining these two passages, to avoid Plato's doctrine of the pre-existence of the soul to which he is completely opposed. As it is to Justin and Irenaeus to Athanasius too, the immortality of the soul is a gift of God. (On Athanasius' familiarity with the doctrine of the world's preservation by God's will see further *C.G.* 41, *infra*, 136 f.).

> "For this is the reason that it considers and thinks about the immortal and eternal things, since it is immortal, too. And as, since the body is mortal, its senses, too, consider mortal things, in the same way the soul, since it contemplates and considers immortal things must be immortal as well and live always. For the thoughts and ideas about immortality never leave it, remaining in it and becoming so to speak a torch in it for the certainty of immortality. So for this reason it also has the idea of the contemplation of God and becomes its own path taking the knowledge and concept of God's Word not from outside but from itself."

The rhetorical argument by analogy is applied here: Everybody agrees that the body is mortal and perceives temporary things; it is also clear that the soul thinks eternal things; hence the soul must be immortal just as the body is mortal. Athanasius may feel justified in drawing the conclusion that the soul is immortal since it thinks immortality, because he adheres to the (generally accepted) tenet that there is a similarity between the object which is known and the subject which knows, see e.g. *De Inc.* 57: ὥσπερ γὰρ εἴ τις ἐθελήσειεν ἰδεῖν τὸ τοῦ ἡλίου φῶς, πάντως τὸν ὀφθαλμὸν ἀποσμήχει καὶ λαμπρύνει, σχεδὸν ὅμοιον τῷ ποθουμένῳ ἑαυτὸν διακαθαίρων, ἵνα οὕτως φῶς γενόμενος ὁ ὀφθαλμὸς τὸ τοῦ ἡλίου φῶς ἴδῃ ... (cp. on this tenet A. Schneider, Erkenntnis des Gleichen durch Gleiches in antiker und patristischer Zeit, *Beiträge zur Geschichte der Philosophie des Mittelalters, Supplementband II (Festgabe zum 70. Geburtstage Clemens*

Baeumkers) Münster i.W. 1923, pp. 61-76 and J. H. Waszink in his edition of Calcidius, p. 100). For further examples of the theory that the soul is immortal since it thinks about immortality see L. Leone, *op. cit.*, p. 65, – of particular importance is Lactance, *Div. Inst.* 7, 9: *apparet animam non interire neque dissolvi, sed manere in sempiternum, quia Deum qui sempiternus est et quaerit et diligit*, cp. H. W. A. van Rooijen-Dijkman, *De vita beata, Het zevende boek van de Divinae Institutiones van Lactantius, Analyse en bronnenonderzoek*, Leiden 1967, pp. 74 ff. God has given the soul the possibility to contemplate eternity by creating the soul in His image, therefore God also gives to the soul the possibility to become like what it contemplates, *viz.*, immortal. In grasping this faculty the soul uses itself as a road towards God and immortality.

CHAPTER 34

Refutation of idolatry and exhortation to turn towards the true God on the basis of the immortal soul.

Translation and Commentary:

> (34) "So we say, as was said before, as they denied God and worship what is lifeless, in the same way believing that they do not have a rational soul, they receive the punishment for their folly from the fact that they are counted among the irrational beings."

Here Athanasius refers to Greek idolators who deny that man has a soul. It is hardly conceivable that Athanasius here has any school of philosophers in mind, since no Greek philosopher denies this (the Epicureans only deny that man has an immortal soul). What he here seems to suggest is that those who do take part in idolatry behave like people who do not believe that they have a rational soul and thereby debase themselves to the level of animals which lack reason. (The heretics who according to Athanasius deny that man has a soul in his view follow the views and behaviour of these Pagan idolators, see *C.G.* 30, *supra*, 101 f.).

> "And therefore as soulless beings worshipping soulless beings they are worthy of pity and guidance."

It is in fact going a considerable step further to suggest that the idolators are soulless than to say that they are irrational (like animals). Since Athanasius wants to say that the idolators are like their idols, and since the idols are soulless (see *C.G.* 14-15, *supra*, 58 ff.) he claims (in a rhetorical way) that the idolators are soulless. He here ironically agrees with them that they have no soul as they claim. – On the idea that they deserve pity (which is no excuse for them) see *supra*, 55.

> "But if they think they have a soul and are rightly proud of their rationality, why, as if they had no soul, do they dare to act against reason and do they think what one ought not to think but make themselves greater than even the Divine? For although they have an immortal and to them invisible soul they picture God in what is seen and mortal."

Those who are attacked here are probably the Platonists: they are proud of their rationality (ἐπὶ τῷ λογικῷ μέγα φρονοῦσι), cp. what is said about Plato, *C.G.* 10: πολλὰ καυχησάμανος ὡς περὶ θεοῦ διανοηθείς and about the Platonists, *C.G.* 19: βαθύτερα λέγειν νομίζοντες, in *C.G.* 20 he shows that despite the excuses with which they come forward they picture God in what is visible, see *supra*, 69 ff.

> "Or why, as they turned away from God, do they in the same way not take refuge in Him again? For they can, as they turned away in their mind from God and shaped what is not as gods, in the same way rise with the mind of their soul and turn again towards God."

His opponents are here invited to do the opposite of what original man and his descendants did, see *C.G.* 3-4, *supra*, 20 ff., especially 24.

> "And they can turn back when they have cast off the pollution of all desire which they have put on and wash themselves until they have cast off every strange addition to their soul and show it only as such as it was made in order to be able to contemplate in it the Word of the Father in whose image they were also created in the beginning."

This self-purification has clearly ethical implications (as also idolatry leads man to a morally wrong way of life), see *De Inc.* 57: ... ὁ θέλων τῶν θεολόγων τὴν διάνοιαν καταλαβεῖν, προαπονίψαι καὶ προαποπλῦναι τῷ βίῳ τὴν ψυχὴν ὀφείλει ... A. Hamilton, Athanasius and the Simile of the Mirror, *Vigiliae Christianae* (34) 1980, pp. 15 f. suggests that Athanasius here has in mind Plotinus, *Enneads* 1, 6, 5, 43 ff.: οἷον εἴ τις δὺς εἰς πηλὸν ἢ βορβορον τὸ μὲν ὅπερ εἶχε κάλλος μηκέτι προφαίνοι, τοῦτο δὲ ὁρῷτο, ὃ παρὰ τοῦ πηλοῦ ἢ βορβόρου ἀπεμάξατο· ᾧ δὴ τὸ αἰσχρὸν προσθήκη τοῦ ἀλλοτρίου προσῆλθε καὶ ἔργον αὐτῷ, εἴπερ ἔσται πάλιν καλός, ἀπονιψαμένῳ καὶ καθηραμένῳ ὅπερ ἦν εἶναι. This could well be the case: Athanasius is attacking the Platonists here, he might well do so in reminding them of what they say themselves and in thereby challenging them to put their thoughts into practice. In addition there seem to be more similarities between Plotinus, *Enneads* 1, 6 Περὶ τοῦ καλοῦ and the *Contra Gentes De Inc. Verbi*: See apart from *C.G.* 8 which Hamilton, *op. cit.*, p. 15 compares with *Enneads* 1, 6, 5, 25 ff., 36 ff., the parallels quoted *supra*, 100, and the text from *De Inc.* 57 quoted *supra*, 111, where it says that if the eye wants to see the sun it should clean itself and become like the sun. This can be compared with Plotinus' famous lines in *Enneads* 1, 6, 9, 30 ff.: οὐ γὰρ ἂν πώποτε εἶδεν ὀφθαλμὸς ἥλιον ἡλιοειδὴς μὴ γεγενημένος, οὐδὲ τὸ καλον ἂν ἴδοι ψυχὴ μὴ γενομένη. Γενέσθω δὴ πρῶτον θεοειδὴς πᾶς καὶ καλὸς πᾶς, εἰ μέλλει θεάσασθαι θεόν τε καὶ καλόν (although this parallel is not a cogent proof that Athanasius knew this treatise, since Plato, *Rep.* 508A says something similar, cp. also the quotation from Posidonius given by Sextus Empiricus, *Adv. Mathem.* VII 93: ὡς τὸ μὲν φῶς, φησὶν ὁ Ποσειδώνιος ..., ὑπὸ τῆς φωτοειδοῦς ὄψεως καταλαμβάνεται, see K. Gronau, *Poseidonios und die jüdisch-christliche Genesisexegese*, Leipzig-Berlin 1914, pp. 170 ff., Irenaeus comes also fairly close, *Adv. Haer.* 4, 36, 6: ὥσπερ οἱ βλέποντες τὸ φῶς, ἐντός εἰσι τοῦ φωτός, καὶ τῆς λαμπρότητος αὐτοῦ μετέχουσιν· οὕτως οἱ βλέποντες θεόν, ἐντός εἰσι τοῦ θεοῦ, μετέχοντες αὐτοῦ τῆς λαμπρότητος.

> "For it was made in God's image and created in His likeness as also the divine Scripture indicates when it says in the name of God: '*Let us make man in our image and likeness*' (*Gen.* 1:26). Hence, too, when it casts off all pollution of sin which has been poured over it and keeps pure only what is in the image, then naturally when this shines forth it contemplates as in a mirror the Image of the Father, the Word, and considers in Him the Father, of whom the Saviour also is the Image."

On man's creation in God's image which enables him to contemplate the Image of God see *supra*, 20. Because the soul is an image of God's Image, i.e. the Word, the soul can see God in itself as in a mirror (in which God's Image is reflected). This simile appears repeatedly in Athanasius, see *C.G.* 2, 8, and is derived from Christian tradition, see e.g. Theophilus, *Ad Aut.* 1, 2, Clement of Alexandria, *Quis dives salvetur* 21, 7.

> "Or if the instruction on the part of the soul is not enough through what disturbs the soul's mind from outside and causes the soul not to see what is more, then it is also possible to receive knowledge of God from what is visible, since creation through its order and harmony indicates and loudly proclaims as with letters its Lord and Maker."

The pollution of the soul from outside is the fact that the bodily world distracts the soul from contemplating God, see *C.G.* 3-8, *supra*, 20 ff. - This sentence leads to the next part of the treatise: God's revelation through the harmony of the universe. In *De Inc.* 11-13 Athanasius deals with four ways of knowing God: the first one is in the fact that man was created in God's image (this was discussed so far in the *Contra Gentes*), the second one is through the harmony of the universe (this will be discussed in *C.G.* 35-45a), the third one is through the law and the prophets of the Old Testament (this will be discussed in *C.G.* 45b-46), the fourth one is through the incarnation of the Word (this will be discussed in the bulk of the *De Incarnatione Verbi*). This is not a chronological order in the sense that the one stage supersedes the other one: original man who before the fall lives according to his destination of being created in God's image already contemplates God's providence over the universe, see *C.G.* 2, *supra*, 18, of this original man it says that he has his eyes in order to see the harmony of creation, see *C.G.* 4, *supra*, 25. There is a history of God's adaptation to human weakness and in this sense the stages follow each other, but this is a consequence of human weakness, even after the incarnation of the Word the other ways of receiving knowledge of God should still be gone by man. If man had not fallen from his original state only the first two ways would have been necessary, after the fall God showed two new ways without blocking the two original ones. – On the loud proclamation of God by creation see *C.G.* 1, *supra*, 9.

Part IV

(35-46)

THE CREATOR AND CREATION

1) 35-45a

GOD'S REVELATION THROUGH THE HARMONY OF THE UNIVERSE

Introduction

In this part Athanasius proves that there is a Divine Logos who created and governs the universe which constitutes a harmony of the opposite. He discusses three questions: Firstly *whether* there is a Divine Logos (35-39), secondly, *who* this is (40a), thirdly, *how* this Logos is and works (40b-45a). This is a rhetorical scheme, see e.g. *Quintilian, Inst. orat.* 3, 6, 80: *Credendum est igitur his ... tria esse, quae in omni disputatione quaerantur, an sit quid sit quale sit* (cp. H. Lausberg, *op. cit.*, pp. 83 f., Tertullian works with the questions *quis sit* and *qualis sit*, see *Adv. Marc.* 1, 17, 1, cp. G. C. Stead, Divine Substance in Tertullian, *Journal of Theological Studies* (14), 1963, pp. 57 ff.).

The question whether there is a Divine Logos is answered with a reference to the works of the Logos. Invisible in His nature the Logos makes Himself known through the order of the universe (35), through instituting the natural laws (which had been taken as a proof that the elements of the world are not divine, see *C.G.* 27), and through forcing what is opposite into a peaceful harmony (36-37). The oneness of the Divine Logos is of special importance. The order of all things points to *one* ruling Logos, a plurality of gods would cause great anarchy. The idea that a plurality of gods created one world is completely unacceptable, since this would imply weakness in the Divine: the gods would need cooperation. The theoretical possibility that one God could have created more than one world is left open (perhaps in order to avoid a position which conflicts with Origen says), but the fact is that there is one Logos who created and rules one world. The images which must illustrate this (the city, lyre and boat) are all traditional ones which appear in Pagan and Christian writers (38-39).

A brief answer is given to the question of who this Logos is: Jesus Christ (40a). He cannot be compared with a perishable human word nor with the Stoic λόγος σπερματικός. He is the imperishable, powerful Word of God who created the world out of nothing and prevents the world from being dissolved into nothing again (40b-41). When Athanasius describes extensively how the Word of God is at work he resumes the arguments and images which he used when he proved that the world is not divine and that there must be a divine Logos. This is not a clumsy repetition of what was said before, but an effort to make it clear that Christ is indeed the Divine Logos about whose existence the human mind can be sure from the harmony of the universe. There is one particularly speculative element in these expositions about the creative activities of the Logos: He created all things together with one command, there is no sequence of moments in the divine act of creation (42-44). – As the universe reveals the Divine Logos, so the Divine Logos reveals the Father. Athanasius speaks about the relation between the Logos and the Father in a way which does not exclude subordination altogether (which seems to be another indication that Arianism was not yet a formal heresy at the time Athanasius wrote his apologetic treatise, since if it had been one might expect that Athanasius would exclude subordination).

Chapter 35

The works of creation reveal the Creator.

Translation and Commentary:

(35) First Athanasius discusses the question of *whether* there is a Creator. This is shown to be the case through the harmony of the universe.

"For since God is good and loves men and cares about the souls which were made by Him, since He is by nature invisible and incomprehensible, existing beyond all created substance and since because of this human race would be devoid of knowledge of Him, because creation is out of nothing, but He is uncreated, – for this reason God ordered in His own Word creation in such a way that, since He is by nature invisible, He might be known by men at least through His works."

On God's goodness see *C.G.* 41, *infra*, 135 f., on God as ἐπέκεινα πάσης γενητῆς οὐσίας ὑπάρχων see *C.G.* 2, *supra*, 16. In *C.G.* 29 Athanasius had used God's invisibility as an argument that the visible parts of creation cannot be divine (see *supra*, 95), now he argues that the visible creation can point towards the invisible Creator. This is a familiar theme in Athanasius, see e.g. *De Inc.* 11, 18, 32, 54. In his polemics against the Arians Athanasius stresses that revelation through creation leads to knowledge of the Creator who is ἀγένητος, not to God as the Father of the Son, see *De Decr.* 29, 31 (PG 25, 469 ff.), *Contra Arianos* 1, 34 (PG 26, 81B); 2, 42 (PG 25, 237 ff.) especially 1, 33 (PG 26, 81A): Καὶ οὗτοι μὲν ἀγένητον λέγοντες μόνον ἐκ τῶν ἔργων σημαίνουσιν αὐτόν, καὶ οὐκ ἴσασι καὶ αὐτοὶ τὸν Υἱόν, ὥσπερ Ἕλληνες, cp. Hilary of Poitiers, *De Trin.* 3, 22. – Revelation of the invisible God through the visible world is a popular topic in Pagan and Christian writers, see e.g. Ps.-Aristotle, *De mundo* 399 b 21 f.: πάσῃ θνητῇ φύσει γενόμενος ἀθεώρητος (sc. ὁ θεός) ἀπ' αὐτῶν τῶν ἔργων θεωρεῖται, Irenaeus, *Adv. Haer.* 2, 4, 5: *Invisibilis quidem poterat eis esse propter eminentiam, ignotus autem nequaquam propter providentiam*, 2, 8, 1, Aristides, *Apol.* 1, 1, Theophilus, *Ad Aut.* 1, 7, Eusebius, *Dem. Evang.* 4, 5, Lactance, *Div. Inst.* 1, 2. – On the Stoic background of the word διακοσμεῖν used for the ordering of the world see J. Geffcken, *op. cit.*, p. 33.

"For often the artist, even if he is not seen, is known from his works. And as they say about Phidias the sculptor that his works through their symmetry and mutual proportion of their parts reveal to those who look at them Phidias even if he is not present, in the same way one must know from the order of the cosmos its Maker and Creator, God, even if He is not seen by the bodily eyes."

For Phidias' fame as a sculptor cp. Origen, *Contra Celsum* 8, 17. In itself Polycleitos would be more suitable to be quoted as an example of a sculptor characterized by symmetry, since he wrote a book on rhythm and proportion. Athanasius may simply name the most famous Greek sculptor as an example and ascribe to him the symmetry which he needs in this context (Phidias and Polycleitos are both named by Origen in *Contra Celsum* 8, 17). – What is very important to Athanasius is that the sculptor is more than his work (see *supra*, 65 f., 72 f., and *infra*, 151), so if this comparison is applied to God as Creator it means that creation is not divine.

> "For God did not misuse His invisible nature (let nobody come forward with this excuse) and leave Himself completely unknown to men. But, as I said before, He ordered creation in such a way that even if He is not visible by nature, He nevertheless is known from His works."

It is probably Marcion who is attacked here. The orthodox Christians firmly rejected his claim that God was unknown before Christ and referred as a proof to God's revelation in creation, see e.g. Irenaeus, *Adv. Haer.* 4, 11, 1, Tertullian, *Adv. Marc.* 1, 17 f.

> "And I do not say this on my own authority, but on the authority of what I learned from the divinely inspired men, of whom one is Paul who writes in this way to the Romans:"

On the divinely inspired men, θεόλογοι, i.e. the Biblical writers, see *C.G.* 1, *supra*, 10 f., and *De Inc.* 57.

> "For His invisible attributes are visible ever since the creation of the world, since the eye of reason detects them in the things He made' (*Rom.* 1:20). And in frankness he tells the Lycaonian people: 'We, too, are men of like nature to you, preaching to you to turn from the vanities to the living God who made heaven and earth and sea and all that is in it, who in the previous generations allowed all nations to go their ways. Yet He did not leave Himself without some witness through His kindness, giving us rain from heaven and fruitbearing seasons, filling our hearts with good and joy" (*Acts* 14:15-17).

These are the usual texts which must prove God's revelation through creation; on the interpretation of these texts see B. Gärtner, *op. cit.*, pp. 73 ff., 133 ff.

> "For who, seeing the circling of heaven and the course of the sun and the moon and the positions and revolutions of the other stars which are opposed and different, but in the difference all preserve a common order, does not think that they do not order themselves, but that there is another Maker who orders them? And who seeing the sun rise day and the moon shine by night, waning and waxing unchangeably according to an exactly equal number of days, and that of the stars some cross and variously change their paths and others move unchangeably, would not get the idea that there is certainly a Creator who steers them?"

In *C.G.* 27 and 29 (see *supra*, 90 ff., 96) the nature of these elements was taken as a proof that the heavenly bodies are not divine themselves, now they are taken as a proof that the heavenly bodies have been ordered by and are governed by God their Creator. The idea behind this is: The elements are not divine but reveal their Creator. The harmonious movements of the heavenly bodies are often taken as a proof of the existence of the Divine, see e.g. Plato, *Leges* X 886A, Ps.-Aristotle, *De mundo* 399 a 1-14, Cicero, *De nat. deor.* 2, 2, Clement of Rome, *Ad Cor.* 20, Eusebius, *Praep. Evang.* 7, 10. – On the general theme that the universe is a hormony see also Plato, *Timaeus* 30A, Albinus, *Epit.* 13, 3, Irenaeus, *Adv. Haer.* 2, 2, 3 and *infra*, 121, *C. G.* 36.

CHAPTER 36

The harmony of the opposite proves the existence of a Creator.

Translation and Commentary:

(36) "Who, seeing that what is opposite in nature has been put together and keeps a concordant harmony, for example seeing fire mixed with water and dry with the wet, and that these are not in conflict with each other, but make one thing as if the body consisted of one substance, who would not think that He who has put these together is outside them?"

In *C. G.* 27 it had been argued that the nature of these things is such that they need each others' help, in *C. G.* 29 that they destroy each other, see *supra*, 90 ff., 96 f., here in *C. G.* 36 the fact that the nature of these things is prevented from exerting the power of destroying the opposite is taken as a proof for God's existence, – for more examples of this commonplace in Christian and Pagan literature see J. H. Waszink's edition of Tertullian's *De anima*, pp. 155 f. (to which could be added Tertullian, *Adv. Marc.* 2, 29, 4, Irenaeus, *Adv. Haer.* 2, 11, 1; 2, 37, 2 and Ps.-Aristotle, *De mundo* 396 a 33 ff.: ἐκ τῶν ἐναντίων ἀρχῶν συνεστηκὼς ὁ κόσμος, λέγω δὲ ξηρῶν τε καὶ ὑγρῶν, ψυχρῶν τε καὶ θερμῶν ... τὸ ἄρρεν συνήγαγε πρὸς τὸ θῆλυ, and 396 b 23 ff.). The putting together into harmony of what is of an opposite nature is an indication of God's omnipotence. In the present chapter Athanasius resumes arguments about natural laws: these laws have been instituted by an almighty God. We have seen (*supra*, 90) that Christians also express scepticism about these natural laws, since they want to safeguard God's omnipotence. To Athanasius these laws are an indication of God's omnipotence. In his polemics against the Arians Athanasius says that one cannot explain the substance of heaven, the sun, the stars, wood and water, but because of this one does not deny their existence, – so one should not investigate curiously into the Trinity, but simply believe in it, see *Ad Ser.* 1, 18.

"Who, seeing that winter gives way to spring and spring to summer and summer to autumn, and that these are opposite in nature, for winter makes cold, summer burns, spring feeds and autumn makes decrease, but that they nevertheless all provide a similar and harmless usefulness to men, who would not consider that there is somebody who is stronger than these who gives the balance to all and steers them all, even if he does not see Him?"

In *C.G.* 29 the fact that the seasons confine each other was taken as a proof that they are not omnipotent and divine, see *supra*, 96 f. Here this confinement is taken as an indication that it has been instituted by somebody who surpasses them in strength.

"Who, seeing that the clouds are supported in the air and that in the clouds the weight of water is bound, does not receive an idea of Him who has bound these and ordered them to happen?"

On the clouds and the rain see *C.G.* 27, *supra*, 91.

"Or who seeing that the earth itself very heavy by nature is founded upon the water and remains immobile on what is by nature mobile does not have the idea that there is a God who has ordered and made this?"

On the earth as founded on the water see *C.G.* 27, *supra*, 91.

"Who, seeing in due season the fruitbearing of the earth, the rains from heaven, the streams of the rivers, the gushing up of the fountains, the birth of animals out of dissimilar beings, and that this does not happen constantly but in defined seasons?"

For fruitbearing and rain see *C.G.* 27, *supra*, 91, on the happening of these things in defined seasons cp. Ps.-Aristotle *De mundo* 397 a 24 ff.: "Ἡ τε γῆ ... κατὰ καιρὸν ἐκφύουσά τε πάντα ... (For the birth out of dissimilar beings see *infra*, 121).

"And in general, who having learned that in what is dissimilar and opposite the balanced and equal order is kept by these things would not think that there is one Power which has ordered and administrates these things according to its pleasing and remaining in its happiness? For by themselves they could not coexist and ever come into being because they are opposite by nature."

In *C.G.* 29 (see *supra*, 96) Athanasius had argued that these opposite things should coexist if they are to be gods, but that was a kind of coexistence in which they would not be confined by each other but all exert their complete power. That coexistence proved to be impossible, but these opposite things can have been put by God Almighty into a coexistence in which they confine each other. – The remark that in extending providence the Logos remains in His happiness could be made against the Epicureans who deny providence because according to them it is incompatible with the blessed state of the gods, cp. Cicero, *De nat.*

deor. 1, 17, 45: *quod beatum aeternumque sit, id nec habere ipsum negotii quicquam nec exhibere alteri*, Lucrece, *De rer. nat.* 1, 44-49 (= 2, 646-651).

> "For water is by nature heavy and downward flowing, but the clouds are light and belong to the elements which are light and ascending. And nevertheless we see that the heavier water is carried in the clouds."

On the clouds and the rain cp. *C.G.* 27, *supra*, 91.

> "Furthermore the earth is very heavy and the water is lighter than it, nevertheless what is heavier is carried by what is lighter and the earth does not sink but remains unmoved."

On the earth which is fixed on the water see *supra*, 91, *C.G.* 27.

> "And the male is not the same as the female and yet they are brought together in unity and one birth of a similar living being is caused by both of them."

Earlier in this chapter (see *supra*, 120) it said that animals are born out of dissimilar beings, now it says that man and female give birth to a similar living being. What Athanasius means to say is that male and female are dissimilar and that these dissimilar beings give birth to a living being which is of a similar species. On male and female see also the quotation from Ps.-Aristotle given *supra*, 119.

> "And to sum up, the cold is opposite to what is warm, the moist is in conflict with what is dry and nevertheless having come together they are not in conflict with each other, but as a result of their harmony they make one body and cause the birth of all things."

What Athanasius here refers to are the four elements of the bodies, the hot, cold, dry, and wet (see *C.G.* 9, *supra*, 44), they constitute one body and guarantee the continuation of life. This has been caused by God in His omnipotence.

CHAPTER 37

Elaboration of the harmony of the opposite and attack on the doctrine of the survival of the fittest.

Translation and Commentary:

> **(37)** "For that which is by nature conflicting and opposite by nature would not have brought itself together, if He who had bound them together were not stronger than they and their master to which also the elements give way and obey as obeying slaves to their master."

For the idea that the binding principle must be more than the elements which are bound together, see also Aristides, *Apol.* 2: Ἰδὼν δὲ τὸν κόσμον καὶ τὰ ἐν αὐρῷ πάντα ὅτι κατὰ ἀνάγκην κινεῖται συνῆκα τὸν κινοῦντα καὶ διακρατοῦντα εἶναι θεόν· πᾶν γὰρ τὸ κινοῦν ἰσχυρότερον τοῦ κινουμένου καὶ τὸ διακρατοῦν ἰσχυρότερον τοῦ διακρατουμένου ἐστίν, cp. J. Geffcken, *op. cit.*, p. 33. – The obedience of the elements is unchangeable, – it is rather interesting to see that when Athanasius is confronted with the question of why God did not appear in a better part of creation than in man he answers that of all parts of creation only man went astray, whilst the other parts remained as they were created, see *De Inc.* 43: Διὰ τί οὖν, ἐὰν λέγωσιν, οὐχὶ δι' ἄλλων μερῶν καλλιόνων τῆς κτίσεως ἐφάνη, καὶ καλλίονι ὀργάνῳ οἷον ἡλίῳ ἢ σελήνῃ ἢ ἄστροις ἢ πυρὶ ἢ αἰθέρι οὐ κέχρηται, ἀλλὰ ἀνθρώπῳ μόνον, γινωσκέτωταν ὅτι ... οὐδὲν ... τῶν ἐν τῇ κτίσει πεπλανημένον ἦν εἰς τὰς περὶ θεοῦ ἐννοίας, εἰ μὴ μόνος ὁ ἄνθρωπος· ἀμέλει οὐχ ἥλιος, οὐ σελήνη, οὐκ οὐρανός, οὐ τὰ ἄστρα, οὐχ ὕδωρ, οὐκ αἰθὴρ παρήλλαξαν τὴν τάξιν, ἀλλ' εἰδότες τὸν ἑαυτῶν δημιουργὸν καὶ βασιλέα Λόγον μένουσεν ὡς γεγόνασιν. – The Epicureans use the fact that the elements (as lifeless beings) cannot obey as an argument against the doctrine of creation, see Cicero, *De nat. deor.* 1, 8, 19: *quem ad modum autem oboedire et parere voluntati architecti aër ignis aqua terra potuerunt?* This is said against the Platonic doctrine of creation which shows some similarity with what Athanasius says here, see Plato, *Timaeus* 32B/C: καὶ διὰ ταῦτα ἔκ τε δὴ τούτων τοιούτων καὶ τὸν ἀριθμὸν τεττάρων τὸ τοῦ κόσμου σῶμα ἐγεννήθη δι' ἀναλογίας ὁμολογῆσαν, φιλίαν τε ἔσχεν ἐκ τούτων ὥστε εἰς ταὐτὸν αὐτῷ συνελθὸν ἄλυτον ὑπό του ἄλλου πλὴν ὑπὸ τοῦ συνδήσαντος γενέσθαι. It appears that Athanasius in the present chapter attacks the Epicurean doctrine about how the cosmos came into being (see *infra*, 123), so when he says here that the elements obey God as slaves obey their master this remark could be directed against the Epicureans.

> "And they do not, paying attention only to their own nature, fight each other. But knowing their Lord who has bound them together they are in harmony with each other, by nature in opposition to each other yet by the will of Him who steers them in harmony."

In *C.G.* 29, see *supra*, 96, Athanasius argued *inter alia* that the mutual opposition of the parts of creation show that these are not divine, since they do harm each other, but what harms is not God, since God only helps. He now shows that God prevents the parts of creation from exerting their faculty to harm each other by forcing them into harmony. (On the 'steering' of God see *infra*, 136 f.).

> "For if the one mixture of these had not come about by a superior order, how could the heavy and the light have been mixed and come together, or the dry and the wet, or the circular and the straight, or the fire and the cold, or in general the sea and the earth, or the sun and the moon, or the stars and heaven, and the air and the clouds, since the nature of each differs from the other? For there should have been a great fight between them, since the one

burns and the other one is cold, and the heavy one is inclined downwards, and the light on the other hand is pulling upwards, and since the sun shines and the air is causing darkness. For the stars, too, would have fought each other, since some have their place higher, others lower. And night would not have given way to day, but it would certainly have remained in fight and conflict with it."

This is a detailed and rhetorical resumption of the argument given in *C.G.* 29, suggesting that one can only be grateful that the parts of creation are not divine but instead ruled by God.

"But if this happens, one would no longer see order but disorder, no longer a system but a lack of it, no longer coherence but complete incoherence, no longer proportion but disproportion. For by the strife and warfare of each either all would be destroyed or only the strongest one would be seen. And that, too, would show the disorder of the universe. For if it were left alone and in lack of help from others, it would make the whole unharmonious. Just as if only a foot or only a hand remained, it would not have kept the integrity of the body. For what kind of cosmos would exist if only the sun gave light or only the moon circled or there were only night or always day? Furthermore what sort of harmony would there be if there were only heaven without the stars or the stars without heaven? And what would be the use, if there were only the sea and if only the earth were fixed without water and the other parts of creation? And how would man or in general a living being have appeared on earth if the elements were in conflict with each other and one was the strongest but unable to put the bodies together? For nothing of all things could consist of only the warm or only the cold or only the wet or dry. But all would be completely in disorder and incoherence! But not even what seems to be the strongest could have existed without the help of the other ones, for this is the way in which it now exists."

If everything destroyed everything all things would be reduced to chaos or to nothing. Strictly speaking it is not logical to say this; it would be logical to say that because of the mutual strife nothing would appear out of nothing or out of chaos. – The cosmos as a whole and the human body necessarily consist of various parts which are in need of each others' help, see *C.G.* 28, *supra*, 93, therefore there could also be no cosmos if not everything had destroyed everything, but the strongest one had prevailed. This could be a polemic against the Epicurean doctrine of the survival of the fittest (which goes back to Empedocles, see Aristotle, *Phys.* II 8, 198b 29 ff.), see for this doctrine e.g. Lucrece, *De rer. nat.* 5, 837 ff. Epicure's doctrine that there is no providence but that things have come into being through chance is attacked by Athanasius in *De Inc.* 2 in a way which shows similarity with what is said here in *C.G.* 37: if that were the case all things would have to be uniform and similar and there should be no variety, all things should only be sun or moon or in man only hand, eye or foot. But since this is not the case, and since there is an ordered variety, this order shows that things did not come into being through chance but through Providence: ... οἱ 'Επίκουροι, οἳ καὶ τὴν τῶν ὅλων πρόνοιαν καθ' ἑαυτῶν οὐκ εἶναι μυθολογοῦντες, ἄντικρυς παρὰ τὰ ἐναργῆ καὶ φαινόμενα λέγοντες· εἰ γὰρ αὐτομάτως τὰ πάντα χωρὶς προνοίας κατ' αὐτοὺς γέγονεν, ἔδει τὰ πάντα ἁπλῶς γεγενῆσθαι καὶ ὅμοια εἶναι καὶ μὴ διάφορα ... ἔδει τὰ πάντα εἶναι ἥλιον ἢ σελήνην, καὶ ἐπὶ τῶν ἀνθρώπων ἔδει τὸ ὅλον εἶναι χεῖρα, ἢ ὀφθαλμόν, ἢ ποῦς. νῦν δὲ οὐκ ἔστι μὲν οὕτως ... ἡ δὲ τοιαύτη διάταξις οὐκ αὐτομάτως αὐτὰ γεγενῆσθαι γνωρίζει, ἀλλ' αἰτιάν τούτων προηγεῖσθαι δείκνυσιν.

Chapter 38

The harmony of the cosmos proves that there is one Creator.

Translation and Commentary:

(38) "So since there is not a lack of system but a system in the universe and not lack of symmetry but symmetry and not disorder but order and a harmonious construction of the world, one must consider and receive an idea of the Lord who has brought and bound this together and has created harmony in them."

This is the factual opposite of the hypothetical situation discussed in the previous chapter, see *supra*, 121 ff.

> "For even if He is not seen with the eyes, on account of the order and harmony of what is opposite it is nevertheless possible to get an idea of their Ruler, Governor and King."

See on this *C.G.* 35, *supra*, 118.

> "For as if we saw that a city which consists of many and different people, small and great, rich and also poor, old and young, men and women, is inhabited in an orderly way and that those who live in it are different but in harmony with each other, and that the rich do not oppose the poor, nor the great the small, nor the young the old, but all at peace in equality, - if we saw that we certainly have the idea that the presence of a ruler regulates the harmony even if we do not see him. For disorder is an indication of anarchy, but order points to the leader."

The same comparison is given in an elaborated way in *C.G.* 43, see *infra*, 141, it is a popular comparison, see Theophilus, *Ad Aut.* 1, 5: Εἶτα βασιλεὺς μὲν ἐπίγειος πιστεύεται εἶναι, καίπερ μὴ πᾶσι βλεπόμενος, διὰ δὲ νόμων καὶ διατάξεων αὐτοῦ καὶ ἐξουσιῶν καὶ δυνάμεων καὶ εἰκόνων νοεῖται, cp. further Ps.-Aristotle, *De mundo* 400 b 13 ff., Cicero, *De nat. deor.* 2, 31, 78. (It could be that Athanasius puts this comparison into contrast with what happens in polytheism: there is a conflict within one and the same city, see *C.G.* 23: ἔστι δὲ ὅπου καὶ μία χώρα, καὶ μία πόλις πρὸς ἑαυτὰς στασιάζουσι περὶ τῆς τῶν εἰδώλων δεισιδαιμονίας). Irenaeus applies the same idea to the Roman empire and its emperor, see *Adv. Haer.* 2, 4, 6: *Aut nunquid hi qui sub Romanorum imperio sunt, quamvis nunquam viderint Imperatorem, sed valde et per terram, et per mare separati ab eo, cognoscent propter dominium eum qui maximam potestatem habet principatus*, cp. W. C. van Unnik, Irenaeus en de Pax Romana, *Kerk en Vrede, Feestbundel voor Prof. dr. J. de Graaf*, Baarn 1976, p. 211 (Van Unnik erroneously refers this quotation to *Adv. Haer.* 2, 6, 2).

> "For also when we see the harmony of the limbs in the body that the eye does not fight the ear and that the hand is not in conflict with the foot but that each fulfils its function without conflict, we certainly understand from this that the soul which governs the limbs is in the body even if we do not see it."

Man's senses all have a natural impulse (see *C.G.* 31, *supra*, 103), these can easily come into conflict with each other, therefore the soul has to constrain them into harmony (cp. *C.G.* 4 and 31, *supra*, 25 f., 103 f.).

> "In the same way we must in the order and harmony of the universe apprehend God the Ruler of the universe and the fact that He is one and not many. And this orderly arrangement and the harmony of all things in concordance does not show many but one Ruler and Governor of it, the Word. For if there were many rulers of creation, such an order of all things would not be preserved. But all things would be in disorder because of the many rulers, because each one tries to pull all things towards his own will and because each one fights the other one. For as we said that polytheism is atheism, similarly government by many must be anarchy. For since each one tries to abolish the rule of the other one nobody would appear to govern any more, but there would be anarchy with all. And where there is no ruler, there certainly disorder appears."

A plurality of gods means a fight between these gods, this was said repeatedly before, see *C.G.* 6, 23, 29. The general statement that polytheism is anarchy was not made in this way before, Athanasius may regard it as a summary of the argument given in *C.G.* 23 (J. C. M. van Winden draws our attention to Origen, *Contra Celsum* 1, 1, who speaks about the 'godless anarchy' of the Scythians, see the quotation given *supra*, 85). For the disorder which is caused by the absence of one Ruler see *C.G.* 37, *supra*, 122 f.: the disorder which the world would represent without one Ruler would be an image of the disorder between the many gods. (Cp. for the argument given here Philo, *De conf. ling.* 170, and *Corpus Hermeticum* 11, 9). Pagan authors also defended polytheism by saying that the supreme God rules over divine beings, as kings on earth, e.g. Hadrian, rule over human beings, see W. den Boer, Συγγράμματα, pp. 174 f.

"And on the other hand the one order and concordance of the many, different beings shows that the Ruler, too, is one."

The one world proves that there is one God, this argument will be elaborated in *C.G.* 39, see *infra*, 127 ff. The one world consists of many different parts, since what is caused must be less than its cause and since plurality is less than the one (see *supra*, 47, 22), the Creator must certainly be one (and must in difference from the world *not* consist of many parts, cp. *C.G.* 22, 28, *supra*, 78, 93 f.).

"For as when somebody hears at a distance a lyre which consists of many different strings and admires their harmonious symphony, because not only the bass produces its sound, nor only the high one, nor only the middle one, but in equal balance all sound together, and certainly understands from this that the lyre does not move itself, but that it is not played by many either, but that there is one musician who has skillfully combined the sound of each string to the harmonious symphony, – even if he does not see him. Similarly since the order in the whole world is completely harmonious, and since what is above is not in conflict with what is below nor what is below with what is above, but one order of all things is produced, then it follows that one thinks that the Ruler and King of the whole creation is one and not many, He who illuminates and moves all things with His own light."

The image of the musician and the lyre was used for the soul and the body, now it is applied to God and the world, this could be an indication that Athanasius saw man as a μικρὸς κόσμος, – which is the underlying idea of Plato's *Timaeus*. This metaphor for God and the world was a popular one (which goes back to Heraclitus: παλίντροπος ἁρμονίη ὅκωσπερ τόξου καὶ λύρης, Diels, *F.V.S.*, 22 B 51), see apart from the quotations from Philo given by P. Th. Camelot, *op. cit.*, p. 181, also Athenagoras, *Leg.* 16, Irenaeus, *Adv. Haer.* 2, 37, 2: *Quia autem varia et multa sunt quae facta sunt, et ad omnem quidem facturam bene aptata, et consonantia: quantum autem spectat ad unumquodque eorum, sunt sibi invicem contraria et non convenientia: sicut citharae sonus per uniuscuiusque distantiam consonantem unam melodiam operatur, ex multis et contrariis sonis subsistens.*

Chapter 39

The oneness of the cosmos proves that there is one Creator.

Translation and Commentary:

(39) "For we must not think that there are many rulers and makers of creation, but for the sake of correct piety and truth it is right to believe that its Creator is one and that this is the case since creation itself clearly shows this. For this is a sure indication that the Maker of the universe is one, that there are not many worlds but one world."

It appears that there is only one world, this one world points towards one Creator, cp. Eusebius, *Praep. Evang.* 3, 13, 7: οὕτω δῆτα καὶ ἐπὶ τοῦ σύμπαντος κόσμου, ἑνὸς μὲν ὄντος καὶ ἐκ μιᾶς τῆς σωματικῆς ὕλης συνεστῶτος εἰς μέρη δὲ πλεῖστα διῃρημένου ... οὐ πολλὰς χρῆ ὑποτίθεσθαι δημιουργοὺς δυνάμεις, μόνην δὲ μίαν θεολογεῖν, τὴν ὡς ἀληθῶς θεοῦ δύναμιν καὶ θεοῦ σοφίαν.

"For if there were many gods, there ought to be many different worlds."

This is the opposite of what was said in the previous chapter: the one world reveals the one Creator.

"For it would not be becoming that the many produced only one world nor that the one world were made by many gods because of the absurdities which appear from this. In the first place because if the one world had been made by many gods, there would be weakness on the part of the makers, because only one work had been produced by many. And from this would appear a not insignificant indication of the imperfect skill to create of each one. For if one were strong enough, the many would not supplement their mutual shortcomings. But to say that in God there is a shortcoming is not only impious, but the limit of all godlessness."

Athanasius, of course, argues on a purely hypothetical basis: If many gods create one world, then they must supplement their weakness, if one God had enough power to create a world such mutual assistance would not be necessary. But to say that God is weak and not perfect is absurd, see *C.G.* 22, *supra*, 78.

"For also amongst men one would not call an artist perfect, but weak, if he did not produce one work on his own, but together with many. But if each could produce the whole, but all made it because of their companionship in what was made, such a thing would be ridiculous if each one worked for glory lest he were suspected of inability. Now it is most absurd to say that there is vainglory in the gods."

If a human artist needs help he has no perfect skill. Athanasius goes on to discuss the possibility that each artist can make the whole on his own, but that they all take part in this activity in order not to seem unable. The implication of this is that only one world can be created, i.e. that a plurality of worlds is impossible and that every god, although able to produce the whole himself, must content himself with a part. He does not refrain from taking part in this activity since he seeks glory (which is in fact vainglory). But this is a striving after honour unworthy of gods. Even amongst men the seeking of glory is rejectable, instead man should seek immortality, see *De Inc.* 47: ... Χριστὸς ... ἔπεισεν ... μηδὲν μὲν ἡγεῖσθαι τὴν ἐπὶ γῆς δόξαν, μόνης δὲ τῆς ἀθανασίας ἀντιποιεῖσθαι. (Often actions were meant in order to secure immortal fame after death, see on this subject A. D. Leeman, *Gloria. Cicero's waardering van de roem en haar achtergrond in de hellenistische wijsbegeerte en de Romeinse samenleving*, Rotterdam 1949, pp. 71 ff., A. J. Vermeulen, *The Semantic Development of Gloria in Early-Christian Latin*, Nijmegen 1956, pp. 39 ff. To this kind of glory Christians were opposed since they expected immortality as a gift from God, cp. J. H. Waszink, *Tertullian über die Seele*, Artemis Zürich-München 1980, pp. 310 f. and A. D. Leeman, *op. cit.*, pp. 79 f.). - Not only Christians stressed that God did not create the world in order to acquire an honour which He does not need (see e.g. Irenaeus, *Adv. Haer.* 4, 25, 1; 2, 5, 1), but the Platonists also stressed this, see the quotation given by Clement of Alexandria from Plato (which cannot, however, be found in the works of Plato), *Strom.* 5, 11, 75, 3: Οὐ γὰρ χρείας ἕνεκεν ὁ θεὸς πεποίηκεν τὸν κόσμον, ἵνα τιμὰς πρός τε ἀνθρώπων καὶ πρὸς θεῶν τῶν ἄλλων καὶ δαιμόνων ... καρποῖτο, - this statement is in line with Plotinus, *Enn.* 2, 9, 4, 12-14: Τί γὰρ ἂν ἑαυτῇ καὶ ἐλογίζετο γενέσθαι ἐκ τοῦ κοσμοποιῆσαι; Γελοῖον γὰρ τὸ ἵνα τιμῷτο (cp. 2, 9, 11); Celsus says something similar when he asks in connection with the incarnation whether God before the incarnation thought Himself to be underrated and therefore wanted to make Himself known, and then goes on to say that the Christians (who hold this view according to him) ascribe to God a very mortal ambition, see Origen, *Contra Celsum* 4, 6: ... πολλὴν <δή> τινα καὶ πάνυ θνητὴν φιλοτιμίαν τοῦ θεοῦ καταμαρτυροῦσι. - In his polemics against the Arians Athanasius argues against the Arian doctrine that Christ was God's tool when He created the world by pointing out that this implies weakness on the part of God, see *Contra Arianos* 2, 29 (PG 26, 208B): ... ἀσθένειαν δὲ (sc. περὶ τὸν θεὸν εἰσάγουσιν οἱ ἄφρονες) ὅτι μὴ μόνος ἠδυνήθη ποιῆσαι, συνεργοῦ δὲ ἢ ὑπουργοῦ χρείαν ἔσχε. Christians used to argue against many creators by saying that this implies weakness and imperfection in God, see e.g. Irenaeus, *Adv. Haer.* 2, 1, 4, Lactance, *Div. Inst.* 1, 3, 3: ... *necesse est imbecillos esse, siquidem singuli sine auxilio reliquorum tantae molis gubernaculum sustinere non possunt. deus autem ... ex omni utique parte perfectae consummatae virtutis est: quod si verum est, unus sit necesse est.*

> "Furthermore, if each one were able to create the whole work, why is there a need of the many, since one is sufficient for the whole?"

The only reason which could be given appeared to be ridiculous: all gods wanted to share in the glory of their product. Since the possibility that they needed each others' help is also excluded one can only conclude that a plurality of gods is superfluous.

> "Furthermore it would appear impious and absurd, if the work is one, but the makers different and many, when it is a natural law that the one and perfect is superior to the different things."

On this natural law see *C.G.* 3, *supra*, 21.

> "And this, too, must be known, that if the world had been made by many it would also have different movements and dissimilar to itself. For looking towards each of its makers it would also have different movements. And in this difference, as has been said before, there would again be disorder and chaos in the universe."

The makers would be different, therefore also the movements instituted by them and this leads to chaos in the universe, see *C.G.* 37, *supra*, 122 f. The difference in the world which is apparent, can only lead to harmony if all obey one Creator.

> "For also a ship which is steered by many will not sail in straight course if there were not one pilot who held the helm."

For the argument that there can only be *one* helmsman in a boat cp. Lactance, *De ira dei* 11, 4. The comparison between God and the world and the helmsman and a boat is very popular, see Plato, *Politicus* 272E ff. (on Athanasius' use of this passage see *C.G.* 41, *infra*, 137), Ps.-Aristotle, *De mundo* 400 b 6 ff.: καθόλου δὲ ὅπερ ἐν νηῒ ὁ κυβερνήτης ... τοῦτο θεὸς ἐν κόσμῳ, Numenius, *fragm.* 18 (ed. Des Places), Theophilus, *Ad Aut.* 1, 5, Tertullian, *Apologeticum* 11, 5; 47, 7 (with a reference to Plato), Athenagoras, *Leg.* 22,12 (cp. J. Geffcken, *op. cit.*, p. 210), Clement of Alexandria, *Strom.* 7, 2, 5, 4, Eusebius, *Praep. Evang.* 7, 3, 3.

> "Nor will a lyre which is played by many produce a harmonious sound if there is not one artist playing it."

See on this comparison *C.G.* 38, *supra*, 126.

> "So since there is one creation and one cosmos and one order of this cosmos, one must draw the conclusion that its King and Lord Creator is one."

This is the general conclusion from what has been said so far in this chapter. But now Athanasius adds something with which he wants to prove that the one God could have produced more worlds if He had wanted to, God's power is not so limited that He could only have produced one world. God had a special reason for creating only one world:

> "For because of this the Creator Himself has made the whole world one, lest because of the coexistence of many worlds one presumed that there are also many creators, but in order that, since there is only one work, one also believed in only one Maker of it. And not because there is only one Creator, for this reason there is only one cosmos, for God could also make other worlds, but because the world which has been made is one, one must also believe that its Maker is one."

The creation of only one world is God's adaptation to human weakness which easily turns to polytheism and idolatry (for further examples of God's adaptation as seen by Athanasius see E. P. Meijering, *Orthodoxy and Platonism in Athanasius*, pp. 50 and 120). It could be that Athanasius here opposes Plato's doctrine in *Timaeus* 31A/B that the Demiurge did not create an infinite number of worlds, because He wanted to make the sensible world as similar as possible to its example, i.e. the intelligible world of ideas. That world being one, the sensible world had to be one as well (31A: πότερον οὖν ὀρθῶς ἕνα οὐρανὸν προσειρήκαμεν, ἢ πολλοὺς καὶ ἀπείρους λέγειν ἦν ὀρθότερον; ἕνα, εἴπερ κατὰ τὸ παράδειγμα δεδημιουργημένος ἔσται. This passage from Plato's *Timaeus* was fairly well known, see Albinus, *Epit.* 12, 3, Clement of Alexandria, *Strom.* 5, 12, 79, 3-4, Plutarch, *De plac. philos.* 879A, quoted by Eusebius, *Praep. Evang.* 15, 33, cp. D. T. Runia, *Philo of Alexandria and the Timaeus of Plato*, VU Boekhandel 1983, pp. 143 ff.). Athanasius may have had the feeling that if this is the case the ideas function as a law to the Creator. In leaving the possibility open that God could have created more worlds Athanasius manages not to depart too far from Origen who actually taught that God created more worlds in a series one after another, and who comes forward with this doctrine when he wants to show that God's omnipotence was at no time idle, see *De Princ.* 3, 5, 3: *Sed solent nobis obicere dicentes: Si coepit mundus ex tempore, quid ante faciebat deus quam mundus inciperet? Otiosam enim et immobilem dicere naturam dei impium est simul et absurdum vel putare quod bonitas aliquando bene non fecerit et omnipotentia aliquando non egerit potentatum ... Nos vero consequenter respondebimus ... quoniam non tunc primum, cum visibilem istum mundum fecit deus, coepit operari, sed sicut post corruptionem huius erit alius mundus, ita et antequam hic esset, fuisse alios credimus* (cp. *De Princ.* 1, 4, 3, – Athanasius always makes great efforts to interpret even embarassing statements by Origen *in meliorem partem*, cp. E. P. Meijering, *Orthodoxy and Platonism in Athanasius*, p. 129).

CHAPTER 40

The Creator of the world is the Father of Jesus Christ. Jesus Christ is the Word of the Father.

Translation and Commentary:

(40) Having dealt with the question of *whether* there is a Creator of the world and having answered this question affirmatively Athanasius now asks *who* this Creator is (see on these distinctive questions *supra*, 115).

"Who could this be? For this, too, must certainly be made clear and said, lest one, led astray by ignorance about Him, supposed somebody else (to be the Word) and fell back into the same godlessness as that which was discussed before. But I believe that nobody harbours doubts about this. For if our argument has shown that the so called gods in the writings of the poets are no gods, and if it has proved that those who deify creation err, and if in general it has shown that Pagan idolatry is godlessness and impiety, then certainly if these are demolished, the pious worship must be with us, and He who is adored and announced by us, He alone must be the true God, He who is both the Lord of creation and Maker of all that is.''

The question who the Creator is is answered with the argument from the opposites (see on this *supra*, 31): If Pagan idolatry does not have the true God as its object, then Christian faith must have Him as its object. – If this question is answered in the wrong way, in the sense that the Word of God is not identified correctly, then the same idolatry appears as with those who deify creation. This means that those who believe in a creative Word of God (who is not Christ) are not on a higher level than those who adore men and animals. This rule is not applied consistently by Athanasius: Whilst he attacks the deification of creation he makes use of belief in a creative Logos for apologetic purposes (see *infra*, 132 ff.).

"Who then is He other than the most holy One and beyond all created substance, the Father of Christ who like a supreme pilot through His own Wisdom and His own Word, our Lord and Saviour Jesus Christ, guides and orders the universe to our salvation and creates as it appears to Him to be good."

On God as beyond (created) substance see *C.G.* 2, *supra*, 16, on the comparison between God and a pilot see *C.G.* 39, *supra*, 129, on the ordering of the universe see *C.G.* 35-39, *supra*, 117 ff. Athanasius here adopts philosophical terminology about God and His Providence, hereby suggesting *inter alia* that Christ and God His Father are the God about whom the Pagans speak when they refer to the providential harmony of the universe (cp. Origen, *De Princ.* 1, 3, 1: *tamen a nonnullis etiam ipsorum* (sc. *Graecorum*) *habita eius videtur opinio, cum verbo Dei vel ratione creata esse omnia confitentur*).

"And it is good as it is created and as we see that things are created, since this, too, is what He wants."

On God's will behind creation see *infra*, 135 ff.

"And nobody could disbelieve this. For if the movement of creation were without reason and the universe were carried about haphazardly, then one would also rightly not have believed what is being said by us. But if it exists through reason, wisdom and skill and has been arranged with complete order, then necessarily He who stands at its head and arranged it can be nobody else but the Word of God.''

The orderly movement of the universe reveals the one creating Word, see *C.G.* 38-39, *supra*, 124 ff. That one cannot reasonably doubt this is later on used by Athanasius as an argument in favour of the incarnation, see *De Inc.* 41 f. The Greeks believe that there is a Word of God through which God created and rules the world which is a body. If this Word is in the (body of the) world as a whole, then it is not irrational to believe that it is also in part of the world, *viz.*, the human body of Jesus, *De Inc.* 41 f.: εἰ ὁμολογοῦσιν εἶναι Λόγον Θεοῦ, καὶ τοῦτον ἡγεμόνα τοῦ παντός, καὶ ἐν αὐτῷ τὸν Πατέρα δεδημιουργηκέναι τὴν κτίσιν, καὶ τῇ τούτου προνοίᾳ τὰ ὅλα φωτίζεσθαι καὶ ζωογενεῖσθαι καὶ εἶναι ... εἰ τοίνυν ἐν τῷ κόσμῳ σώματι ὄντι ὁ τοῦ Θεοῦ Λόγος ἐστί, καὶ ἐν ὅλοις καὶ τοῖς κατὰ μέρος αὐτοῦ πᾶσιν ἐπιβέβηκε, τί θαυμαστὸν ἢ τί ἄτοπον εἰ καὶ ἐν ἀνθρώπῳ φαμὲν αὐτὸν ἐπιβεβηκέναι. Athanasius here seems to put forward in a modified way an argument produced by Celsus who asks why the Jews (and Christians) call the whole of the universe God, but then deny that parts of it (the stars) are divine, see Origin, *Contra Celsum* 5, 6: Πρῶτον οὖν τῶν Ἰουδαίων θαυμάζειν ἄξιον, εἰ τὸν μὲν οὐρανὸν καὶ τοὺς ἐν τῷδε ἀγγέλους σέβουσι, τὰ σεμνότατα δὲ αὐτοῦ μέρη καὶ δυνατώτατα, ἥλιον καὶ σελήνην καὶ τοὺς ἄλλους ἀστέρας ἀπλανεῖς τε καὶ πλανήτας, ταῦτα παραπέμπουσιν· ὡς ἐνδεχόμενον τὸ μὲν ὅλον εἶναι θεόν, τὰ δὲ μέρη αὐτοῦ μὴ θεῖα. The modification in Athanasius' argument is that he does not claim that the universe is God, and therefore also parts of the universe (an idea to which Athanasius is completely opposed, see *C.G.* 27, *supra*, 88 ff.), but that the Word of God is in the universe and can therefore also be in a part of it.

> "But I do not mean the word involved and innate in every creature, which some also use to call seminal, which is lifeless and without power to reflect and think anything, but at work only by an extrinsic art according to the skill of him who applies it."

Having answered the question *whether* there is a Word of God and *who* this is, Athanasius now deals with the question *how* this Word is: He could here have in mind the Stoic doctrine of the λόγοι σπερματικοί which are immanent in all things and are contained in the one λόγος σπερματικός (see the quotations given by C. J. de Vogel, *Greek Philosophy III*, Leiden 1959, pp. 65 f.). What he opposes here is a λόγος σπερματικός immanent in an individual thing. He will contrast this with the powerful creative Word of God. It is interesting to see that Justin Martyr who adopts the Stoic term λόγος σπερματικός for Christ interprets it not as the word sown but as the sowing Word, and this is a meaning to which Athanasius (if it were explained to him) would not be opposed, since this is what he will advocate in the present chapter (cp. J. H. Waszink's paper, Bemerkungen zu Justins Lehre vom Logos Spermatikos, *Mullus*, pp. 380 ff., and further M. Mühl, Der λόγος ἐνδιάθετος und προφορικός von der älteren Stoa bis zur Synode von Sirmium 351, *Archiv für Begriffsgeschichte* (7) 1962, p. 54).

> "Nor in the way in which human race has the word consisting of syllables and expressed in the air."

Athanasius says elsewhere of the human word which consists of syllables and is expressed in the air that it is lifeless and perishable, see *Contra Arianos* 2, 35 (PG 26, 221B): Καὶ ὁ μὲν τῶν ἀνθρώπων λόγος ἐκ συλλαβῶν ἐστι συγκείμενος, καὶ οὔτε ζῇ, οὔτε τι ἐνεργεῖ, ἀλλὰ μόνον ἐστὶ σημαντικὸς τῆς τοῦ λαλοῦντος διανοίας, καὶ μόνον ἐξῆλθε καὶ παρῆλθε μηκέτι φαινόμενος, ἐπειδὴ οὐδὲ ἦν ὅλως πρὶν λαληθῇ (for similar statements made by Augustin about human words see E. P. Meijering, *Augustin über Schöpfung, Ewigkeit und Zeit. Das elfte Buch der Bekenntnisse*, Leiden 1979, pp. 28 f., see also Irenaeus, *Adv. Haer.* 2, 16, 4).

> "But I mean the living and acting God the very Word of Him who is good and God of all things who is different from what is made and from all creation, but who exists as the own and only Word of the good Father who ordered this universe and illuminates it with His providence."

As living and acting this Word differs from the human words. On the titles αὐτολόγος and ἀγαθός see *C.G.* 46, *infra*, 149 f.

> "For being the good Word of the good Father, He ordered Himself the order of all things, putting opposite things together and ordering one harmony out of these."

The activities described in *C.G.* 37-38, *supra*, 121 ff., are here ascribed to Christ, the Word of the Father.

> "He, being the Power of God and the Wisdom of God, turns heaven, has suspended the earth and by His own will placed it resting on nothing."

On the revolution of heaven see *C.G.* 27, *supra*, 91, cp 118 f. There it also said that the earth is placed on the water, here in *C.G.* 40 Athanasius says that the Word placed the earth on nothing. In both cases the event is miraculous: the earth is suspended and does not sink (either into the water or into nothing) *through the will of the Logos*.

> "Illuminated by Him the sun warms the whole earth, and the moon receives its measure of light."

In *C.G.* 27 it was proved that the moon and the stars are not divine, since they receive help (which probably means: their light, see *supra*, 91) from the sun: now it is also stressed that the sun receives its light from the creative Word of God.

> "Through Him the water is also suspended in the clouds, rains flow over the earth, the sea is confined and the earth is covered with verdure in all kinds of plants."

On the clouds, rain and the fertility of the earth see *supra*, 91, *C.G.* 27.

> "And if somebody in unbelief enquired about what is being said, whether there is a Word of God at all, such a man would if he has doubts about the Word of God be mad."

In his polemics against the Arians he says something similar about the Arians as he says here about those who doubt the existence of a Word of God: they who deny the Word of God are devoid of reason, see *De Decr.* 2 (PG 25, 425D/428A): Τὸν γὰρ τοῦ Θεοῦ Λόγον ἀρνούμενοι εἰκότως καὶ λόγου παντός εἰσιν ἔρημοι. (Athanasius likes to use the argument that if there is no Word of God, then God would be ἄλογος, i.e. without a Word and – with a typical play of words – stupid, – the implication is very serious, since the Arians are stupid, which means that without a Word God would be like the Arians, – the apex of absurdity, see *Contra Arianos* 1, 14 (PG 26, 41C), 19 (PG 26, 52D), 24, 25 (PG 26, 61 f.); 2, 32 (PG 26, 216 B); 3, 63 (PG 26, 456B), *De Decr.* 15 (PG 25, 449B).)

> "Nevertheless he has the proof from what is seen, that all exists through the Word and Wisdom of God and that nothing of what exists would have been established if it had not come into being through a Word, and divine Word at that, as has been said."

The existence in harmony and order is the proof of the existence of the Word of God.

Chapter 41

The reason why God created and rules the world through His Word.

Translation and Commentary:

> **(41)** "But being the Word, He is not, as I said before, composed of syllables as in the case with men, but He is the exact Image of His Father. For men, consisting of parts and stemming from nothing, have a word of a composed and dissolvable nature."

See on this *supra*, 133, *C.G.* 40, on the theory that what stems from nothing, i.e. what has a beginning, is also dissolvable see *C.G.* 33, *supra*, 110 f.

> "But God is being and not composed, therefore also His Word is being and not composed, but as the one and only begotten God, proceding as good from the Father as from a good source He orders and contains all things."

On the rejection of the idea that God is composed of parts see *C.G.* 22 and 28, *supra*, 78, 94. For the (popular) comparison of the relation of the Father and the Son with the well and the river, see also *Contra Arianos* 1, 14 (PG 26, 41C), 19 (PG 26, 52B), 27 (PG 26, 68B), *Ad Ser.* 2, 2 (PG 26, 609B). Athanasius likes this comparison taken from nature since it is an indication of the eternity of this relation: a well is never without its river. On the expression that the Son procedes from the Father as from a good source cp. *De Inc.* 3: ὁ Θεὸς γὰρ ἀγαθός ἐστι, μᾶλλον δὲ πηγὴ τῆς ἀγαθότητος ὑπάρχει.

> "And the reason why the Word of God came to created things at all is really wonderful and reveals that it was not becoming to have happened otherwise than as it also is. For the nature of the created things is, since it came into existence out of nothing, a fluid, weak and mortal one when it is considered by itself."

For the fluidity and weakness of created things see also *Contra Arianos* 1, 28 (PG 26, 69A): Ἄνθρωποι μὲν γὰρ παθητικῶς γεννῶσι, ῥευστὴν ἔχοντες τὴν φύσιν. This seems to be a familiar qualification given in Platonism to the material world, see e.g. Albinus, *Epit.* 11, 2, who calls the bodies, παθητὰ ... καὶ ῥευστὰ ... καὶ οὐκ ἀεὶ κατὰ τὰ αὐτὰ καὶ ὡσαύτως ἔχοντα, οὐδὲ μόνιμα καὶ ἔμπεδα, Numenius, *fragm.* 8 (ed. Des Places): ... τὸ σῶμα ῥεῖ καὶ φέρεται ὑπὸ τῆς εὐθὺ μεταβολῆς (cp. *fragm.* 11 - on this doctrine of the fluidity of the body of the world as an internal danger to the world as it was expressed by Neo Platonists see J. H. Waszink, *Studien zum Timaioskommentar des Calcidius I*, Leiden 1964, pp. 72 f.). - It should be noted that this doctrine of the fluidity of matter is more understandable in Platonism which teaches creation out of chaotic matter than in the Christian doctrine which presupposes the creation out of nothing, since one might ask why God did not create the world in such a way that such a threat did not exist. (J. C. M. van Winden draws out attention to the fact that this doctrine cannot easily be brought into harmony with the doctrine that God created all things in a perfect state right in the beginning, but some Christians also taught that God in the beginning created the first 'seeds' of all things, and this latter doctrine can more easily be combined with the doctrine of the fluidity of matter whcih is an internal threat to the world. As far as we can see Athanasius does *not* provide this latter doctrine).

> "But the God of all things is good and supremely beautiful by nature. Therefore He also loves men, for someone who is good would not be envious of anyone. Hence He does not begrudge anyone his existence, but wants them all to be in order to be able to show His love of men."

Athanasius here quotes (as he also does in *De Inc.* 3) the well known passage in Plato's *Timaeus* 29E: Λέγωμεν δὴ δι' ἥντινα αἰτίαν γένεσιν καὶ τὸ πᾶν τόδε ὁ συνιστὰς συνέστησεν. ἀγαθὸς ἦν, ἀγαθῷ δὲ οὐδεὶς περὶ οὐδενὸς οὐδέποτε ἐγγίγνεται φθόνος (see for further examples in which this passage from Plato's *Timaeus* is quoted by Christian writers Ch. Kannengiesser, *Athanase d'Alexandrie, Sur l'Incarnation du Verbe* (S.C. 199), Paris 1973, pp. 270 f.). H. Dörrie, Was ist "spätantiker Platonismus?" – Überlegungen zur Grenzziehung zwischen Platonismus und Christentum, *Theologische Rundschau*, N.F. 36 (1971), pp. 294 ff. (= *Platonica Minora* 1976, p. 516, a brief repetition is given in, Die Andere Theologie, *Theologie und Philosophie* (56, 1) 1981, p. 23 note 70) argues that a Platonist could not possibly agree with Athanasius' interpretation of this sentence from Plato's *Timaeus*: According to Athanasius this applies to the highest God who is the Creator, according to the Platonists it applies to the second god who is called 'good', since he participates in the idea of the Good (see Plato, *Rep.* 509B) which transcends being. What Dörrie here presents as *the* Platonic interpretation of this text is the interpretation given to it by the Neo Platonists and by Numenius, see *fragm.* 20 (ed. Des Places), but there are also Platonists who identify the Creator with the highest God, see e.g. Apuleius, *De Platone et eius dogmate* 1, 11, Albinus, *Epit.* 12, 1; 27, 1, Varro as quoted by Augustin, *De civ. Dei* 7, 28, – for further details see E. P. Meijering, *God Being History. Studies in Patristic Philosophy*, Amsterdam/Oxford/New York 1975, pp. 27 f. – For Athanasius' statement that God created men in order to show them His love cp. Irenaeus, *Adv. Haer.* 4, 25, 1: *Igitur initio non quasi indigens Deus hominis, plasmavit Adam, sed ut haberet in quem collocaret sua beneficia*, and Tertullian, *Adv. Marc.* 2, 3, 1-2.

> "So seeing that all created nature according to its own structure is fluid and dissolvable, lest it experienced this and the universe were dissolved again into non-being, therefore, having made all things and having given creation its substance through His own eternal Word, He did not leave it to be carried away by its nature and be afflicted, lest it be in danger of disappearing again into non-being, but as a good God He governs and establishes through His own Word, who is also God, the whole world, in order that creation illuminated by the leadership, providence and ordering of the Word could remain in existence, since it participated in the really being Word out of the Father and is helped by Him to its existence, lest it experienced what it would have experienced if the Word did not preserve it, I mean non-being, "the Word is the Image of the invisible God, the first-born of all creation. For through Him and in Him all exists, visible and invisible, and He is the head of the church" (*Col.* 1:15-18), as the servants of the truth teach in the holy writings."

So creation through and participation in the really existing Word of God preserves the fluid world from a relapse into non-being. Now it is clear why the Word of God must be unlike the perishable human word: such a perishable word could not preserve the world from perishing. In *De Inc.* 3 Athanasius presents a similar argument as to why man was created in God's image: God saw that man, created out of nothing could not live for ever, therefore He made man through the participation in God's image participate in the power of the Word that man may be able to live the blessed life in paradise: ... τὸ ἀνθρώπων γένος ἐλεήσας, καὶ θεωρήσας ὡς οὐχ ἱκανὸν εἴη κατὰ τὸν τῆς ἰδίας γενέσεως λόγον διαμένειν ἀεί ... κατὰ τὴν ἑαυτοῦ εἰκόνα ἐποίησεν αὐτούς, μεταδοὺς αὐτοῖς καὶ τῆς τοῦ ἰδίου Λόγου δυνάμεως, ἵνα ὥσπερ σκιάς τινας ἔχοντες τοῦ Λόγου καὶ γενόμενοι λογικοὶ διαμένειν ἐν μακαριότητι δυνηθῶσι, ζῶντες τὸν ἀληθινὸν καὶ ὄντως τῶν ἁγίων ἐν παραδείσῳ βίον, cp. G. Florovsky, Creation in Saint Athanasius, *Studia Patristica* VI, Berlin 1962, pp. 46 f. - Here in *C.G.* 41 Athanasius makes use of a passage from Plato's *Politicus, viz.*, 273D/E (this is again a well known text from Plato, see P. Courcelle, Tradition néoplatonicienne et traditions chrétiennes de la 'Région de Dissemblance' (Platon, Politique 273), *Archives d'Histoire doctrinale et littéraire du Moyen Age*, 1957, pp. 5-33, E. Gilson, *Regio Dissimilitudinis* de Platon à Saint Bernard de Clairvaux, *Medieval Studies* (9) 1947, pp. 108 ff.). Athanasius quotes this passage explicitly in *De Inc.* 43 and it appears that he alludes to it here in *C.G.* 41, this becomes clear when we compare the three relevant texts:

Plato, *Politicus* 273D/E	Athanasius, *De Inc.* 43	Athanasius, *C.G.* 41
ἵνα μὴ χειμασθεὶς ὑπὸ ταραχῆς διαλυθεὶς εἰς τὸν τῆς ἀνομοιότητος ἄπειρον ὄντα πόντον δύῃ (sc. ὁ κόσμος)	... ὁ ... Πλάτων φησὶν ὅτι ὁρῶν τὸν κόσμον ὁ γεννήσας αὐτὸν χειμαζόμενον καὶ κινδυνεύοντα εἰς τὸν τῆς ἀνομοιότητος δύνειν τόπον, καθίσας ἐπὶ τοὺς οἴακας τῆς ψυχῆς βοηθεῖ, καὶ πάντα τὰ πταίσματα διορθοῦται	ἵνα δὲ μὴ τοῦτο πάθῃ, καὶ πάλιν εἰς τὸ μὴ εἶναι ἀναλυθῇ τὸ ὅλον ... οὐκ ἀφῆκεν αὐτὴν (sc. τὴν κτίσιν) τῇ ἑαυτῆς φύσει φέρεσθαι καὶ χειμάζεσθαι, ἵνα μὴ κινδυνεύσῃ πάλιν εἰς τὸ μὴ εἶναι

Both the quotation in *De Inc.* 43 and the allusion in *C.G.* 41 are fairly free (the words καθίσας ἐπὶ τοὺς οἴακας τῆς ψυχῆς in *De Inc.* 43 are obviously caused by Plato, *Politicus* 272E: οἷον πηδαλίων οἴακος ἀφέμενος, a passage alluded to by Numenius, *fragm.* 18, ed. Des Places), but in the quotation Athanasius at least feels obliged to maintain the words 'the place of dissimilarity' whilst in the allusion he speaks of non-being, this latter formulation is, of course, in line with the doctrine of the creation out of nothing instead of (as the Platonists teach) out of chaotic matter. As is not unusual (see *supra*, 59) Athanasius quotes a Biblical text (*Col.* 1:15-18) in order to corroborate a theory which he found in philosophy.

Chapter 42

The Word of the Father establishes the harmony of the universe.

Translation and Commentary:

> (42) "So He, the almighty and perfectly holy Word of the Father, having come to all things and everywhere having spread out His powers and having illuminated all visible and invisible things, He contains and encloses them in Himself, having left nothing void of His power, but gives life and preservation to all things everywhere, to each thing individually and to all things together."

The power which the Word of God spreads out is the power to create all things and to keep them in being, see *C.G.* 41.

> "And by mixing the principal elements of all perceptible being, which are the hot and the cold, the wet and the dry, he ensures that they are not in conflict with each other, but form one concordant harmony. Through Him and His power fire does not fight what is cold nor wet what is dry. But although they are by themselves opposed to each other they have come together as friends and kin, they give birth to visible things and they become the principles of existence for the bodies."

In *C.G.* 37, *supra*, 121 ff., the same was said when it was argued that there must be a divine Principle which has ordered the harmony of the opposite, now it is repeated in order to show that this divine Principle is the Word of the Father.

> "In obedience to this Word, God, what is on earth receives life and what is in heaven subsists."

On the obedience of the elements of the world and the heavenly bodies see *C.G.* 37, *supra*, 122.

> "And through Him the whole sea and the great ocean have their own movement within their own bounds."

See on this *C.G.* 27 and 40, *supra*, 92, 133 f.

> "And all dry land is covered with verdure in all kind of different plants, as I said before."

This was said before in *C.G.* 40, *supra*, 134.

> "And lest I dwell too long by naming each with its manifest name there is nothing of what is and comes into being which does not have its origin and

subsistence in Him and through Him, as also the theologian says: 'In the beginning was the Word and the Word was with God and the Word was God, all has been made through Him and without Him nothing was made."

The clear revelation in Scripture makes long and boring expositions superfluous, cp. *C.G.* 1, *supra*, 10.

"For as a musician, tuning his lyre and combining skillfully the bass and the high tones, the middle ones and the other ones produces the sound of a single melody, – similarly the Wisdom of God, containing the universe like a lyre and combining what is in the air with what is on earth and what is in heaven with what is in the air and combines the whole with the parts and moves them with His command and will and thereby makes beautifully and harmoniously one world and its one order, Himself remaining unmoved with the Father, but moving all things with His own ordering as each thing pleases His own Father."

Again, this comparison was used when the question was answered whether there is a divine Principle behind the harmony of the one universe (see *C.G.* 38, *supra*, 126), it is repeated now in order to show that this divine Principle is the Word of the Father. The act of creation and the extension of providence do not affect the essence of the Word which remains unmoved by this, something similar is said of the act of the incarnation, see *De Inc.* 17 (see also *supra*, 134 ff.).

"For what is incredible in His divinity is that with one and the same expression of will He moves around and orders all things together and not with intervals, but all things at once, what is straight and what is curved, what is above, in the middle, below, what is wet, cold, warm, what is visible and invisible, each according to its nature. For together with this same nod the straight is moved as straight and the circular as circular, and what is in the middle is moved as it is. What is warm is warmed, what is dry is dried, and all things are given life and exist through Him according to their nature. And through Him a wonderful and truly divine harmony is established."

The claim that in the acts of creation and preservation the Word of God remains unmoved is corroborated by saying that the Word creates, orders and preserves all things with one command simultaneously. In his polemics against the Arians who teach that Christ is the mediator in creation who learned from the Father how to create Athanasius stresses that the act of creation does not take place in the course of time, but in one moment, see *Contra Arianos* 2, 24 (PG 26, 197C/200A): οὐδὲ γὰρ οὐδὲ ὑπέρθεσιν ἔχει, ὅπερ ἂν ἐθελήσῃ γενέσθαι, ἀλλὰ μόνον ἠθέληκε, καὶ ὑπέστη τὰ πάντα, 2, 31 (PG 26, 000): τὸ γὰρ δόξαν καὶ βουληθὲν εὐθὺς ἐγίνετο τῷ Λόγῳ. This is a fairly common view on God's creative activities, see e.g. Irenaeus, *Adv. Haer.* 1, 6, 1: *qui* (sc. *universorum Deus*) *simul ut cogitavit*, *perfecit it quod cogitavit, Corp. Herm.* 8, 12: *voluntas enim Dei ipsa est summa perfectio, utpote cum voluisse et perfecisse uno eodemque temporis puncto conpleat,* Basil, *Hexaem.* 1, 2, Ambrose, *Hexaem.* 1, 3, 8, Augustin, *Conf.* 11, 7, 9, - on Philo's views on this matter see H. A. Wolfson, *Philo. Foundations of Religious Philosophy in Judaism, Christianity and Islam I*, Cambridge (Mass.) 1968[4], pp. 311 f. - When one holds the view that God's creative activity is beyond time it seems difficult to avoid as a consequence a view to which the Christians were strongly opposed: the Neo Platonic doctrine of the eternity of the world which wants to exclude the idea that God - rather arbitrarily - 'once upon a time' decided to create a world, - for Athanasius' unsatisfactory treatment of this question see *Contra Arianos* 1, 29 (cp. E. P. Meijering, *Orthodoxy and Platonism in Athanasius*, pp. 86 f.).

CHAPTER 43

Comparisons for the relation between the Word of God and the universe.

Translation and Commentary:

> (43) "And in order that such a great thing may be known from an example, let what is being said be compared with a large choir. So as the choir consists of different men, children, women, old people and people who are still young, and as when the leader conducts each sings according to his nature and power, the man as a man, the child as a child, the old man as an old man, the young as a young man, and all produce one harmony;"

Of the three comparisons given in this chapter only this one has not yet been produced by Athanasius, it seems to be a familiar one in this context, see Ps.-Aristotle, *De mundo* 399 a 14 ff.: Καθάπερ δὲ ἐν χορῷ κορυφαίου κατάρξαντος συνεπηχεῖ πᾶς ὁ χορὸς ἀνδρῶν, ἔσθ' ὅτε καὶ γυναικῶν, ἐν διαφόροις φωναῖς ὀξυτέραις καὶ βαρυτέραις μίαν ἁρμονίαν ἐμμελῆ κεραννύντων, οὕτως ἔχει ἐπὶ τοῦ τὸ σύμπαν διέποντος θεοῦ, and 400 b 7-8: ... ὅπερ ... ἐν χορῷ δὲ κορυφαῖος ... τοῦτο θεὸς ἐν κόσμῳ.

> "or as our soul moves at the same time our senses according to the function of each so that they are all moved together when there is one object, and the eye sees, the ear hears, the hand touches, the smell smells, the taste tastes, and often also the other limbs of the body so that also the feet walk;"

This comparison also occurred when it was shown that there must be a divine Principle behind the harmony of the opposite (see *C.G.* 38, *supra*, 125, cp. also *supra*, 138), now it is used in order to describe how the Word of the Father rules the universe, but there is a different emphasis: In *C.G.* 38 it was stressed that because there is a soul the different parts do not fight each other (as the various parts of the universe are not in conflict with each other), now it is stressed that the soul governs the various parts of the body at the same time (as the Word created and preserves all things together and with one and the same command, see *C. G.* 42, *supra*, 139).

> "or in order to make clear what is being said in a third example, it is above all like a big city which has been built and is governed by the presence of the ruler and king who had it built. For when he is present and in command and surveys all things, all in obedience hasten, some to the fields, others to the aqueducts in order to draw water, one goes in order to collect provisions another goes to the senate, another to the assembly, the judge goes to judge and the ruler to legislate, the artist walks straight towards his work, the sailor to the sea, the carpenter to build, the doctor to cure, the builder to build, the one goes to the field, the other one comes from the field, some go around the city, others leave the city and again go into it. And all this happens and occurs because of the presence of the one ruler and his orders. Similarly it is with the whole of creation, even if the example is inadequate yet one must understand it in a broader sense. For by one nod of the Word, God, all things are ordered together, and each thing does its own actions and by all together one order is established."

Again, this comparison also occurs in *C. G.* 38, *supra*, 124, it is repeated here in an amplified way (in fact, this example is elaborated most extensively of the three examples, this is in accordance with the fact that it is referred to as the most suitable one), and as in the previous comparison the emphasis is not laid on the fact that the various activities are not in conflict with each other, but that they happen at the same time. – In *De Inc.* 55 Athanasius compares the routing of the demons by Christ with revolutionaries who stand up when the king seems to be absent when he is hidden in his palace, but who are abandoned by their followers as soon as the real king appears again, – the underlying idea is here, too: Christ puts an end to chaos (cp. *supra*, 81 f., 124 f., *C. G.* 23, 38). – On the inadequacy of images for God taken from human realm see *C. G.* 8, *supra*, 42.

CHAPTER 44

The ruling power of the Father's Word behind what happens in the world.

Translation and Commentary:

> **(44)** "For by the order and the powers of the all-commanding and leading divine and paternal Word heaven revolves, the stars move, the sun shines, the moon rotates, the air is illuminated by Him, the ether is warmed and the winds blow."

R. W. Thomson, *op. cit.*, p. 121, translates: "the air is illuminated by the sun", this translation would be in line with what is said in *C.G.* 27: the air is warmed by the ether and ether is illuminated by the sun. But we regard it as more likely that Athanasius wants to say that the air is illuminated by the Word (as he had said in *C.G.* 40 that the sun receives its light from the Word, see *supra*, 133). In *C.G.* 27 Athanasius had given a description of the laws by which nature is governed (which show that the various parts of nature are not divine), now he shows that the Father's Word has instituted these laws, so it is He who causes the natural events.

> "The mountains stand reaching to the heights, the sea swells, the living beings in it are fed, the earth, remaining unmoved, bears fruit, man is formed and lives and dies, and simply all lives and moves. The fire burns, the water chills, springs gush forth, rivers flow, seasons and times pass, rains come down, clouds fill, hail is formed, snow and ice freeze, birds fly, serpents move, fish swim, the sea is sailed, the earth is sown and bears fruit in due seasons, plants grow, some are young others ripe, what grows becomes old and wanes, some disappear, others are born and become visible. And all this, and even more than this which because of its multitude we cannot mention, the Word of God, acting incredibly and wonderously, illuminates and grants life, He moves and orders them with His command, producing the world as one, not leaving outside Himself even the invisible powers."

In *C.G.* 27 it was shown that nature is governed by laws, *C.G.* 40 that these laws prove that there is a ruling Principle, now it is shown that this Principle is the Word of the Father. – On the *one* world see *C.G.* 38-39, *supra*, 126 ff. The invisible powers which are also created seem to be the angels, cp. *Sermo maior de fide* 26 (PG 26, 1280C) where the angels are called κτίσεις ἀόρατοι.

> "For since He is their Maker and has concluded these, too, in the universe, He contains them and gives them life by his order and providence. And there could not be a reason for disbelief in this. For as through His providence the bodies grow and the rational soul moves and has the power to reason and live, – and this needs no long proof for we see it happen – similarly the Word of God Himself with one and a single command, with His own power moves and contains the visible world and the invisible powers, giving to each its own function, so that the divine powers move more in a divine way and the visible things in the way they are also seen to be moving."

The argument for the creation of the invisible and more divine beings, i.e. the angels, runs as follows: As the Word in man creates a visible body which can only perceive, but also an invisible soul which has a greater power, *viz.*, to reason, similarly in the universe the Word creates visible things and the invisible beings which move in a more divine way. (On the oul's power to move and to reason – a power which has been given to it by the Creator – see *C.G.* 4 and *C.G.* 31-33, *supra*, 26, 102 ff. In this context it is significant that according to Athanasius one of the activities of the soul during the sleep of the body is that it meets angels, see *supra*, 109).

> "And He Himself above all things, becoming the Leader and King and Structure of all things works all things to the glory and knowledge of His Father, almost teaching and speaking through the works which He does: 'From the greatness and beauty of the creatures by analogy their Creator is seen' (*Wisdom* 13:5)."

The Logos, giving structure to the universe, is called Structure Himself. – Christ's works in creation speak out and reveal God, see on this *C.G.* 1 and 27, *supra*, 9, 89. The works which Christ does to the glory and knowledge of the Father could here be meant as an allusion to *John* 14:11-14 (*John* 14:9 will be quoted in the next chapter). – *Wisdom* 13:5 is used in a similar way by Hilary of Poitiers, *De Trin.* 1, 7.

Chapter 45a

The relation between the Word and the Father.

Translation and Commentary:

> **(45a)** "For as it is possible, looking up to heaven and seeing its order and the light of the stars, to form an idea of the Word who orders this, similarly thinking of the Word one must also think of God His Father proceding from whom He is rightly called Interpreter and Messenger of His Father."

As the harmony of the universe reveals something behind it, *viz.*, the ordering Word, so the Word reveals something behind Him, *viz.*, the Father. The titles 'interpreter and messenger' (ἑρμηνεὺς καὶ ἄγγελος) underline this revealing function of the Word. When Athanasius says that the Word is rightly called 'interpreter and messanger' he indicates that he adopts existing terminology, – he may have in mind Dionysius of Alexandria whom he quotes in *De sententia Dionysii* 23 (PG 25, 516A) as saying: ... ὁ Πατὴρ τὸν Υἱὸν Λόγον ἑρμηνέα καὶ ἄγγελον ἑαυτοῦ ἔχει. This title implies an inferiority of the Word (certainly since it says that *as* the universe reveals the Word, *so* the Word reveals the Father), in his polemics against the Arians Athanasius denies that the Son is an angel (see e.g. *Contra Arianos* 1, 62 (PG 26, 141)), although he does not mean to say here in *C.G.* 45 that the Son is *merely* an angel, it is significant that he does not feel obliged to qualify this title by saying explicitly that the Son may be *called* a messenger but that He *is* more than a messenger. (This seems to be an indication that the apologetic treatise was written before the Arian controversy).

"And one could also see this from what is the case with us. For if we, when a word comes forward from people have an idea that its source is the mind, and concentrating on the word see by reasoning that the mind is expressed by it, all the more by a greater imagination and with an incomparable superiority seeing the power of the Word, we also apprehend His good Father, as the Saviour Himself says: 'He who has seen Me has seen the Father' (*John* 14:9).''

The same comparison is made in *Contra Arianos* 3, 3 (PG 26, 328B): Ἔστι δὲ καὶ ὁ Πατὴρ ἐν τῷ Υἱῷ ... ὡς ἐν τῷ λόγῳ ὁ νοῦς, he adopts this comparison from Dionysius of Alexandria, see *De Sententia Dionysii* 23, 24, especially 23 (PG 25, 513C/516A): ὅ γε νοῦς ποιεῖ τὸν λόγον ἐν αὐτῷ φανείς· καὶ ὁ λόγος δείκνυσι τὸν νοῦν ἐν αὐτῷ γενόμενος· καὶ ὁ μὲν νοῦς ἐστιν, οἷον λόγος ἐγκείμενος· ὁ δὲ λόγος νοῦς προπηδῶν ... καὶ ἔστιν ὁ μὲν οἷον πατὴρ ὁ νοῦς τοῦ λόγου, ὢν ἐφ' ἑαυτοῦ· ὁ δὲ καθάπερ υἱός, ὁ λόγος τοῦ νοῦ. – The reason why Athanasius here in *C. G.* 45 stresses that the procession of the Word from the Father far surpasses the procession of the word from the mind is not that he wants to safeguard the equality of Father and Son, but the fact that all images for the Divine taken from the human realm are inadequate, see *C. G.* 8, *supra*, 42, and the fact that the human word is a perishable expression of the mind whilst the Word of the Father is eternal, see *C. G.* 40 and 41, *supra*, 132, 134.

"The whole divinely inspired Scripture, moreover, proclaims this more clearly and more adequately, from where we, too, take the courage to write to you, and you, reading these Scriptures, can have the proof of what is said. For an argument which is confirmed by more adequate ones has an irrefutable proof.''

The legitimation for Athanasius' words is taken from Christian writers before him and even more from Scripture, see *C. G.* 1, *supra*, 10. This remark leads to the second section of this part of the treatise.

2) 45b-46

SCRIPTURAL TESTIMONY TO GOD'S REVELATION THROUGH THE HARMONY OF THE UNIVERSE

Introduction

Having proved from the harmony of the universe that there is a Divine Logos and that He is Jesus Christ, Athanasius now proves the same from Scripture. Scripture testifies that man should turn away from idolatry and only adore the true God (45b). This God is one, He created the world in His Word or Wisdom, as especially becomes clear from *Gen.* 1:26 and *Prov.* 8:27. Athanasius stresses that the Word is not divine by participation, but by essence (hereby using the language of Origen). Opposition against a divinity of Christ which only implies participation in God's being need not be directed against the Arians but can be directed against Gnostics and Paul of Samosata. Athanasius remains close to the Origenistic tradition by saying that Christ is αὐτοσοφία etc., but by avoiding the term αὐτοαγαθός (which Origen applied to the Father and not to the Son).

CHAPTER 45b

Scriptural warning against idolatry.

Translation and Commentary:

(45b) "So from the beginning the divine Word made sure to remind the Jewish people of the abolition of the idols saying: 'You will not make for yourself an idol nor image of anything which is in heaven above and on earth below' (*Ex.* 20:4), and it indicates the reason for their abolition by saying in another place: 'The idols of the gentiles are silver and gold, the works of men's hands. They have a mouth and will not speak, they have eyes and will not see, they have ears and will not hear, they have a nose and will not smell, they have hands and will not touch, they have feet and will not walk' (*Psalm* 113:12-15)."

See on this *C.G.* 14-15, *supra*, 58 ff.

"And He was not silent in the instruction about creation, but well aware of its beauty, lest somebody looking at their beauty worshipped them not as works of God but as gods He fortified men by saying: 'And do not looking up with your eyes and seeing the sun and the moon and the whole order of heaven be misled and worship them which the Lord your God has assigned to all people beneath heaven' (*Deut.* 4:19). He has assigned them, not to become gods for them, but that through their function the Gentiles may know God the Creator of all things, as has been said."

The assignment of the various parts of creation to their particular function must make all men, i.e. especially the Gentiles, make know God the Creator. Athanasius here refers back to the argument given in *C.G.* 27, 40, 42, and 44 that the specific functions of the parts of creation show that they are not omnipotent, i.e. not divine, but that they are subjected to laws instituted by their Creator. This can be understood by anyone who observes nature. – On the beauty of nature by which man ought not to be induced to deify it see *supra*, 89 f.

"For in ancient times the Jewish people had a fuller teaching, because they had the knowledge of God not only from the works of creation, but also from divine Scriptures. But trying to pull away men in general from the error of idols and irrational imagination He says: 'You will not have other gods except Me' (*Ex.* 20:3).''

It seems strange that Athanasius first says that the Jews have a fuller knowledge of God than the Pagans, since they know God not only from creation but also from Scripture and then with a quotation from Scripture proves that God wants all men to turn away from idolatry. The solution to this apparent contradiction could be that according to Athanasius the prophets were sent only *to* the Jews and rejected by them, but that they were sent not only *on behalf of* the Jews, but of all men in order to teach all men, see *De Inc.* 12: οὐδὲ γὰρ διὰ Ἰουδαίους μόνους ὁ νόμος ἦν οὐδὲ δι' αὐτοὺς μόνους οἱ προφῆται ἐπέμποντο, ἀλλὰ πρὸς Ἰουδαίους μὲν ἐπέμποντο καὶ παρὰ Ἰουδαίων ἐδιώκοντο· πάσης δὲ τῆς οἰκουμένης ἦσαν διδασκάλιον ἱερὸν τῆς περὶ Θεοῦ γνώσεως, καὶ τῆς κατὰ ψυχήν πολιτείας.

"It is not since other gods exist that He forbids them to have these, but lest somebody, having turned away from the true God, started to deify for himself what is not, as are the so called gods mentioned by the poets and prose-writers who have been shown not to be gods, and the very text in which He says 'You will not have other gods' (*Ex.* 20:3) shows that they are no gods, since it refers to the future. But what occurs in the future, this is not at the time when it is being said."

In this exegesis of *Ex.* 20:3 Athanasius clearly differs from Origen (of course, without saying to), who takes the future tense as a proof that these gods exist and explains it that God wants that these existing gods should not be gods to the Jews, see *In Exodum Homilia* VIII 2: *Si dixisset: non sunt dii praeter me, absolutior sermo videretur. Nunc autem quia dicit: "erunt tibi non dii alii praeter me", non negavit quia sint, sed ne illi sint cui haec praecepta dentur inhibuit.* – Athanasius claims to have shown that these are no gods, this in itself is true, but he sometimes also argues as if they did exist, e.g. when he said that the idols deceived and beguiled those who adored them, see *supra*, 85, 87.

CHAPTER 46

Scriptural instruction about God and His Word.

Translation and Commentary:

(46) "So having abolished the godlessness of the gentiles or idols, was the divine instruction silent and did it just leave mankind drift deprived of knowledge of the Divine?"

The godlessness of the Gentiles is that the Gentiles do not adore the true God, the godlessness of the idols is the fact that they are no gods, as was shown in the previous chapter.

> "Not at all, but it anticipates men's mind by saying: 'Hear, Israel, the Lord, your God, is one' (*Deut.* 6:4) and again: 'You will love the Lord your God with all your heart and with all your strength' (*Deut.* 6:5) and again: 'You will worship the Lord your God, and Him alone you will serve and to Him you will cleave' (*Deut.* 6:13).''

These texts must show that Scripture, too, teaches that there is only one God as can also be shown by reason (cp. *C.G.* 6, *supra*, 32, where also *Deut.* 6:4 is quoted).

> "And that also the providence and ordering of the Word in all things and towards all things is testified to by the whole divine Scripture, the following texts quoted now are sufficient to prove what we say, where the divinely inspired writers say: 'You have established the foundations of the earth and it stands firm, by your command stands fast the day' (*Psalm* 118:90-91) and again: 'Sing to our God on the harp, to Him who surrounds the heaven with clouds, prepares rain for the earth, makes grass and verdure spring up in the hills in order to serve men and gives food to the herds' (*Psalm* 146:7-9).''

These texts confirm what was said in *C.G.* 27, 40, 42, and 44 about the natural laws instituted by God.

> "But through whom does He give except through whom all things were made? For through whom they were made, through Him also the providence of all things must be. Now who could this be other than the Word of God, about whom He also says elsewhere: 'By the Word of God heavens were founded and by the breath of His mouth all their power' (*Psalm* 32:6).''

It had been shown that the order of the universe had been established not so much by God as by the Word of God. This, too, must now be proved with Scriptural texts.

> "For Scripture also says that all things were made in Him and through Him, persuading us, too, when it says: 'He spoke and they were made, He commanded and they were created' (*Psalm* 32:9). As also the in all respects great Moses confirms in the beginning of his book about creation, explaining what is said and saying: 'And God said: Let us make man in our image and likeness' (*Gen.* 1:26). For also when He undertook the creation of heaven and earth and all things, the Father said to Him: 'Let heaven be made and let the waters be brought together, and let the dry land be seen, and let the earth bring forth plants and all living creatures' (*Gen.* 1; 6, 9, 12, 20).''

It is, of course a common exegesis of *Gen.* 1:26 to refer the plural to the Father and the Son (and the Holy Ghost), see e.g. Justin Martyr, *Dial.* 62, Theophilus, *Ad Aut.* 2, 18, Irenaeus, *Adv. Haer.* 4, 34, 1; 5, 1, 3; 5, 15, 4. Athanasius thinks that, since heaven sea and earth are not addressed directly, it is the Son who is addressed in these commandments (see further *infra* in this chapter).

> "From this one could also refute the Jews for not reading Scripture genuinely. For with whom, one might say to them, was God speaking, that also in His commandment He should speak? For if He commanded what was being created and spoke with them, His words were superfluous, for it did not yet exist, but was about to be created. But nobody speaks to what does not not exist, nor does one order and speak to what has not yet been created in order to come into being. For if God gave His order to what was about to be created, He should have said: 'Become, heaven, and, Become, earth, sea, and, Come forward, plants, and, Be made, man'."

In his polemics against the Arians Athanasius rejects the idea that lower beings were created by higher ones, or that the things which were created could have received the commandment to come into being directly from God, his own doctrine being that all things were created by the Word, see *Contra Arianos* 2, 21 (PG 26, 192A): τίς ἡ χρεία τοῦ Λόγου, δυναμένων τῶν ὑποβεβηκότων παρὰ τῶν ὑπερεχόντων γίνεσθαι; ἢ ὅλως δυναμένου καὶ κατὰ τὴν ἀρχὴν ἑκάστου τῶν γενομένων ἀκοῦσαι παρὰ τοῦ Θεοῦ· Γενοῦ, καί, Ποιήθητι· καὶ οὕτως ἂν ἕκαστον ἐδημιουργεῖτο. Ἀλλ' οὐδὲ γέγραπται τοῦτο, οὔτε δυνατὸν ἦν. Τῶν γὰρ γινομένων οὐδέν ἐστι ποιητικὸν αἴτιον· πάντα γὰρ διὰ τοῦ Λόγου γέγονεν.

> "But now He did not do that, but He orders by saying: 'Let us make man', and, 'Let the plants come forth', from which it appears that God was speaking with somebody nearby about these things. So somebody had to be with Him with whom He also spoke when He made the universe."

As was in the first part of this section first shown that there is a Word of God and then the question was answered who this Word is (see *supra*, 115, 130), so it is now proved with Biblical texts that there is a creative Word of God, and now it is asked who this Word is:

> "Now who could this be but His Word? For with whom could one say that God speaks other than with His own Word? Or who was with Him when He made all that was created other than His own Wisdom who says: 'When He made heaven and earth I was with Him' (*Prov.* 8:27). And in naming heaven and earth it includes all that is made in heaven and earth. And being with Him as Wisdom, and as Word seeing the Father, it made, formed and ordered the universe."

Again this is the familiar text quoted in connection with Christ as the creative Word of God, see e.g. Justin Martyr, *Dial.* 129, 3, Theophilus, *Ad Aut.* 2, 10, Origen, *De Princ.* 1, 2, 1, Irenaeus, *Adv. Haer.* 4, 34, 3, see further E. Evans, *Tertullian's Treatise against Praxeas*, London 1948, pp. 220 ff., J. H. Waszink, *Tertullian, The Treatise against Hermogenes*, Maryl.-London 1956, pp. 131 ff., for Athanasius' exegesis of *Prov.* 8:22,

which provided difficulties since Wisdom says: 'The Lord *created* Me' cp.
E. P. Meijering, *Orthodoxy and Platonism in Athanasius*, pp. 98 ff. - The
ordering activity of the Word which was first shown from the harmony of
creation is now shown from Scripture as well.

> "And being the Power of the Father He gave the strength for existence to
> all things, as also the Saviour says: 'All that I see the Father do, I do similarly' (*John* 5:19)."

What is referred to here is the special power to create out of nothing
and to preserve in existence what has been created, see *C. G* 41, *supra*, 135
ff.

> "And His holy disciples teach that through Him and towards Him all
> things have been made (cp. *Col.* 1:16) and that, being a good Offspring of a
> good Father and the true Son, He is the Power of the Father and the
> Wisdom and the Word, being this not by participation nor are these
> properties added to Him from outside as is the case with those who participate in Him and are illuminated by Him and receive strength and reason
> in Him, but He is Wisdom itself, the Word itself, the own Power itself of the
> Father, Light itself, Truth itself, Righteousness itself, Virtue itself, and
> indeed Stamp, Effulgence and Image (of the Father)."

What is attacked here seems to be the Arian doctrine, since this is the
way in which Athanasius also presents and attacks the Arian doctrine
about Christ, see e.g. *Contra Arianos* 1, 18 (PG 26, 49A): ... ἔδει τοῦτο
οὕτως ἀεὶ εἶναι, ἵνα μὴ τὸ καλὸν καὶ ἡ ἀλήθεια ἐπιγένηται, καὶ ἐκ προσθήκης
συνίσταται τὸ τῆς θεολογίας πλήρωμα, 3, 6 (PG 26, 333A): τὰ λεγόμενα περὶ
τοῦ Πατρὸς ταῦτα λεγόμενα περὶ τοῦ Υἱοῦ οὐ κατὰ χάριν ἢ μετοχὴν ἐπιγενόμενα
τῇ οὐσίᾳ αὐτοῦ, see further 1, 25 (PG 26, 64B); 1, 28 (PG 26, 72A); 2, 82
(PG 26, 320C); 3, 60 (PG 26, 449A), *Epist. ad ep. Aeg. et Lib.* 13 (PG 25,
568C). But it is not necessary to suppose that Athanasius is here in *C. G.*
46 implicitly attacking the Arians; he may be opposing Paul of Samosata,
- in one of the fragments of the disputations with Paul of Samosata it says
that his view leads to the belief *ut non substantia sit in eo filius dei, sed sapientia
secundum participationem* (see *Reliquiae sacrae* II, ed. M. J. Routh, S.T.P.,
Oxford 1814, p. 476). Or Athanasius may be attacking the Valentinians
who according to Irenaeus teach that Jesus and the heavenly Christ were
united through participation, see *Adv. Haer.* 3, 16: *qui autem a Valentino
sunt, Jesum quidem qui sit ex dispositione, ipsum esse qui per Mariam transierit, in
quem illum de superiori Salvatorem descendisse, quem et Christum dici ... participasse autem cum eo qui esset ex dispositione de sua virtute et de suo nomine.* (For
further opposition against the Gnostics see *C. G.* 6, *supra*, 32 ff.). The
doctrine of Jesus' sonship by participation was obviously not limited to
the Arians, so that Athanasius' polemical remarks against it here need
not be an attack on the Arians. - Regarding the titles αὐτολόγος etc., one

may think of Origen as background (see e.g. *Contra Celsum* 3, 41; 5, 39, see on this matter further G. Gruber, ΖΩΗ. *Wesen, Stufen und Mitteilung des wahren Lebens bei Origenes*, München 1962, pp. 104 ff.). It is interesting that Athanasius does not call the Son αὐτοαγαθός, but only the good Offspring of the good Father. We regard it as unlikely that he was opposed to this title for the Son, but he may avoid it, since in calling the Son such he would unnecessarily deviate from Origen, who calls the Father αὐτοαγαθός and the Son ἀγαθός, see *De Princ.* 1, 2, 13, *In Ioann.* 13, 25, 36, *In Matth.* 15, 10. (Here influence by Numenius may be traced, as R. M. Grant does, The Book of Wisdom at Alexandria, *Studia Patristica* (7) 1966, p. 467, cp. G. C. Stead, The Platonism of Arius, *The Journal of Theological Studies* (15) 1964, p. 21, see *fragm.* 16 (ed. Des Places): ὁ μὲν πρῶτος θεὸς αὐτοαγαθόν, ὁ δὲ τούτου μιμητὴς δημιουργός, cp. *fragm.* 19, 20).

"To sum up, He is the perfect Fruit of the Father, the only Son and the precisely similar Image of the Father."

In his polemics against the Arians Athanasius will stress that Christ is the Father's eternal Fruit (see e.g. *Contra Arianos* 2, 2) and the Father's eternal Image (see e.g. *Contra Arianos* 2, 82).

PERORATION
(47)

Having shown that God created the world in His Word Athanasius gives a brief summary of what has been said about the Father and His Word. He who still adores creation rather than the Creator is inexcusable in his stupidity and will, if he is not converted to God's truth, face eternal punishment.

Chapter 47

Concluding observations.

Translation and Commentary:

(47) "Now who who could give an account of the Father in order to be able to find out about the powers of this Word, too?"

In the beginning of the treatise it was said that a necessary brevity in the expositions would be observed (see *C.G.* 1, *supra*, 10), now it is stressed that the subject is in fact inexhaustible, in other words: certainly not all that can be said has been said. Similarly he says towards the end of the *De Incarnatione Verbi* that it is impossible to relate all the achievements of the incarnation as it is impossible to count all the waves of the sea, see *De Inc.* 54: Καὶ ὅλως τὰ κατορθώματα τοῦ Σωτῆρος τὰ διὰ τῆς ἐνανθρωπήσεως αὐτοῦ γενόμενα τοιαῦτα καὶ τοσαῦτά ἐστιν ἃ εἰ διηγήσασθαί τις ἐθελήσειεν, ἔοικε τοῖς ἀφορῶσιν εἰς τὸ πέλαγος τῆς θαλάσσης καὶ θέλουσιν ἀριθμεῖν τὰ κύματα ταύτης.

> "For as He is the Word and Wisdom of the Father, so He also condescends to created beings, He appears in order to make known and give an idea of His Begetter, being Holiness itself, Life itself, the Door, Shepherd and Way, King, Leader and Saviour for all, life-giving and light and the Providence of all things."

All this refers to Christ's revelation of God in creation which has been described so far. The relation between the Father and the Son could only be expressed with inadequate images (see *supra*, 144, *C.G.* 45), the works in creation are too many in order all to be summed up (see *C.G.* 44, *supra*, 142).

> "So the Father, having out of Himself such a good and creative Son, did not hide Him from what was created but reveals Him every day to all through the substance and life of all He brings about."

On the rejection of the idea that God hid Himself see *C.G. 35, supra*, 118, on the daily revelation of the Son through creation see *C.G.* 1, *supra*, 9.

> "And in Him and through Him He also reveals Himself, as the Saviour says: 'I am in the Father and the Father is in Me' (*John* 14:10). So that necessarily the Word is in Him who generated Him, and that He who is generated eternally lives with the Father."

The special aspect of divine generation, in which it differs from human generation, is that it takes place beyond time, see the quotation from *Contra Arianos* 1, 28 given *supra*, 135.

> "But although this is so and nothing is outside Him, but heaven and earth and all that is in them depend on Him, nevertheless men in their stupidity have removed knowledge of and worship of Him and honoured what is not more than what is and instead of the really being God they deified what is not 'worshipping creation instead of the Creator' (*Rom.* 1:25), doing something which is stupied and impious."

This sentence resumes what was said in the beginning: the true knowledge and worship of God displays itself in creation, see *C.G.* 1, *supra*, 9, (the only difference being that in the opening sentence of the treatise Athanasius spoke about γνῶσις and θεοσέβεια and here he speaks about γνῶσις and εὐσέβεια) but men ignore it. – On giving honour to what is not see *supra*, 25 f., on the really being God *supra*, 22 f. – Athanasius often accuses the Pagans of idolatry in the sense that they give more honour to creation than to the Creator, see e.g. *C.G.* 8, *De Inc.* 11, *Contra Arianos* 2, 14 (PG 26, 177A); 3, 16 (PG 26, 356A/B), *Epist. ad ep. Aeg. et Lib.* 4 (PG 25, 545B) (in the last three instances the same charge is made against the Arians who say that Christ is merely a creature and nevertheless serve Him, and in doing so relapse into Paganism). This is, of course, a traditional charge against Paganism, see e.g. Philo, *De opif. mundi* 7 f., Aristides, *Apol.* 3, 2, Irenaeus, *Adv. Haer.* 2, 8, 2.

> "For it is as if somebody admires the works more than the artist and, speechless because of the buildings in the city, despises their architect."

On this comparison between God and the world and the artist and his products see *supra*, 127 f., on the comparison between the world and a city see *supra*, 124, 141 on the idea that the idolators gaze in admiration at the world see *C.G.* 27, *supra*, 89 f.

> "Or as if one praises the musical instrument, but wants to get rid of him who put it together and tuned it."

This musical instrument is the lyre, see *supra*, 126, 129.

> "Stupid and completely blind men."

This blindness is no excuse, see *supra*, 36.

> "For how could they at all have known the house or ship or lyre, if the shipbuilder had not constructed it or the architect had not built it or the musician had not put it together?"

For the comparison of the world with a ship see *C.G.* 39, *supra*, 129.

> "Just as he who reasons in this way is mad, yea beyond all madness, similarly they give me the impression of not being healthy in their mind who do not recognize God and do not worship His Word, the Saviour of all, our Lord Jesus Christ, through whom the Father orders and contains all things and extends His providence over all things."

This was shown extensively in *C.G.* 35-45a.

> "And you having your pious faith in Him, o Christian, rejoice and become hopeful, because the fruit of the pious faith in Him is immortality and the kingdom of heaven if only the soul is disposed according to his laws."

Rejoicing in the Word of God was one of the characteristics of original man, see *C.G.* 2, *supra*, 17, the Christian believer can return to this state and thereby regain immortality. This will be described extensively in the second half of the apologetic treatise, *De Incarnatione Verbi*. The gift of immortality is linked with the condition that the believer keeps God's commandments, here expressed in the words ἐὰν κατὰ τοὺς αὐτοῦ νόμους ἡ ψυχὴ κεκοσμημένη γένηται (these words evoke again what was said in *C. G.* 32: not the senses but the soul which governs the senses can obey the laws). A. von Harnack's description of the 'physische Erlösungslehre' of the Greek fathers, *viz.*, that this is like an ellipse with moral life and the gift of deification through the incarnation and the sacraments as its two poles applies to Athanasius as well, see *Lehrbuch der Dogmengeschichte* II, Berlin 1909[4], p. 57, cp. p. 157.

> "For as for those who live according to Him the reward is eternal life, so for those who walk the opposite way which is not the one of virtue there is great shame and merciless danger on the day of judgement, because although they know the way of the truth they did the opposite of what they knew."

On the way of truth, which is the way of virtue see *C. G.* 5 and 30, *supra*, 29, 99. The great shame for the unbelievers on the day of judgement contrasts with the unashamed frankness of original man (see *C. G.* 2, *supra*, 19) to which the Christian believer can return. That there is no excuse for the unbelievers has been shown throughout in this treatise: they could have known better (see especially *supra*, 36, 42 f., 152). For the double final judgement cp. *De Inc.* 56: ... κρινεῖ δὲ (sc. ὁ Χριστὸς) τοὺς πάντας, πρὸς ἃ ἕκαστος ἔπραξε διὰ τοῦ σώματος, εἴτε ἀγαθά, εἴτε φαῦλα· ἔνθα τοῖς μὲν ἀγαθοῖς ἀπόκειται βασίλεια οὐρανῶν, τοῖς δὲ τὰ φαῦλα πράξασι, πῦρ αἰώνιον καὶ σκότος ἐξώτερον.

SOME FINAL OBSERVATIONS

Athanasius' apologetic treatise *Contra Gentes - De Incarnatione Verbi* is an example of 'preaching to the converted':
The reader is a Christian, so what he is presented is a reaffirmation of the faith he already has. This does not mean that he finds nothing new in the treatise. He does not find a new faith, but he may find some new arguments which corroborate it, - new not in the sense that they were never expressed before, but in the sense that they were so far unknown to the reader. In learning about these arguments the reader's φιλομάθεια could be satisfied. More or less the same applies to the writer of the treatise, Athanasius. He, too, reaffirms his faith by corroborating it with reasonable arguments which he had found in the writings of Christian theologians before him. By writing them down and expressing them in his own way these (to theologians) well known arguments became his own. He puts these arguments into a scheme (which was not unknown either) which is the pattern of the whole treatise. There are four ways of revelation: Man is created in God's image and can therefore know God, man can know God through the harmony of the universe, man can know God through Scripture (the Old Testament), these three ways of revelation are dealt with in the *Contra Gentes*, the fourth way is knowledge of God through the incarnation of the Word of God, - this is discussed in the *De Incarnatione Verbi*. All the arguments which had been produced more or less *ad hoc* by Christian apologists here reappear in a systematic exposition of Christian faith.

A. von Harnack once observed that when one wants to describe the development of a movement one need not take the beginning as the point of departure of description, but that one can also begin with the end (quoted by O. Ritschl, *Dogmengeschichte des Protestantismus*, Leipzig 1908, p. VI). Athanasius' apologetic treatise certainly does not mark the end of the apologetic tradition in Christian theology, but his treatise was written at a time when Paganism no longer posed a threat to the church: Christianity had been declared a *religio licita*, and in the *De Incarnatione Verbi* Athanasius proudly describes how the risen Christ has triumphed over Pagan idolatry and philosophy and how more and more people are converted to Christian faith. Athanasius not only had the feeling that the war between Christianity and Paganism would be won by Christianity (this had firmly been believed by all apologists ever since the beginning) but that it was obvious that it had already been won by Christianity, or rather by the risen Christ who draws the masses to the true faith. This fairly new situation leads to a different kind of apology. When we look back from Athanasius' apologetic treatise to earlier ones by other Christian writers we see that apology has received the character of dogmatics. The traditional apologetic arguments now appear as stones in a dogmatic building, they no longer function *ad hoc* but are part of a well considered system. These arguments can still be used in discussions with Pagans, but their primary function is to prove to the Christians themselves that Christian faith is not unreasonable and never has been, as appears from the fact that these are the arguments with which earlier generations of Christian theologians had defended Christian faith.

When these arguments were used against Pagans (at least against Pagan intellectuals), this, too, was to a certain degree 'preaching to the converted'. These Pagan intellectuals would agree that God is beyond all created substance, that He is incorporeal and unchangeable, many of them would even agree that the harmony of the universe points towards a Divine Logos which (or who) rules the world. What they would not, of course, agree with is that this Divine Logos is Jesus Christ (as Athanasius argues in the *Contra Gentes*) and that this Logos became man (as he argues in the *De Incarnatione Verbi*). Athanasius certainly knew how far philosophers would agree with him, and he will have gone to great lengths in saying things about God and His Logos with which they agreed in order to make them (and himself and his Christian readers) believe that it is a reasonable step from this common ground to the specifically Christian faith in Jesus Christ as God's Logos. He will undoubtedly have convinced the Christians that this is the case, but whether he would have convinced many Pagan readers must be doubted: They would not have regarded this as a reasonable step but as an irrational leap, – the gulf between reason and faith is wider than apologists believed. Efforts should certainly be made to bridge it, but when such bridges have been built, these are constantly in danger of collapsing and need constant maintenance. When this has been noticed not only the continuity but also the discontinuity in the long tradition of Christian apology becomes apparent.

INDICES

I. INDEX OF QUOTATIONS FROM ANCIENT AUTHORS

ALBINUS

Epitome
3, 1	17
5, 5	108
9, 1	25
11, 2	135
12, 1	136
12, 3	94, 130
13, 3	119
17, 4	103
24	101
25, 7	103
26, 3	24
27, 1	136
27, 4	42
31, 1	103 f.

AMBROSE

Hexaemeron
1, 3, 8	140

APULEIUS

De Platone et eius dogmate
1, 11	136

ARISTIDES

Apologia
1, 1	117
1, 2	47, 93
2	121 f.
3 ff.	92
3, 2	79, 152
3, 3	90
8, 4-6	54
9, 3-4	52
9, 6	52
9, 6-7	53
10, 2	93
10, 9	55
11, 5	87
12	44
12, 2	49
13, 7	52, 53

ARISTOTLE

De caelo
294 a 29	91
296 a 24 ff.	92

Physica
194 a 21	68
198 b 29 ff.	123

Topica
5, 4, 5 (132 b 1 ff.)	68

Ps.-ARISTOTLE

De mundo
396 a 33 ff.	119
396 b 11 f.	68
396 b 23 ff.	119
397 a 24 ff.	120
399 a 1-14	119
399 a 14 ff.	140
399 b 21 f.	117
400 b 6 ff.	129, 140
400 b 13 ff.	124

ATHANASIUS

Ad Maximum Philosophum
1	11

Ad Serapionem
1, 1	4
1, 16	95
1, 17	10
1, 18	10, 119
1, 19	10
2, 2	135
4, 5	10
4, 6	19
4, 14	13

Contra Arianos

1, 14	134, 135		
1, 16	54, 78		
1, 17-18	93		
1, 17	95		
1, 18	149		
1, 19	134, 135		
1, 21	19		
1, 23	95		
1, 24	134		
1, 25	134, 149		
1, 27	135		
1, 28	135, 149, 151		
1, 29	42, 140		
1, 30 ff.	32		
1, 33	117		
1, 34	117		
1, 52	24		
1, 56	2		
1, 62	143		
2, 2	150		
2, 12	13		
2, 14	152		
2, 17	42		
2, 21	2, 148		
2, 24	35, 139		
2, 25	9		
2, 26	35		
2, 29	128		
2, 31	139		
2, 32	134		
2, 34	54, 78		
2, 35	133		
2, 39	34		
2, 40	2		
2, 41	93		
2, 42	117		
2, 67	97		
2, 76	106		
2, 82	149, 150		
3, 1	10		
3, 3	144		
3, 6	149		
3, 8	50, 75		
3, 16	75, 152		
3, 18-21	107		
3, 19	87		
3, 31 f.	13		
3, 32	42		
3, 35	11		
3, 60	149		
3, 62	24, 51		
3, 63	95, 134		
3, 65	61		
3, 66	24		

Contra Gentes

1	1, 9 ff., 36, 47, 118
2	15 ff., 29, 36, 41, 59, 109, 114, 117, 131
3	20 ff., 41, 82
4	15, 23 ff., 40
5	27 ff., 41, 59
6	1, 18, 29 ff., 36, 59, 79, 80, 125
7	15, 22, 29, 32, 34 ff., 57, 82, 83
8	15, 28, 40 ff., 113, 114, 152
9	27, 43 ff., 88
10	45, 46, 47 ff., 78, 113
10 f.	44
11	15, 46, 50 ff., 78
12	12, 48, 51, 52, 53 ff.
13	12, 44, 47, 56 ff., 79
14	50, 58 ff.
15	45, 60 f.
16	61 ff.
16 ff.	44
17	65 ff.
18	67 ff., 73
19	69 ff., 113
20	71 ff., 113
21	74 ff.
22	45, 57, 77 ff., 126, 127
23	12, 22, 36, 79 ff., 124, 125
24	34, 82 ff.
25	83 ff.
26	12, 52, 86 ff.
27	9, 43 f., 88 ff.
28	52, 53, 78, 90, 93 ff., 126
29	33, 95 ff., 117, 119, 120 ff., 125
30	1, 29, 59, 99 ff.
31	23, 29, 40, 102 ff.
31-32	26
32	26, 52, 105 ff., 153
33	108 ff.
34	9, 16, 18, 24, 41, 112 ff.

35	16, 109, 117 ff.	33	11
35 ff.	18	40	36, 75
35-39	115	41	41
35-45a	114	41 f.	132
36	119 ff.	43	10, 122, 137
37	121 ff.	46	12, 13, 81
37 f.	30	47	49, 106, 127
38	124 ff.	48	11, 13
39	IX, 22, 93, 126 ff., 131	49	11, 68
		50	13
40	16, 115, 130 ff.	51	53, 81
40b-45a	115	53	11, 56
41	16, 117, 134 ff.	54	11, 117, 151
42	138 ff.	55	141
43	140 ff.	56	5, 10 f., 153
44	109, 141 ff.	57	18, 111, 113, 118
45a	143 f.		
45b	145 f.		
45b-46	114	*De sententia Dionysii*	
46	4, 146 ff.	23	143, 144
47	10, 42, 57, 89, 150 ff.	24	144

De Synodis
35   2

De Decretis Nicaenae Synodi

2	134		
8	35	*Epistula ad episcopos Aeg. et Lib.*	
11	73, 78	4	75, 152
12	42	13	149
15	134	16	34, 54, 78
19	2		
20	87	*Epistula ad Marcellinum*	
24	19	27	100
28	16, 32		
29	117	*Vita Antonii*	
31	117	16	10
		20	99, 103
De Incarnatione Verbi		22	15
1	10, 11, 13, 30	45	19
2	1, 30, 31, 123	73	69, 76
3	17, 50, 135, 137	74	11 f., 55, 109
5	28, 86	74 ff.	11
11	117, 152	75	12
11-13	114	79	12
12	55, 146		
13	18	*Sermo maior de fide*	
15	42	26	142
17	139		
18	117		
18 f.	13	ATHENAGORAS	
26-30	12		
27 ff.	106	*Legatio*	
28	22	1	44, 80
29	36, 71	6, 2	43
30	13	6, 3	91
31	19, 60	8	33
32	9, 28, 36, 117	8, 2	78

14	80		158, 7	47
15, 3	57		255, 2, 2	26
16	126		255, 6, 6	26
18, 1	70			
20, 3	53			
21	52		BASIL	
22	62			
22, 12	129		*Hexaemeron*	
28, 3	81 f.		1, 2	146
30, 3	49			
32, 1	53			

CALCIDIUS

ATTICUS

Timaeus translatus (ed. Waszink)
57   109
256   105

Fragments (ed. Baudry)
4   110

CICERO

AUGUSTIN

De natura deorum
1, 1, 2   80

Confessiones
11, 4, 6   9, 40
11, 7, 9   140
13, 20, 28   47
13, 31, 46   47

1, 6, 14   80
1, 8, 19   122
1, 17, 45   121
1, 25, 71 ff.   78
1, 33, 92   78

De civitate Dei
7, 28   136
10, 14   26
12, 1, 3   47

2, 2   119
2, 22, 57-58   68
2, 23, 60   67
2, 24, 63 f.   62
2, 24, 64 ff.   63
2, 28, 70   54

De diversis quaestionibus LXXXIII
28   47

2, 31, 78   124
2, 32   109
2, 33, 86   47
3, 17, 43 ff.   69
3, 24, 62   64

De Genesi contra Manichaeos
1, 2, 4   47

De Trinitate
1, 10, 20   26

De officiis
1, 4, 11   103
3, 25, 95   23

De vera religione
18, 35   47

Tusculanae Disputationes
1, 38, 91   106
1, 39, 94   106

Enarrationes in Psalmos
26, 8 (II)   47
39, 8   47
91, 8 (I)   106
102, 22   106
120, 10   106

CLEMENT OF ALEXANDRIA

Paedagogus
2, 1, 1-2   28
2, 9, 82, 3   109
2, 10, 83-115   27
2, 34   28
2, 67, 2   28

Sermones
51, 14, 23-24   26
96, 4, 4   47
108, 3   106
124, 4   106

Protrepticus

2, 24, 3	49
2, 26, 1	45
2, 27	53
2, 37, 4	49
2, 79	44
3, 42, 3	84
3, 42, 9	85
3, 43	85
3, 44, 2	45
4, 49, 1	46
4, 51	46, 61
4, 51 f.	72
4, 52	62
4, 54 ff.	46
4, 57, 5	56
5, 66, 1 ff.	88
7, 73	62
10, 102, 3	45
11	20

Quis dives salvetur

21, 7	114

Stromateis

1, 16, 74 ff.	69
2, 23, 137, 1	27
3, 3, 12 ff.	27
4, 5, 21, 1 ff.	26
5, 8, 52 f.	28
5, 11, 75, 3	128
5, 12, 79, 3-4	130
5, 32-38	90
6, 12, 99, 6 f.	26
7, 2, 5, 4	129
7, 6, 31 ff.	83
7, 12, 78, 6	18
7, 14, 84	18

CLEMENT OF ROME

Ad Corinthios

20	119
46	4

PS.-CLEMENTINE HOMILIES

3, 7, 2	102
17, 7	102

CORPUS HERMETICUM

Asclepius 8, 12	140
Asclepius 37	74
Poimandres 11, 9	125

EPISTULA AD DIOGNETUM

2, 2	56

EUSEBIUS

Demonstratio Evangelica

3, 3	43
3, 6	12
4, 5	117

Praeparatio Evangelica

1, 4	80, 81
1, 5, 2	11
1, 6	88
1, 9	81, 88
1, 9, 18	46
2, 1	44, 81
2, 2	67
2, 4	53
2, 6	46
3, 10, 21	49
3, 13, 7	127
4, 8 ff.	83
4, 15	85
4, 16	85
5, 3	45
7, 2	20, 45
7, 2, 6	46
7, 3	90
7, 3, 3	129
7, 10	119
7, 18, 3	102
10, 6	69
13, 14	49
13, 18	43
14, 16, 8	91
15, 29	91
15, 33	130

GREGORY NAZIANZEN

Orationes

20, 7	47
20, 10	47
25, 15	47
40, 23	47

Orationes theologicae

3, 15	47
4, 7	47
5, 14	47

GREGORY OF NYSSA

De anima et resurrectione (PG 46)
25A   9

In sanctum Pascha (GNO IX)
257   9

HERACLITUS

FVS
22 B 51   126

HERODOTUS

Historiae
1   81

HILARY OF POITIERS

De Trinitate
1, 1   22
1, 2   103
1, 4   80
1, 7   47, 143
1, 18   9
2, 2   95
2, 5   10
3, 7   93
3, 8   50
3, 13   106
3, 22   117
4, 14   9, 10
4, 36   9
5, 1   95
5, 21   9
6, 17   9
6, 19   93
6, 22   95
7, 30   9
7, 38   9
8, 2   95
9, 44   10
9, 59   103
10, 4   4
11, 1   10
12, 26   10
12, 53   92

Enarrationes in Psalmos
2, 14, 15   93
129, 1   92
129, 3   95

HIPPOLYTUS

Philosophumena
8, 8   91

Refutatio
1, 19, 1   25
1, 25, 1   32

IRENAEUS

Epideixis
3   16

Adversus Haereses
1, 6, 1   95, 139
2, 1   33
2, 1, 2   35
2, 1, 4   96, 128
2, 2, 3   119
2, 4, 4   51
2, 4, 5   117
2, 4, 6   125
2, 5, 1   106, 128
2, 8, 1   117
2, 8, 2   152
2, 11, 1   119
2, 14, 1   35
2, 15, 3   78, 95
2, 16, 4   78, 95, 133
2, 18, 3   25
2, 18, 4   51
2, 37, 2   119, 126
2, 37, 3   47
2, 40, 1   10
2, 41   10
2, 41, 2   90, 92
2, 42, 2   78, 95
2, 46, 1   35, 95
2, 46, 2   35
2, 46, 4   35
2, 50   105
2, 51-52   21
2, 52   105
2, 56, 1   47, 110 f.
3, 8, 3   47
3, 12, 14   34 f.
3, 16   149
4, 2   33
4, 11, 1   118
4, 21, 2   95
4, 25, 1   107, 128, 136
4, 25, 3   93
4, 29   93
4, 31-32   93

4, 34, 1	147		1, 21	87
4, 34, 3	148		2, 1, 5	21
4, 34, 5	9		2, 2, 14	57
4, 36, 6	114		2, 2, 23 f.	56
4, 49, 2	93		2, 4	79
4, 53, 1	4		2, 5, 5	90
4, 60, 2	27		2, 5, 14	89
4, 61, 1	107		3, 8, 29	90
4, 62	47		3, 12, 4	106
4, 64, 3	36		6, 25	83
5, 1, 3	147		7, 9	112
5, 15, 4	147			

Epitome
6	46
18	83
63	31

JUSTIN MARTYR

Apologia I
9, 2	56
10, 1	93
13, 1	93
43, 8	107
44	31

LUCRECE

De rerum natura
1, 44-49	121
1, 305	95
2, 646-651	121
5, 837 ff.	123
6, 43 ff.	93

Apologia II
13	87

Dialogus cum Tryphone
4, 1	16
5, 1-6, 2	110
5, 4	110
62	147
129, 3	148

MAXIMUS OF TYRE

Orationes
11, 5a-b	80

PS.-JUSTIN

Cohortatio ad Graecos
2	52, 53
3	62
6	109
20	31
22	18

MINUCIUS FELIX

Octavius
19, 10	62
21, 8	49
30	87

NOVATIAN

De Trinitate
6, 36	95

LACTANCE

De ira dei
11, 4	129

NUMENIUS

Divinae Institutiones
1, 2	117
1, 3	54
1, 3, 3	128
1, 10	53
1, 11, 45 ff.	49
1, 18	67

Fragments (ed. Des Places)
2	17
8	135
11	135
16	150
18	129, 137

19	150	3, 5, 3	130
20	136, 150		
47	108	*In Joannem*	
		2, 13	25
		13, 25, 36	150

ORIGEN

In Matthaeum

Contra Celsum		15, 20	150
Praefatio 2	9		
1, 1	71, 85, 125		
1, 5	57, 58		
1, 9	11, 14, 86	PAUL OF SAMOSATA	
1, 17	53		
1, 48	105	*Reliquiae sacrae* (ed. Routh)	
1, 67	10	II, p. 476	149
3, 22	10		
3, 41	150		
3, 43	49	PHILO	
3, 76	57		
4, 6	128	*De confusione linguarum*	
4, 14	11	170	125
4, 28	12		
4, 48	53	*De decalogo*	
4, 66	31	16, 79	45
5, 6	89, 132		
5, 10	90	*De opificio mundi*	
5, 39	150	7 f.	152
6, 3-4	49	25	18
6, 10	43		
7, 62	57	*De posteritate Caini*	
8, 17	117 f.	3-4	78
8, 21	93		
		De somniis	
In Exodum Homiliae		II 1	105
8, 2	146		
		De specialibus legibus	
De Principiis		1, 13	43
Praefatio 8 ff.	78		
1, 1	78		
1, 1, 5	36		
1, 1, 7	105	PLATO	
1, 1, 9	20		
1, 2, 1	148	*Cratylus*	
1, 2, 13	150	397C	88
1, 3, 2	131		
1, 3, 6	100	*Epistula VII*	
1, 3, 8	28	341C	49
1, 4, 3	130		
1, 7, 3	89	*Leges*	
1, 8, 4	24	667 D/E	62
2, 1, 1	22	886A	119
2, 3, 6	111	888E ff.	68
2, 9, 2	25	896E-899B	88
2, 11, 7	20		
3, 1, 3	103	*Phaedo*	
3, 4, 1	101	86E ff.	104

Phaedrus
   245C   24, 108, 110 f.
   246/247   28

Politicus
   272E   137
   272E ff.   129
   273D/E   137

Republic
   327A   49
   331C   23
   376 ff.   61
   378B/C   54
   508A   114
   508C ff.   36
   509B   16, 136
   514 ff.   42
   580D   101
   597   68
   617E   31

Theaetetus
   176A/B   17

Timaeus
   28A   25
   29E   30, 136
   30A   119
   31A/B   130
   32B/C   122
   32D   94
   32D-34B   94
   37C   25
   41A/C   43, 110 f.
   69C   28
   86D   104
   92A   44

PLOTINUS

Enneads
   1, 6, 5, 25 ff.   113
   1, 6, 5, 36 ff.   113
   1, 6, 5, 43 ff.   113
   1, 6, 8, 3 f.   100
   1, 6, 9, 7   100
   1, 6, 9, 30 ff.   114
   1, 8, 14, 3   24
   2, 9, 4, 12-14   128
   2, 9, 9, 30 ff.   89
   2, 9, 11   128
   4, 3, 11   71, 75
   4, 3, 11, 1-6   74
   5, 8, 1, 35-36   73

PLUTARCH

De animae procreatione in Timaeo
   1013C   108
   1015C   31
   1016A   109

De placitis philosophorum
   879A   130

PORPHYRY

De abstinentia
   2, 36   85
   2, 54 f.   85
   2, 58   85

Epistula ad Marcellam
   24   31

Sententiae
   33, 3   17

QUINTILIAN

Institutio oratoria
   3, 6, 80   115
   8, 6, 73 f.   66

SEXTUS EMPIRICUS

Adversus Mathematicos
   7, 93   114

TERTULLIAN

Ad nationes
   1, 10, 39   52

Ad Scapulum
   2, 8   93

Ad uxorem
   1, 2   27

Adversus Hermogenem
   18, 5   47

Adversus Judaeos
   5, 3 ff.   93

Adversus Marcionem

1, 3, 3	34
1, 3 ff.	34
1, 4, 5-6	96
1, 11, 3	33
1, 11, 5	68
1, 11, 9	35
1, 13, 2	47
1, 15, 4	32
1, 16, 1	35
1, 17, 1	115
1, 17 f.	118
1, 18, 3	9
2, 2, 4	50
2, 3, 1-2	136
2, 4, 5	107
2, 9, 7	47
2, 18, 3	93
2, 29, 4	119
4, 8, 3	96

Apologeticum

5, 1	46
7-8	86
9, 1	86
9, 5	84
9, 16	87
10, 4	49
10, 10	49
11, 5	129
14, 2	54
14, 3	52
17, 2-3	9
21, 7 f.	53
21, 8	52
24, 7 f.	80
25, 8	51
47, 7	129

De anima

3, 1	32
5, 6	95
6, 11 f.	109
9, 4	109
24	21
42, 3	110
43, 12	105
45, 1	105
46, 11	105
50, 1	110
53, 3	28

THEOPHILUS

Ad Autolycum

1, 2	36, 114
1, 5	124, 129
1, 7	117
1, 9	53
1, 10	49
2, 2	46
2, 3	47, 106
2, 10	93, 148
2, 18	147
2, 27	17
3, 3	53
3, 8	53

XENOPHANES

FVS

1, 24	95
21, A 31	34

II. INDEX OF SUBJECTS AND NAMES

Achilles 64 f.
Adam 19
adultery 51 f., 54 f.
Aidoneus 54
Aigaion 52
Alcmene 53
allegory 62
Ammon 45, 83
anamnesis 21
Anaximanes 91
angels 2, 15, 17 f., 142
animals (worship of) 44 f.
Anoubis 77
anthropomorphism 78

Antinous 45 f., 86
Antiope 53
antiquity (appeal to) 48
Aphrodite 48, 54, 87
Apis 83
Apollo 47, 62, 67
Apollodorus Mythographus 48
arbitrariness 24, 28 f.
Arcas 54
Ares 54, 62, 84, 87
Arians 1 f., 19, 116, 143, 149
Aristaios 68
art 68 ff., 117, 127
Artemis 48, 49, 53, 67, 84

INDICES

artist 46, 50, 56, 60, 67 ff., 73, 152
asceticism 14, 27, 29
Asclepius 67
Athena 47, 52, 54, 67
audacity 27, 44

brevity 3, 10

Carneades 69
Carpocrates 2
cause 47
cave (simile of) 42
Charybdis 77
choir (simile of) 140
Chrysippus 91
city (simile of) 124, 141
Constantine 46
contemplation 16 f., 100 f.
corporeality (of God) 78 f.
creation 9 ff.
Cronos 52, 62, 85
cross 11 f.
curiosity 10
Cybele 86

Danaë 53
deification 43 ff.
Demeter 47, 67
demons 12, 141
desires 18, 40
devil 21
Diodorus 81
Diomedes 54, 64
Dion of Prusa 70
Dionysus 45, 53, 54, 83
Dioscuri 53
dogmatics 155
dreams 104 f., 109
dualism 21

elements 43 f., 90 ff., 121 ff.
Epicureans 30, 51, 78, 92 f., 101, 112, 120, 122
etymology 63
Euhemerism 44, 46
Europa 53
evil 14 ff., 29 ff.
exile 1 ff.
exordium 2 f.

fall (man's) 20 f.
fate 51 f.
fear (of death) 12, 22
fig-leaves 40
fluidity (of creation) 135
form (and matter) 72 f.

Ganymede 51
glory 127 f.
Gnostics 1 f., 30
goodness (God's) 16 ff., 135 f.

Hadrian 45, 86
harmony of the universe 115 ff.
Hecabe 64
Hector 64
Hephaistos 47, 54, 62, 67
Hera 47, 52, 54, 62, 64, 67, 69, 85
Heracles 53, 54
Hermes 45, 47, 53
Hippocentaur 77
Homer 68 f.
homosexuality 86
Horus 45, 49
hyperbole 66 f.

ideas 25
idolatry 15 ff., 38 ff.
idols 13
image (God's) 15 ff., 70
images (of gods) 56 ff.
imitation 85
immortality 17, 98 ff.
incarnation 11 f.
invention 68 f.
Isis 45, 48

Jews 146
Jupiter Latiaris 85

Korax 68
Kore 48

"Lasterkatalog" 28
laws (natural) 90 ff., 142, 147
Leda 53
Leto 53
logos spermatikos 116, 132 f.
Lycurgus 68
lyre (simile of) 104, 126, 129, 139

Maia 53
mantics 105
Marcion, Marcionites 1 f., 15, 27, 30, 32, 118
marriage 27
matter 30
Metrodorus 91 f.
mirror (the soul as) 20, 114
mysticism 14
myths 61 ff.

Neotera 48

Nestor   64
Nicene Synod   4

Odysseus   64
omnipotence (god's)   33, 96, 119 ff.
Omphele   55
one and many   22
Osiris   45, 49

Palamedes   68
passibility (of God)   54
Perseus   53, 54
Phidias   117 f.
planets   43, 88 ff.
Platonists   15 ff., 71 ff., 89, 113
poets   60 ff.
Polycleitos   117 f.
Poseidon   47, 52, 62, 67
Posidonius   92, 114
prayer   26
pre-existence (of the soul)   24, 44, 98 ff.
prostitution (sacred)   86
providence   18

reason (and faith)   11, 155
reductio ad absurdum   64
revelation (four ways of)   114, 154
Rhea   87

sacrifices   82 ff.
Sarpedon   52
Sceptics   51, 62, 64 f., 69, 78, 80
Scripture   3, 10, 32, 139, 144

Scylla   77
self-castration   86
self-purification   113 f.
self-sufficiency (God's)   91, 93 f.
Semele   53
sin   14 ff.
sleep (and death)   110
Solon   68
'sons of God'   10
sorites   69
soul (and movement)   24, 98 ff.
Stoics   51, 62, 64, 117
sun (simile of)   13, 36
survival of the fittest   123

taedium   3
Thales   91
Thersites   64 f.
Theseus   48
Thetis   52
transmigration (of souls)   44
tripartition (of the soul)   28, 100 f.
Triptolemus   68
Trojan war   51, 53 f.
Typhon   49

will (man's)   23 ff., 103 f., 107
will (God's and Christ's)   24, 51
women (esteem of)   48

Zeno   68
Zeus   45, 47, 49, 51, 53, 62, 64, 65, 67, 69, 83, 87

III. INDEX OF MODERN AUTHORS

Andresen, C.   10, 42
Armstrong, A. H.   21, 25, 27, 71, 73, 74, 75, 77

Baeumker, C.   30
Berkhof, H.   IX
Boer, W. den   46, 60, 71, 125

Camelot, P.Th.   10, 13, 15, 16, 19, 23, 44, 49, 53, 80, 83, 86, 100, 101, 108, 126
Chadwick, H.   89
Courcelle, P.   100, 137

Daniélou, J.   42
Diels, H.   91 f.
Dodds, E. R.   47
Dörrie, H.   31, 136
Düring, I.   68, 92, 105

Evans, E.   148

Flasch, K.   73
Florovsky, G.   137

Gärtner, B.   46, 58, 93, 118
Geffcken, J.   44, 49, 51, 52, 53, 54, 56, 62, 70, 78, 79, 85, 87, 92, 93, 117, 122
Giesecke, A.   4
Gilson, E.   137
Görgemanns, H.   24, 36
Grant, R. M.   13, 34, 95, 150
Gronau, K.   114
Gruber, G.   150

Hager, F. P.   30
Hamilton, A.   113
Harl, M.   28, 29

Harnack, A. von 153, 154

Jaeger, H. 19
Joly, R. 19
Joosen, J. C. 62

Kannengiesser, Ch. 1, 4, 136
Karpp, H. 24, 36
Kehrhahn, T. 3
Koch, H. 40

Lausberg, H. 3, 13, 115
Leeman, A. D. 127
Leone, L. 23, 24, 44, 45, 53, 67, 71, 83, 87, 88, 100, 102, 108, 112
Louth, A. 19

Marrou, H. I. 106
Merki, H. 17
Merlan, P. 22
Meijering, E. P. 4, 10, 42, 47, 130, 133, 136, 140, 149
Michel, O. 28
Moreau, M. 106
Mühl, M. 133
Müller, C. W. 17
Munz, P. 22

Neumann, K. J. 60
Norden, E. 93

Osborn, E. F. 22
Owen, E. C. E. 15

Pépin, J. 62, 110
Pohlenz, M. 106
Prestige, G.-L. 54

Quispel, G. 102

Recheis, P. A. 19
Ritschl, O. 153
Roldanus, J. 100
van Rooijen-Dijkman, H. W. A. 112
Routh, M. J. 149
Ruhbach, G. 11
Runia, D. T. 130

Schneider, A. 111
Schoemann, J. B. 16
Stead, G. C. 2, 31, 48, 55, 62, 72, 102, 115, 150

Taylor, A. E. 110
Theiler, W. 25, 47
Thomson, R. W. IX, 13, 30, 33, 46, 49, 55, 83, 141

Unnik, W. C. van 125

Vermeulen, A. J. 128
Vogel, C. J. de 21, 65, 132

Waszink, J. H. 17, 21, 23, 25, 28, 32, 40, 42, 96, 105, 109, 110, 112, 119, 128, 132 f., 135, 148
Wehrli, F. 105
Whittaker, J. 16
Windelband, W. 87
Winden, J. C. M. van 1 f., 4, 10, 11, 16, 42, 110, 135
Wolfson, H. A. 25, 140

Zeller, E. 21